Flourishing in Tensions

Flourishing in Tensions

Embracing Radical Discipleship

MICHAEL BRÄUTIGAM

WIPF & STOCK · Eugene, Oregon

FLOURISHING IN TENSIONS
Embracing Radical Discipleship

Copyright © 2022 Michael Bräutigam. All rights reserved. Except for brief quotations in critical publications or reviews, no part of this book may be reproduced in any manner without prior written permission from the publisher. Write: Permissions, Wipf and Stock Publishers, 199 W. 8th Ave., Suite 3, Eugene, OR 97401.

Wipf & Stock
An Imprint of Wipf and Stock Publishers
199 W. 8th Ave., Suite 3
Eugene, OR 97401

www.wipfandstock.com

PAPERBACK ISBN: 978-1-6667-3529-1
HARDCOVER ISBN: 978-1-6667-9222-5
EBOOK ISBN: 978-1-6667-9223-2

09/07/22

Unless otherwise indicated, Scripture quotations are from the Holy Bible, English Standard Version® (ESV®). Copyright © 2001 by Crossway, a publishing ministry of Good News Publishers. All rights reserved.

Scripture quotations marked MSG are taken from the Message, copyright © 1993, 2002, 2018 by Eugene H. Peterson. Used by permission of NavPress. All rights reserved. Represented by Tyndale House Publishers, Inc.

Scripture quotations marked NIV are taken from the Holy Bible, New International Version®, NIV® Copyright © 1973, 1978, 1984, 2011 by Biblica, Inc.™ Used by permission. All rights reserved worldwide.

To Donald Macleod

Contents

Acknowledgments ix
Abbreviations xiii
Introduction 1

1. Embracing Tensions — 9

I: DENY YOURSELF

2. Understanding the Self — 31
3. Embracing Newness — 47
4. Practicing Self-Denial — 61

II: TAKE UP YOUR CROSS

5. Cross-Bearing and Christ's Suffering — 79
6. Sharing in Christ's Sufferings — 97
7. Taking Up the Cross — 114

III: FOLLOW ME

8. Following Personally — 133
9. Following Together — 157
10. Seeking the Friend's Face — 182

Concluding Remarks 197
Bibliography 205
Subject Index 223
Scripture Index 237

Acknowledgments

I BEGAN THIS PROJECT during writing leave in Switzerland in the second half of 2019, just a few months before the COVID-19 pandemic struck and changed our lives. I am grateful to the leadership team of Melbourne School of Theology (MST)/Eastern College for granting me this sabbatical. I especially appreciate the support of Rosemary Wong, the Board, and the executive team, Tim Meyers, Peter Riddell, Justin Tan, Peter Tyrrell, and Jude Long. Professor Christiane Tietz welcomed me warmly as visiting fellow at the theological faculty of the University of Zurich, and I am deeply indebted to her and her team. I thoroughly enjoyed my time researching and writing in Zurich. I want to express my gratitude to librarians Regula Wegman and Ute Beck, who were extraordinarily kind and helpful as I was trying to locate various resources.

This book is dedicated to my friend and teacher, Donald Macleod. Donald has taught me theology, and I have always admired how he uniquely combines intellectual rigor and reverential awe—both in the classroom and in his writings. He possesses the rare gift to express the most profound theological truths in accessible language and with pastoral sensitivity. I am still striving to follow his example here. I am also thankful to my teachers in psychology at the University of Trier. While writing the chapter on self-denial, I again realized how much of my thinking had been shaped by my psychology professors in the late 1990s and early 2000s. A particular note of gratitude goes to Professor Sigrun-Heide Filipp, whose lectures on the psychology of the self proved highly stimulating, and much of what I am sharing in this chapter is based on her teaching. I am indebted to my students in the theology, psychology, and church history classes. This book has grown out of my conversations with these bright students, and I am grateful for their constant reminder to focus on questions of meaning and purpose when it comes to discipleship.

I owe a particular note of gratitude to MST's executive principal, Tim Meyers, who accentuates in his regular chapel messages the importance of personal transformation in our lives as followers of Jesus Christ. I gladly share his ideal of a transformative theology that not only feeds our minds but aims at character transformation. It is a particular privilege when one can also call their colleagues friends. Over the past years, I have benefited enormously from conversations with my friends and colleagues. A particular note of thanks to Gillian Asquith, Peter Botross, Andrew Brown, Angelo Cettolin, Richard Coombs, Mark Durie, Greg Forbes, Chris Green, Matt Jacoby, Kirk Franklin, Delle Matthews, David Ng, Eric Oldenburg, David Reimer, Nathan Runham, Richard Shumack, and Jacqui Stok. Jason Lam, Bonhoeffer scholar par excellence, has offered helpful feedback regarding an earlier draft of this manuscript. Throughout the development of this book, I enjoyed exchanging many ideas with Tom Kimber, and I am grateful to him for his friendship and for taking the time to talk through many of the themes presented here. Tom's clear focus on spiritual formation, and, in particular, his constant reminder to seek silence and solitude in our walk with Christ, has found its way, especially into the last chapter. I also would like to thank my friends from the Centre for Theology and Psychology, in particular, John Andersen, Kuruvilla George, Chris Groszek, Lidia Lae, Judy Lillis, Chris MacLeod, Lisa Miller, Katherine Thompson, and Judy Wilkie. Your friendship and your enthusiasm are constant sources of encouragement to me.

I would also like to extend my gratitude to friends and colleagues who have taken the time to read an earlier version of the manuscript and offered helpful feedback: Ross Cooper, Mark Elliott, Mathis Grossmann, Ernie Laskaris, Lisa Miller, and Ruth Nicholls, thank you for making this a much stronger piece. Bruce Pass, your valuable suggestions have helped me improve this work in so many places. This book is now much stronger, and I am extremely grateful to you for your astute comments and, of course, your friendship and encouragement throughout this process. It has been refreshing to talk theology with you (with an East German accent!) during various lockdowns.

English is my second foreign language, and I am always grateful to learn from English grammar experts, of which Diana Summers is a formidable specimen. Diana has not only done an excellent job proofreading the manuscript, but given her German and Latin expertise, she was also able to assist me with essential questions of translation. I am also indebted to Greta Morris, who has again excelled in her editing and typesetting skills. Thanks to Matt Wimer and George Callihan at Wipf and Stock for taking on another project. It is such a smooth experience working with you. Finally, Jenni, thank you for your patience and long-suffering. While I was working comfortably from a café or library in Zurich, you cared for sick children in various Swiss hospitals. You are more than an essential worker—you are a true heroine.

Melbourne, June 2022
Michael Bräutigam

Abbreviations

CD	Karl Barth, *Church Dogmatics*. 14 vols. in 13 parts. Translated and edited by G. W. Bromiley and T. F. Torrance. Edinburgh: T. & T. Clark, 1956–75
KD	Karl Barth, *Die kirchliche Dogmatik*. 4 vols. in 13 parts. München: Chr. Kaiser, 1932; Zürich: Evangelischer Verlag Zürich, 1938–65
DBW	*Dietrich Bonhoeffer Werke*. Edited by Eberhard Bethge et al. 17 vols. München and Gütersloh: Christian Kaiser/Gütersloher Verlagshaus 1986–99
DBW 1	*Sanctorum Communio: Eine dogmatische Untersuchung zur Soziologie der Kirche*. Dietrich Bonhoeffer Werke. Vol. 1. Edited by Joachim von Soosten. München: Chr. Kaiser Verlag, 1986
DBW 4	*Nachfolge*. Dietrich Bonhoeffer Werke. Vol. 4. Edited by Martin Kuske and Ilse Tödt. München: Chr. Kaiser Verlag, 1989
DBW 8	*Widerstand und Ergebung*. Dietrich Bonhoeffer Werke. Vol. 8. Edited by Christian Gremmels et al. Gütersloh: Chr. Kaiser/Gütersloher Verlagshaus, 1998
DBWE	*Dietrich Bonhoeffer Works* in English. 17 vols. Edited by Wayne Whitson Floyd Jr. Minneapolis, MN: Fortress, 1996–2014
DBWE 1	*Sanctorum Communio: A Theological Study of the Sociology of the Church*. Dietrich Bonhoeffer Works. English Ed. Vol. 1. Edited by Clifford Green. Translated by Reinhard Krauss and Nancy Lukens. Minneapolis, MN: Fortress, 1998

DBWE 2	*Act and Being: Transcendental Philosophy and Ontology in Systematic Theology.* Dietrich Bonhoeffer Works. English Ed. Vol. 2. Edited by Wayne Whitson Floyd, Jr. Translated by H. R. Rumscheidt. Minneapolis, MN: Fortress, 1996
DBWE 3	*Creation and Fall: A Theological Exposition of Genesis 1–3.* Dietrich Bonhoeffer Works. English Ed. Vol. 3. Edited by John W. de Gruchy. Translated by Douglas Stephen Bax. Minneapolis, MN: Fortress, 2004
DBWE 4	*Discipleship.* Dietrich Bonhoeffer Works. English Ed. Vol. 4. Edited by Geoffrey Kelly and John D. Godsey. Translated by Barbara Green and Reinhard Krauss. Minneapolis, MN: Fortress, 2001
DBWE 5	*Life Together and Prayerbook of the Bible.* Dietrich Bonhoeffer Works. English Ed. Vol. 5. Edited by Geoffrey Kelly. Translated by Daniel Bloesch and James Burtness. Minneapolis, MN: Fortress, 1996
DBWE 6	*Ethics.* Dietrich Bonhoeffer Works. English Ed. Vol. 6. Edited by Clifford Green. Translated by Reinhard Krauss et al. Minneapolis, MN: Fortress, 2006
DBWE 8	*Letters and Papers from Prison.* Dietrich Bonhoeffer Works. English Ed. Vol. 8. Edited by John W. de Gruchy. Translated by Isabel Best et al. Minneapolis, MN: Fortress, 2010
DBWE 11	*Ecumenical, Academic, and Pastoral Work: 1931–1932.* Dietrich Bonhoeffer Works. English Ed. Vol. 11. Edited by Victoria J. Barnett et al. Translated by Anne Schmidt-Lange et al. Minneapolis, MN: Fortress, 2012
DBWE 12	*Berlin: 1932–1933.* Dietrich Bonhoeffer Works. English Ed. Vol. 12. Edited by Larry Rasmussen. Translated by Isabel Best and David Higgins. Minneapolis, MN: Fortress, 2009
DBWE 15	*Theological Education Underground: 1937–1940.* Dietrich Bonhoeffer Works. English Ed. Vol. 15. Edited by Victoria J. Barnett. Translated by Victoria J. Barnett et al. Minneapolis, MN: Fortress, 2012
DBWE 16	*Conspiracy and Imprisonment: 1940–945.* Dietrich Bonhoeffer Works. English Ed. Vol. 16. Edited by Mark S. Brocker. Translated by Lisa E. Dahill and Douglas W. Stott. Minneapolis, MN: Fortress, 2006

Inst.	John Calvin, *Institutes of the Christian Religion*. 2 vols. Edited by John T. McNeill. Translated by Ford Lewis Battles. Philadelphia, PA: Westminster, 1960 (cited by book, chapter, and section)
LW	Martin Luther, *Luther's Works*. Edited by Jaroslav Pelikan et al. 75 vols. Philadelphia, PA: Fortress/St. Louis, MI: Concordia, 1955–
WA	Martin Luther, *D. Martin Luthers Werke: Kritische Gesamtausgabe* (Weimarer Ausgabe). 120 vols. Weimar: Hermann Böhlaus Nachfolger, 1883–2009 (cited by volume number, page number, and lines)
WA Br	Martin Luther, *D. Martin Luthers Werke: Kritische Gesamtausgabe. Briefwechsel*. 18 vols. Weimar: Hermann Böhlaus Nachfolger, 1930–85 (cited by volume number, page number, and lines)
WA Tr	Martin Luther, *D. Martin Luthers Werke: Kritische Gesamtausgabe: Tischreden*. 6 vols. Weimar: Hermann Böhlau, 1912–21 (cited by volume number, page number, and lines)

Introduction

"Deny yourself, take up your cross, and follow me." Jesus's call to discipleship is radical.[1] It even comes with the risk that one might lose their life (Matt 16:25). Christian discipleship, it seems, is neither glamorous nor for the fainthearted. Faced with this daring call, followers of Christ wonder how they could possibly comply with its demands. Comparing one's comfortable Western lifestyle with the requirements of this audacious call, a substantial gap emerges.[2] There just does not seem to be much that is radical about our lives. Immersed in a culture that runs counter to every element of this call, modern disciples wonder: What does self-denial look like when the pervasive *Zeitgeist* promotes self-esteem and self-improvement? Does not cross-bearing sound foreign, even foolish, in a society that seeks to eradicate pain at all cost? And what does it actually mean to follow Christ today when it is so tempting simply to blend into the surrounding culture of affluence and prosperity? Is a discipleship that fits our culture hand in glove still radical, or are we at risk of adopting what Eugene Peterson called a religious "tourist mindset"?[3]

As the title suggests, this book is about embracing *radical* discipleship. And by that, I do not mean a dualistic form of discipleship that we set up in contrast to culture, where we try to establish a holy discipleship bubble by withdrawing from a world hostile to God. The call of Christ does not

---

1. John Stott, too, uses the term "radical" to denote Christian discipleship. Stott, *Radical Disciple*.

2. To offer an adequate definition of "Western civilization" is frustratingly difficult. Classic definitions that identify certain nations will always fall short of the inherent complexities as mere geographical narrowing will not suffice, as Niall Ferguson observes. "'The West,'" he writes, "is much more than just a geographical expression. It is a set of norms, behaviours, and institutions with borders that are blurred in the extreme." Ferguson, *Civilization*, 15.

3. Peterson, *Long Obedience*, 10.

detach us from this world but makes us live out our calling in a world that is opposed to God. Radical discipleship understood in that way, of course, plunges us into a life of tensions. Yet radical discipleship, the way I envision it, is all about embracing the paradoxical elements of Jesus's call and the tensions to which we are exposed on our way. In fact, Jesus's disciples are called to thrive amid tensions: by denying themselves, they receive new life; by taking up the cross, they gain a new vision of God and self; and by following not their ideas and ideals but Christ, they find true purpose and meaning for their lives.[4]

The key intention of this book is to come alongside the curious believer who sees herself as an unfinished project and desires to mature as a disciple of Jesus Christ.[5] This work seeks to expand our horizon as it encourages us to think about discipleship as an artform that wants to be mastered. It is aimed at serious disciples who want to grow up "and become mature, attaining to the whole measure of the fullness of Christ" (Eph 4:13b). Bidding farewell to confusion and complacency, they seek to go ahead with renewed vigor, a clearer vision of their mission, purpose, and calling. They want to move from lukewarm discipleship to what Dallas Willard called "full-throttle discipleship of Jesus Christ."[6] As Fidelis Ruppert (OSB) describes, they long to experience an authentic existence, freedom, and a "wideness of the heart."[7] They are keen to figure out what Jesus meant when he promised life to his followers, and that in abundance (John 10:10).

As we shall discover through this book, the promise of new, abundant life, is realized in close relationship with Jesus Christ. Christian discipleship dissociated from the person and work of Christ is an impossibility. In fact, Jesus's own life and ministry provide a blueprint for our own movement of self-denial, cross-bearing, and following. We will explore how Jesus, in his threefold office as Prophet, Priest, and King, empowers our own threefold action. Having emptied himself, Christ the Prophet calls us to self-denial, endowing us with a new self; having carried his own cross, Christ the Priest calls

---

4. This basic idea of thriving in tensions is a very Lutheran one, and we, therefore, refer to Luther and Lutheran theologians throughout, in particular, Dietrich Bonhoeffer. "Living between time and eternity, between wrath and mercy, between culture and Christ, the true Lutheran finds life both tragic and joyful," writes H. Richard Niebuhr. "There is no solution of the dilemma this side of death." Niebuhr, *Christ and Culture*, 178.

5. I have borrowed the term "unfinished project" from Tim Meyers, who consistently refers to the disciple in this way in his regular chapel messages at Melbourne School of Theology/Eastern College.

6. Willard, *Renovation*, 25.

7. Ruppert speaks of a "Weite des Herzens." Ruppert, *Geistlich Kämpfen lernen*, 35. Unless otherwise indicated, translations are my own.

us to cross-bearing, giving us new life through his death; and having obeyed the Father perfectly, Christ the King now calls us to follow him, promising to us a whole new network of relationships. By giving heed to Jesus's call, radical disciples grow up and become "a chosen race, a royal priesthood, a holy nation" (1 Pet 2:9). At the end of the day, discipleship is about experiencing profound transformation (even flourishing as the book title suggests) through the Holy Spirit, right in the presence of various tensions. These tensions present themselves to the disciple from within (in the struggle of the new self against the old self with its distorted desires), from without (in the conflict between the new life in Christ against the adversary and the world and its various temptations), and even—most astonishingly—from God himself, but more on this later.[8] The disciple's connection with the Spirit in face of all these tensions, in fact, is what makes discipleship *radical* discipleship.

This radical—in the literal sense that it goes to the root of things—form of discipleship, however, is in crisis and this affects all three core aspects of Jesus's call. There is, first, a crisis of self-denial. Fluctuating between an online and an off-line self, a church self, and an office self (and various other potential selves), contemporary Westerners, and that includes Jesus's disciples today, struggle to arrive at solid identity formation. They constantly wonder whether there lies a stable, authentic self at the core of their being, but neither pastor nor counselor has managed to help them uncover it.[9] Yet how can those unfamiliar with themselves even begin to deny their self? Even to begin to thrive in the tension of self-denial, one first needs to have a firm grasp of the self that Jesus wants us to deny. We can only deny what we know. This sounds like a trivial insight, but it is an important requirement.

Secondly, we observe a crisis of cross-bearing. I struggle to remember hearing a sermon on Jesus's command to take up one's cross in the recent (or even distant) past. We risk ignoring this element of Jesus's call to discipleship. Yet suppression, psychoanalysts tell us, can have negative consequences for our mental health and wellbeing, and so we might as well rise to the challenge as we seek to translate Jesus's command into our own time and context. The call to cross-bearing, of course, creates a serious tension in us. Especially for us today, when pain is considered useless and detrimental; we do everything to eradicate it. It seems that even in the church, we have successfully eliminated any notions of suffering from our conversations. It remains to be seen whether every occasion of suffering counts as cross-bearing, and we will explore this in more detail at the appropriate place.

---

8. See Ford, *Self and Salvation*.

9. Many suffer today from what David Brooks calls a "telos crisis," having no clear vision, no defined purpose, no concrete goals, and no direction. Brooks, *Second Mountain*, 30.

Still, if suffering is pushed to the periphery of our conversation, there can be no fruitful dialogue on cross-bearing. To understand Jesus's call to take up our cross we need at least a basic understanding of a theology of suffering.

Thirdly, there is a crisis of following. The very idea of following evokes a certain resistance among contemporary disciples. Instead of following, our default desire is a preference to go ahead. We ourselves want to determine the direction of our lives and set the agenda even for our Christian walk of life. It is we who want to lead the way, and churches and ministries feed this desire by offering an endless array of leadership courses. I have yet to come across a "follow-ship" course, an offer that sounds far less attractive.[10] Yet the promise issued to those who truly listen to Jesus's call, discarding their felt need for self-determination and material gain, is one of lasting fulfillment as the great shepherd leads them to "green pastures" (Ps 23:2).

The plan for this book is straightforward: we will look at the radical call to discipleship through the prism of Jesus's threefold command found in the Synoptics: "If anyone would come after me, let him *deny himself*, and *take up his cross*, and *follow me*" (Matt 16:24; Mark 8:34; Luke 9:23).[11] These three aspects are not isolated from each other; rather, as François Bovon explains, they form the "three stages of discipleship."[12] We imagine then a cycle where disciples are continuously moving through the three stages. By denying themselves, they find their true self; by taking up their cross they find real life; and by following Christ, they find the great friend. As already mentioned, throughout this work, the person and work of Jesus Christ—in particular, his threefold office as Prophet, Priest, and King—define how we understand the nature of these calls and our mode of discipleship.[13] Before we turn to explore the threefold command to discipleship, it is advisable first to set the stage by examining the complexities of discipleship with a special focus on the discipline of embracing tensions.

---

10. I am grateful to Bruce Pass for raising this important point.

11. For a recent exploration of the theme of discipleship in the Synoptics, see Lészai, *Discipleship*.

12. Bovon talks about "drei Etappen der Jüngerschaft." Bovon, *Das Evangelium nach Lukas*, 481.

13. The notion of Jesus's threefold office (*munus triplex*), of course, is a distinctly Reformed motif that traditionally has been regarded with suspicion by many Lutheran theologians. See Berkhof, *Systematic Theology*, 356–57. However, through the work of Johann Gerhard, as Michael Welker suggests, it received a more favorable response in Lutheran theology and it is thus appropriate to use it here in our framework. Welker, *Quests for Freedom*, ch. 21.

EMBRACING TENSIONS

Jesus's radical call to discipleship obviously provokes tensions. The request to deny oneself and to take up one's cross is particularly hard to digest. It is appropriate, therefore, to deal first with the concrete nature of the tensions that disciples face as they seek to follow in Christ's footsteps. This chapter illustrates how the tendency to avoid and reduce tensions is part and parcel of our human nature. Its implications for our understanding of theology in general, and discipleship in particular, are serious. We look at some of the harmful effects this bias can have on our view of God, of Jesus Christ, and, of course, his cross and the costly grace that is offered to us there through the gospel.[14] This preliminary assessment puts us in a position where we not only recognize the tensions included in Jesus's rigorous call to discipleship, but also enjoy the promise of new life and flourishing that comes with it.

Then in section one of this book, we will offer a careful exploration of the condition of the self so that we will be in the position to distinguish what to affirm and what to deny in ourselves, and from that vantage point we will be able to embrace this tension through which we experience constant renewal of self and newness of life.

I. DENY YOURSELF

What does it mean to deny oneself? One is well advised to ask first: What is the self that we are to deny? This touches on the important questions of our identity and self-understanding as disciples of Jesus Christ. Drawing on insights from biblical theology and social psychology, we note that while we might have considered ourselves to be fairly consistent and decent human beings, psychological evidence suggests that we are rather inconsistent and self-centered. These are the key characteristics of what Scripture identifies as our old self. In contrast to this old self, disciples are promised the attire of a new self. Jesus Christ in his role as Prophet authenticates our new existence through his Spirit and radical disciples approach self-denial with relaxed seriousness as their union with Christ determines their new mode of existence. Embracing the tension of constant rejection of the old self and appropriation of the new self, they adopt a posture of quiet self-awareness. Turning their attention away from self and toward God and neighbor, they flourish in active deeds of love.

---

14. As Bonhoeffer famously put it, "Cheap grace is the mortal enemy of our church. Our struggle today is for costly grace." DBWE 4:43.

In the second part of this work, we will attempt to recover a positive theology of suffering where cross-bearing and flourishing are intimately connected.

II. TAKE UP YOUR CROSS

Like the call to self-denial, "Take up your cross" is provocative and counter-cultural, especially in our "safe space" age where we seek to protect ourselves and our loved ones from every potential risk and hazard. The tension that disciples learn to embrace at this stage is not to avoid difficulties and afflictions but to welcome them as occasions for spiritual growth and maturation. Our own cross-bearing, of course, is always preceded and empowered by Christ in his role as the great high priest, who suffered and gave himself up for us on the cross. As we embrace the ultimate tension by taking up our cross, we receive the Priest's loving action toward us, experience fulfillment amid suffering, and enjoy a new view of God and self. Radical disciples take up their cross when they completely surrender to Christ, and in so doing, are being transformed into the image of their Master through the Holy Spirit.

In the third and final part of this book, we explore how our positive response to Jesus's invitation to follow him leads us into tensions that transform us as we are being turned into friends of God who establish friendship among each other and befriend the world to the glory of God.

III. FOLLOW ME

This is the call that initiates our journey of discipleship, and yet, it is a call to which we listen again and again. "Follow me" touches on a network of relationships. To begin with, the disciple listens to the command of Jesus in his role as King and she follows as an individual. Following Christ is about our intimate fellowship with Jesus and requires a rediscovery of our capacity to listen to him. We hear the voice of the One who is not only King but also the great friend who turns us into friends ourselves. Once on the way of discipleship, they always follow in community, as the fellowship of friends. Jesus calls us individually but brings us together as a community of friends who love one another and also befriend the whole world. Finally, radical disciples in their new mode of existence have a new desire to seek the face of the One they are following. Contemplating the face of Christ, in his humiliation and exaltation, radical disciples experience deep personal transformation.

Of course, the definitive book on discipleship has already been written. Dietrich Bonhoeffer summarized his critique of what he considered a lack of radicality in contemporary Christianity in the book, *Nachfolge* (1937), which literally refers to the act of "following after" Jesus Christ.[15] The book was later translated into English and published as *The Cost of Discipleship* (1948), and it has become a classic resource in Christian theology and spirituality. I gladly echo here the comment of Swiss theologian Karl Barth, who adds to his own reflections on discipleship in his *Church Dogmatics*: "I cannot hope to say anything better on the subject than what is said here . . ." (namely, in Bonhoeffer's *Discipleship*).[16] With this present contribution, I do not seek to offer a theological exploration of Bonhoeffer's *Cost of Discipleship*—this has been done successfully elsewhere.[17] My aim, though, is to offer a fresh reading of Bonhoeffer as I invite other giants of the Protestant faith to the conversation, such as Martin Luther, Adolf Schlatter, and Karl Barth. Martin Stöhr pointed out that Bonhoeffer does not want to be celebrated but needs to be answered, and I seek to follow his suggestion.[18] Much of what I share, then, is inspired and informed by Bonhoeffer's work.[19] I side with Teresa of Avila, who writes in the prologue to her *Interior Castle*, "I'm, literally, just like the parrots that are taught to speak; they know no more than what they hear or are shown, and they often repeat it."[20]

An additional element of this contribution is my intention to invite neighboring disciplines to the table. Psychology is an ideal conversation partner, here. Especially in the field of self-exploration, psychology has a lot to offer, and I will establish connections wherever applicable. While I have written this book predominantly with my theology students in mind, I trust it will also find interested readers in the academy and equip practitioners in various fields of Christian ministry. Anyway, one wonders whether in theology distinctions between experts and novices are appropriate in the first place. I tend to side with Luther here who was convinced that every Christian was a theologian: "We are all called theologians, just as (also we are) all (called) Christians."[21]

---

15. For a brief summary of the various publications and translations of *Nachfolge*, see DBWE 4:29–30.

16. CD IV/2:533–34.

17. Bernd Liebendörfer presents an astute interpretation and application of Bonhoeffer's theology of discipleship for today. Liebendörfer, *Der Nachfolge-Gedanke*. See also Schmitz, *"Nachfolge."*

18. Stöhr, "Bonhoeffer Antworten."

19. My fascination with Bonhoeffer began in 1996 toward the end of my school days at German high school (*Gymnasium*), as I prepared for my oral exam on Bonhoeffer's life and theology, and Bonhoeffer has attracted me ever since.

20. Teresa of Avila, *Collected Works*, 281.

21. This is Bayer's rendering of Luther's dictum originally composed in Latin.

At the end of each chapter the book includes some practical questions for personal reflection. It is hoped that this will bring the content to life and encourage further, deeper reflection on Jesus's invitation to radical discipleship. Discipleship is radical discipleship when the disciple is firmly rooted in the life-giving activity of the spirit of Christ, equipped with a new desire to love God and neighbor. This book will have achieved its purpose when we experience, by the spirit of God, a "breakthrough of God's perfect love and the sight of God—even in this life," as Fidelis Ruppert put it.[22]

Bayer, *Martin Luther's Theology*, 18n8. Luther's full quote in the original goes like this: "Theologi, heisst ein iglicher Christ. Theologia: Gottes wort, Theologus: Gottes worter redet. Das sollen alle Christen sein. Omnes dicimur Theologi, ut omnes Christiani." WA 41:11.9–11.

22. Ruppert refers to "den Durchbruch der vollkommenen Gottesliebe und auf die Gottesschau—schon in diesem Leben." Ruppert, *Geistlich Kämpfen lernen*, 35–36.

1

Embracing Tensions

MOST OF US SHARE an aversion to serious mental effort. This is part and parcel of our fallen human nature. In his book, *Thinking, Fast and Slow*, psychologist Daniel Kahneman explores the reasons why we seem to avoid serious thinking. Why would we rather dodge difficulties and conundrums and simply choose the easiest options available? According to Kahneman, two systems operate in our minds. System one is fast and efficient, it "operates automatically and quickly, with little or no effort and no sense of voluntary control."[1] If asked "what does two plus two equal?" our system one immediately produces the answer "four." So far so good. System two, however, works much more slowly. It is more careful, and it therefore requires considerably more mental energy than system one. Since our organism prefers to save cognitive energy—and let us not forget that our brain consumes about twenty percent of our body's energy, more than any other organ[2]—our default mode goes something like this: "Let's use system one and see how we go." We all enjoy traveling on the avenue of least resistance. There is a catch though: while we might save precious mental energy, we will inevitably make mistakes. If I were to ask you, "How many animals of each kind did Moses take into the ark?" you would probably come up with a rough estimate after a few seconds.[3] When I ask my students this

---

1. Kahneman, *Thinking, Fast and Slow*, 20.
2. Swaminathan, "Why?"
3. For more on what is called the "Moses illusion," see Kahneman, *Thinking, Fast*

question in the classroom, they briefly discuss it amongst themselves and then usually suggest a concrete number. However, ever so often, there is one smart cookie present who interjects, "Wait a minute, it wasn't Moses who built the ark, it was Noah!" Well, of course, it was Noah (Gen 6:14); it was a trick question. But this just goes to show that our minds desperately want to choose the easiest route available. As soon as we hear animals and ark, the matter is settled for system one. Kahneman coined the acronym, WYSIATI to describe this phenomenon, "*What you see is all there is.*"[4] "[M]any people are overconfident, prone to place too much faith in their intuitions," he writes. "They apparently find cognitive effort at least mildly unpleasant and avoid it as much as possible."[5]

This has serious implications for our life and experience: we constantly produce errors. Most of the time we do it unintentionally. We simply cannot help ourselves but to make things appear less complicated and complex than they really are. "The sense-making machinery of System 1 makes us see the world as more tidy, simple, predictable, and coherent than it really is," writes Kahneman.[6] Here are some of the mistakes we make in our everyday life: when we meet someone for the first time and find that person attractive we will, thanks to system one, overestimate other aspects of their personality, such as their IQ for instance.[7] And after reading an article about poisonous spiders, I will, persuaded by system one, overestimate the probability of getting bitten while gardening.[8] The statistics, of course, tell a different story, but studying statistics would involve heavy system two work.[9] The list of errors we make in our judgments due to our preference for using quick system one solutions is long—any decent social psychology textbook will provide a good overview. For our purposes, we draw the important conclusion that there is a real chance that we might have relied on system one too much when it comes to important questions of discipleship as well. Too easily satisfied with what system one serves up, we might not have sufficiently explored the complexities of discipleship, and we are at risk of pursuing a trivial, at worst, cheap, form of discipleship. A number of church historians and theologians, in fact, support this conclusion.

---

and Slow, 73.

4. Kahneman, *Thinking, Fast and Slow*, 85–88.

5. Kahneman, *Thinking, Fast and Slow*, 45.

6. Kahneman, *Thinking, Fast and Slow*, 204.

7. See Nisbett and Wilson, "Halo Effect."

8. This refers to what psychologists call the "availability heuristic." See Kahneman and Tversky, "Availability." Cf. Schwarz et al., "Ease of Retrieval."

9. While it might be not as unlikely in Australia, where almost every animal is out to kill you, I still make a mental shortcut without actually considering the statistics.

THE SCANDAL OF TRIVIALIZATION

The call to discipleship is complex and challenging, and any attempts to reduce its complexity will result in a trivial understanding of discipleship. Writing in the early 1970s, John Stott lamented the growing "anti-intellectualism" he observed in the Protestant church at the time.[10] "Many have zeal without knowledge, enthusiasm without enlightenment," Stott writes. "In more modern jargon," he adds, "they are keen but clueless."[11] A couple of decades later, in the early 1990s, historian Mark A. Noll coined the phrase of the *Scandal of the Evangelical Mind*—also the title of his influential book.[12] According to Noll, at the heart of the scandal was that there was "not much of an evangelical mind."[13] Noll bemoaned North American evangelicals' lack of intellectual engagement with modern culture. Whereas the Protestant tradition always considered "diligent, rigorous mental activity . . . a way to glorify God"—think Luther, Calvin, and Edwards, for instance—"modern evangelicals have not pursued comprehensive thinking under God."[14] To say it with Kahneman, they have failed to engage system two when it comes to thinking rigorously about theological themes. Toward the end of the 1990s, J. P. Moreland published a work that sang a similar tune.[15] Evangelicals, Moreland argues in *Love Your God with All Your Mind*, have neglected the role of reason in their walk with God. "The contemporary Christian mind is starved," he writes, "and as a result we have small, impoverished souls."[16] With a nod to Noll, he underlines that "the 'scandal of the Evangelical mind' is a problem related to *discipleship*."[17] This is spot on. And here lies the most notable—and for our purposes most important—clue in Moreland's contribution: he establishes a direct relationship between attending to one's life of the mind and a healthy view of Christian discipleship.[18] Carl Trueman makes a similar point in his 2011 book, *The Real Scandal of the Evangelical Mind*. As the title suggests, Trueman claims that he has identified the *real* scandal of the evangelical mind.[19] In his view, the real scandal is that

10. Stott, *Your Mind Matters*, 9–10, 21–22.
11. Stott, *Your Mind Matters*, 9.
12. Noll, *Scandal*.
13. Noll, *Scandal*, 3.
14. Noll, *Scandal*, 4.
15. Moreland, *Love Your God*.
16. Moreland, *Love Your God*, 94.
17. Moreland, "About Love Your God" (emphasis added).
18. See, in particular, chapter 3, "The Mind's Role in Spiritual Transformation," in Moreland, *Love Your God*.
19. Trueman, *Real Scandal*.

"evangelicals don't lack a mind, but rather an agreed upon evangel. Although known as gospel people, evangelicals no longer share any consensus on the gospel's meaning."[20] If this is true, and I think Trueman is onto something, it has obvious ramifications for discipleship, for the first thing the disciple needs to understand and to embrace again, day after day, is the costly grace of the gospel.

These scholars all agree on the basic argument that an exclusive system one use leads to an avoidance of tensions and thus a merely partially grasped gospel. Yet half a gospel is no gospel at all. In his 1951 classic, *Christ and Culture*, H. Richard Niebuhr highlights the common paradoxical view (and his observations have not lost any of their relevance today), where gospel and law, Christ and world, are pitted against each other and disciples oscillate between two poles of antinomianism and cultural conservatism.[21]

On one side of the spectrum, the disciple is at risk of sliding into a cheap laissez-faire approach to discipleship where he lives blissfully unaware of God's law and the ways the gospel is supposed to change one's inner being.

However, on the other side of the spectrum, the disciple might feel the need to distance himself from the surrounding culture, trying to eke out an existence as a disciple hermit, unblemished from the profane. In this way, he might perhaps conserve the gospel, but it has no impact on the world anymore and is being rendered meaningless. In both cases, tensions have been successfully reduced, and yet what is left is an ineffective gospel and a caricature of a radical disciple. The disciple's surrounding culture is left unchanged, either through an uncritical assimilation of it or anxious separation from it. By avoiding tensions, in both cases, the disciple makes no impact on the world. The salt has no saltiness (Matt 5:13).

A careful system two use, of course, does not guarantee immunity from lopsided versions of the gospel and discipleship, but it gives at least basic protection, because only with system two involvement will we be able to acknowledge and embrace the tensions contained in the costly gospel through the Holy Spirit. If we fail to balance them carefully, we end up with cheap grace, cheap discipleship, and a distorted vision of God. Dietrich Bonhoeffer incessantly warned his fellow believers of a discipleship that was marked by "cheap grace."[22] The gospel might be simple, but it is not simplistic, and serious reflection is needed as we seek to discover it in all its rich facets.

20. Trueman, *Real Scandal*, back cover.
21. Niebuhr, *Christ and Culture*, 187.
22. As Bonhoeffer famously put it, "Cheap grace is the mortal enemy of our church. Our struggle today is for costly grace." DBWE 4:43. "A Christianity that no longer took discipleship seriously," he writes, "remade the gospel into only the solace of cheap grace." DBWE 4:86.

It seems that a lack of system two involvement is accompanied with a decline in our ability and willingness to tolerate tension and transcendence. When it comes to the Christian faith, satisfaction with quick system one results leads to a trivialization of religion.[23] It is the vital task of theology and the church today to communicate the costly gospel message with clarity and conviction and to prepare believers for costly discipleship. Costly, radical discipleship involves intellectual rigor, that is, willingness to engage in serious system two activity under the guidance of the Holy Spirit.

In which ways is the content of the call to discipleship reduced and trivialized today? This question merits further exploration. I suggest we focus on three key areas: a reduced view of God, and the person and the work of Jesus Christ, which lead to a distorted view of the gospel and discipleship. A clear grasp of the diagnosis is the first step toward recovering costly discipleship.

THE DOMESTICATION OF GOD

In our culture today one observes an increasing move toward a domestication of God.[24] "The transcendent, majestic, awesome God of Luther and Calvin . . . has undergone a softening of demeanor," bemoans Marsha Witten.[25] God might still be important, but he has certainly lost relevance, and with that, we have become ever more irreverent. The awe-inspiring LORD, whose name the Israelites feared to pronounce and in whose presence the prophets trembled and stumbled, has been substituted with a rather nice assistant who helps us toward improving our lives. God is here to help us become more successful, popular, healthy, and rich. Marva Dawn notes,

> The God we have manufactured in our minds is small enough for us to contain Him, to be comfortable with Him. But then we have not understood God's character. If we really let God be GOD, the Sovereign Lord of the cosmos, He will be too vast and mysterious for us ever to be comfortable.[26]

Investigating the spirituality of North American teenagers in the early 2000s, Christian Smith and Melinda Lundquist Denton coined the expression "moralistic therapeutic deism" when it comes to millennials' view of God.[27] The term refers to a God who is available when we need him,

23. Welker, "Selbst-Säkularisierung."
24. See Placher, *Domestication of Transcendence*.
25. Witten, *All Is Forgiven*, 53.
26. Dawn, *Being Well*, 84.
27. Smith and Denton, *Soul Searching*, 162.

but who does not require anything of us.[28] Theirs is the image of God as "a combination Divine Butler and Cosmic Therapist: he is always on call, takes care of any problems that arise, professionally helps his people to feel better about themselves, and does not become too personally involved in the process."[29] Like a helicopter parent, God is expected to wrap us in cotton wool and to protect us from every harm.[30] According to this sanitized caricature, God is convenient, but he is certainly not the God invested with authority to call us into radical discipleship. The Almighty Father has been reduced to a heavenly "nurturing and supportive daddy," as Marsha Witten put it.[31] In the Australian context, Robert Gallagher suggested to "contextualize the gospel" on the continent by comparing the theology of covenant with Australian mateship. "Me and Christ, we'd be mates!" is his slogan, characteristically reflecting an egalitarian motif in Australian thinking where the tendency is to cut down every tall poppy.[32] While this is certainly a creative approach, one clearly recognizes the risk that well-meant contextualization could end up in a limitation of one's view of God. Of course, once God has been emptied of his transcendence, all that is left is his immanence. Contemporary Christianity in the West is being plagued by a lopsided view of God. And lopsided views, as we have seen earlier, are usually the result of a system one that is too quick on the trigger. Thinking about God, though, requires heavy system two involvement, and this means investing mental energy. Radical disciples are called to hold in balance apparent contradictions about God and his perfections.

Regarding the Trinity, swift system one use can easily lead us astray, and errors made here—at the very heart of our Christian faith—can have particularly damaging effects. Holding in balance the distinctness of the divine persons and the unity of the Godhead is challenging. Yet when this fine balance is lost, believers risk swerving toward extremes, overemphasizing one over the other. This has happened time and again in theological history and echoes of it surface powerfully today. Some have placed personhood over unity in the Godhead. Taken too far, this can lead to tritheism, the view that there are three gods, many forms of which have been declared heretical by the church. Others have overemphasized the oneness of God at the expense of the persons' discreteness. This is referred to as modalism,

---

28. Smith and Denton, *Soul Searching*, 163.

29. Smith and Denton, *Soul Searching*, 165.

30. I am borrowing the term "cotton wool generation" from Bastian, *Other Side of Happiness*, 23.

31. Witten, *All Is Forgiven*, 53. James Barr reminded us decades ago that *Abba* isn't to be confused with "daddy." Barr, "Abba Isn't 'Daddy.'"

32. Gallagher, "Me and God," 130.

the assumption that the one God appears in the different modes of Father, Son, and Holy Spirit. Again, various forms of this heresy have flourished throughout the centuries.³³ These distortions, though, are not just old hats; they are alive and well in many vibrant churches today. Here is the all-time favorite sermon illustration of the Trinity: the Trinity is like the three different states of water—solid (ice), liquid (water), and gas (steam). It sounds plausible, yet tragically, one has just committed the modalist error (where the one God simply appears in various modes). Or, others have suggested that God is like the three leaves of the shamrock: each clover represents one person of the Trinity. A great deal of Western Trinitarian reflection drew and continues to draw on these kinds of triads, and these metaphors are certainly helpful to some degree.³⁴ Yet they become problematic when they obscure the personal relations and thus do not adequately account for God's oneness—at worst, we are right down the slippery slope of tritheism. Undoubtedly it is seriously mind-boggling to conceive of one God who is also three. Yet instead of irresponsibly reducing the complexity, radical disciples relish the mystery. They embrace the tension and accept that there are boundaries set by God that their intellect will not transcend.

Another tendency is to reduce the mystery of the Trinity by a social approach. In this case, the theologian infers that the mutual indwelling of the members of the Godhead (*perichoresis*) is analogous to the government of human relationships (in church and society).³⁵ At first glance, it seems not only that the mystery is solved but that it is even applicable to our own life. It almost sounds too good to be true. Yet on closer inspection, Karen Kilby contends, as promising as these attempts sound, we here project our own ideas onto the Trinity and back. Instead, she argues for a careful and yet confident approach, that is, "affirming a doctrine of the Trinity does not depend on being able to answer it, nor does establishing the relevance of the doctrine depend on finding the 'right' answer to it."³⁶ When we have exhausted our system two attempts, it is advisable to refrain from further speculation and to begin worshipping this mysterious God. After rigorous study, there always comes the point when Philipp Melanchthon's recommendation applies: "We ought to worship the mysteries of the Godhead instead of studying them."³⁷

33. Wilhite, *According to Heretics*, 87–104.
34. On this see the important study by Soulen, *Divine Name(s)*.
35. See, for instance, Volf, *After Our Likeness*.
36. Kilby, "Perichoresis and Projection," 444.
37. "Die Geheimnisse der Gottheit [aber] sollten wir lieber anbeten als sie zu erforschen." "*Mysteria divinitatis rectius adoraverimus quam vestigaverimus.*" Melanchthon, *Loci Communes*, 19.

Serious system two thinking processes, therefore, quite naturally usher into worship. "In the ancient Church," Michael Casey writes, "catechetical instruction was supplemented by mystagogy (*mystagogia*—a leading into the mysteries)."[38] As they carefully think about God, disciples are confronted with mystery and assume a posture of reverence.[39] It is for this reason that the important word "worship" made its way into the Athanasian Creed: "And the Catholic Faith is this: That we *worship* one God in Trinity."[40] Of course, in order to worship the one God, we need to know something about him.[41]

Talking and thinking about God, then, leads us not necessarily into solutions, but even deeper into the mystery of God. "While a problem can be solved, a mystery is inexhaustible," writes Daniel Migliore. "A problem can be held at arm's length; a mystery encompasses us and will not let us keep a safe distance."[42] Reverential thinking about God will leave us with a tension—that is to be expected, though, when dealing with mysteries. And surely this can be a little unsettling at times.[43] But we will always be dealing with a "strange God" who makes us feel uncomfortable, as Michael Horton writes:

> The God of the Bible is a strange God—not the kind of God we can manage, manipulate, accommodate, or domesticate to our familiar experience. We cannot find this God by looking within ourselves. His Word is not the same as our inner voice. He cannot be pared down to our size, measured by our speculations, experiences, or felt needs. Rather, he stands over against us, telling us how things actually are . . . God confronts us, disorients us, and pulls us outside of our comfort zones.[44]

This is the God who calls us into radical discipleship. We are reminded of how C. S. Lewis describes this feeling of encountering the mysterious God in *Prince Caspian* from the Narnia series. Upon reuniting with the great lion, Aslan (the Jesus figure in the story), Lucy exclaims, "Aslan, you're

---

38. Casey, *Sacred Reading*, 18.

39. As Casey said, it "is the sobriety of spirit that stems from an experience of the otherness of God which makes us want to subdue self, remain silent, and to submit." Casey, *Sacred Reading*, 26.

40. Schaff, *Greek and Latin*, 66 (emphasis added).

41. Genuine worship, then, happens when the church provides a context where, as Marva Dawn puts it, "meaningful talking, attentive listening, and profound thinking" can take place. Dawn, *Reaching Out*, 13.

42. Migliore, *Faith Seeking Understanding*, 3.

43. "Theologians do not have all the answers, as every good theologian knows," writes Lucy Peppiatt. "All Christians everywhere need to be prepared to be surprised and unsettled by God." Peppiatt, *Disciple*, xv.

44. Horton, *Gospel-Driven Life*, 23.

bigger." "That is because you are older, little one," Aslan responds, "... every year you grow, you will find me bigger."[45] Radical disciples thus embrace the tension of encountering the God who comes so intimately close and is yet so "wholly other,"[46] constantly expanding in their view. God is the God who is utterly different from us, completely other than we are and over and beyond us. "Great is our Lord, and abundant in power; his understanding is beyond measure," exclaims the psalmist (Ps 147:5). Yet, on the other hand, he is so astonishingly close to us, even residing within us through his Spirit (1 Cor 3:16). Disciples who are prepared to follow their Master will grow incrementally in their knowledge of him; they will continually be surprised and at times even be unsettled. Jesus's disciples are, as the apostle Paul put it, "stewards of the mysteries of God" (1 Cor 4:1). Quick system one use might show us only fake or incomplete mysteries. True mysteries, however, are revealed to disciple stewards, who intentionally employ their system two, by carefully studying the Scriptures and prayerfully meditating on the truths revealed in them.

JESUS CHRIST REDUX

Secondly, we observe various attempts today to reduce the complexities of the person and work of Jesus Christ. Hasty system one attempts at solving christological paradoxes have serious implications for discipleship.[47] At worst, they may lead to the christological discipleship dilemma in the sense that the person we are following might not be divine anymore but reduced to an inspired human example. So, we wrestle, together with Bonhoeffer, with the question, "[W]ho is Christ actually for us today?"[48] Radical disciples need to know who it is that calls them to self-denial, to cross-bearing, and to follow-ship.

First and foremost, faithful disciples keep the balance between Jesus's humanity and divinity. This presented a challenge to the church from the very beginning, and it is a challenge for disciples even today. Jewish believers at the time of Jesus were brought up reciting the doctrine that there was only one God: "Hear, O Israel: The LORD our God, the LORD is one" (Deut

---

45. Lewis, *Prince Caspian*, 133.

46. Swiss theologians Adolf Schlatter and Karl Barth reminded us of the God who is "wholly other." See Schlatter, "Der Wert," 263. Barth, *Der Römerbrief*, 47, 59, 66, 76, 223, 435, 498, 522.

47. Bonhoeffer writes, "Christianity without the living Jesus Christ remains necessarily a Christianity without discipleship; and a Christianity without discipleship is always a Christianity without Jesus Christ." DBWE 4:59.

48. Bonhoeffer to Bethge, April 30, 1944, DBWE 8:362.

6:4). Yet since Jesus claimed to be one with God, they had to make room for the news that Jesus Christ was also divine (while avoiding the tritheistic heresy that holds that Jesus was an additional god).[49] Believers from the Greco-Roman background faced the challenge that here was someone who claimed to be God but became human in the incarnation. To them this did not sound attractive at all—from their point of view a god never aspired to become human, only the other way round would make sense.[50] The goal of the philosophy in which they were raised was to get rid of the body and achieve something like a divine status by becoming pure spirit.[51] Both groups were required to endure and even embrace the tension that Jesus Christ was both, truly God and truly human: like the Father in his deity and like us in his humanness. The majority of the Christian church finally agreed on this statement and it was firmly expressed in the Chalcedonian Creed (451).[52]

Orthodox statements of faith such as this are the result of the early church's dealings with attempts to reduce christological tensions. Some movements either overemphasized Jesus's divinity at the expense of his humanity (as in Docetism and Gnosticism),[53] or conversely, they considered Jesus to be a very influential human who lacked divine status (Arianism).[54] Remnants of these distorted Christologies are alive and well today. An example of the former, the docetic distortion, is a prevalent view among many believers today; neglecting Jesus's humanity they seek to be freed from the body and aspire a higher, spiritual existence. "For some," writes Stephen Wellum, "heaven is a place where disembodied spirits enjoy eternal bliss on far-off shores removed from any kind of existence on earth."[55] Yet they leave behind the incarnate Jesus Christ, who lived a perfect human life in our place and who rose triumphantly from the dead with a resurrected body that is the blueprint for the disciple's own "spiritual body" (1 Cor 15:44). For Bonhoeffer, a notable disregard of Jesus's humanity proved detrimental to discipleship in his own time and age and throughout this work we highlight his attempts at correcting this imbalance. The latter, the Arian view, on the

49. Bauckham, *Jesus*, 1–17. See also Hurtado, *One God*; *How on Earth*.

50. On Greco-Roman responses to the exclusive worship of Christ among early believers, see Bauckham, *Jesus*, 139–46.

51. For some Gnostic views on the human body, see Brakke, *Gnostics*, 65–69.

52. Jesus Christ is "truly God and truly man, of a reasonable [rational] soul and body; consubstantial [co-essential] with the Father according to the Godhead, and consubstantial with us according to the Manhood." Schaff, *Greek and Latin*, 62.

53. For a helpful introduction to Docetism, see Wahlde, *Gnosticism*, 62–65.

54. For an introduction to Arianism, see Bray, *God Has Spoken*, 232–72.

55. Wellum, "Heaven," 83.

other hand, is probably more widespread today and manifests itself in various forms. Almost seventy years ago, William Spurrier described three categories of contemporary Arianism, and they are still around today, namely: the view that Jesus was merely a courageous martyr willing to die for his convictions; the view that considers Jesus to have been an archetypical example for his followers to imitate; and connected with that, the view that considers Jesus as no more than an influential religious and moral teacher.[56]

Arianism emerges from the shadow of the past again, gaining influence and prominence in many churches today.[57] Jesus is here portrayed as a helpful (moral) human teacher and an example we ought to emulate.[58] I still remember the days as a young student when the "What Would Jesus Do?" bracelets appeared on everyone's wrists, and they still seem to be around today. Of course, it is a helpful question to ask from time to time, no doubt. And yes, Jesus *is* our example whom we ought to imitate (more on this in chapter 8). But if this is all we ask, and if this is all Jesus is to us, then we are at risk of following an Arian Jesus who is simply there to give us some helpful counsel and direction. Clearly, Jesus is *more* than a (human) moral example and teacher: he is the divine Son of God, vested with authority to call us into radical discipleship, and even more, to empower radical discipleship.

It all went doctrinally downhill when Protestant theologians followed in the wake of the (post) Enlightenment philosophers, primarily Baruch Spinoza, René Descartes, Immanuel Kant, and Georg W. F. Hegel. What they had in common was a distinct focus on the individual subject who had to make up her own mind and use her own reason—*Sapere aude!* (Dare to know!)—was Kant's famous slogan.[59] This shift clearly had an impact on theology, and it rose to the surface, especially in the nineteenth century. This was a time of scientific breakthroughs, discoveries of new territories, economic success, and industrial progress. In a climate where everything counted only when it was observable, quantifiable and, supposedly, empirically verifiable (or at least replicable), theologians at the university struggled as they dealt with what were considered murky topics of revelation. Since humans had emancipated themselves by their use of reason, so it was thought, there was no need anymore for divine revelation.[60] Nineteenth-century theologians, such as Albrecht Ritschl and Wilhelm Herrmann,

---

56. Spurrier, *Christian Faith*, 115–18.

57. As noted by DeVine, *Shalom*, 16.

58. Michael Horton speaks of "an Arian reduction of Christ to a moral example." Horton, *Christian Faith*, 481.

59. Kant, "Beantwortung der Frage," 481.

60. On the background, see Wilson, *Introduction*; McGrath, *Modern German Christology*.

for instance, were desperately trying to make room for faith in a context where only hard facts counted.[61] How does one talk now about the divinity of Christ, of his incarnation or resurrection? That was the challenge that presented itself to theologians at that time. Seeking to carve out a niche in this precarious environment, they increasingly tended to focus more on tangible notions, such as Jesus's moral teachings, and allocate supernatural questions, such as Jesus's divinity and our experience of him, to our private sphere of faith.[62] New Testament scholar Rudolf Bultmann, in a lecture delivered in 1941 on "New Testament and Mythology," captured the sentiment of a worldview where industrial progress is pictured in competition with the traditional, biblical view: "One cannot use electric light and radio, use modern medical and clinical resources in cases of illness, and at the same time believe in the world of spirits and miracles of the New Testament."[63]

Theologians thus moved away from what they considered fruitless discussions about Jesus's divinity and now focused almost exclusively on his humanity instead. The human side of Jesus was considered much more practical and applicable. Again, they did so not because they thought Jesus was not divine, but because they felt that in the cultural climate during that time one could not discuss ideas about Jesus's divinity, his incarnation or resurrection, topics that were beyond the theologian's reach.[64] This tendency ultimately gave way to a divided Jesus Christ. Scholars argued that while one can certainly investigate the historical figure of Jesus, his language and background, for instance, the Christ of faith, however, remains accessible to us only in the world of faith; and this world is not the world of the academy but restricted to our own closet where we shut the door behind us and pray to our Father in heaven (Matt 6:6). Here was the historical Jesus of the academy, and there the Christ of faith of the church.[65] While he might be

---

61. I have dealt with this in more detail elsewhere. See Bräutigam, *Union with Christ*, 61–73.

62. Newbigin, *Foolishness to the Greeks*, 48–49.

63. "Man kann nicht elektrisches Licht und Radioapparat benutzen, in Krankheitsfällen moderne medizinische und klinische Mittel in Anspruch nehmen und gleichzeitig an die Geister- und Wunderwelt des Neuen Testaments glauben." Bultmann, "Neues Testament," 18.

64. "Ritschl and his nineteenth-century contemporaries," writes Richmond, "did not understand Christ's deity in terms of *substance*, nor of *consubstantiality* with God, simply because such terms had become in post-Enlightenment Germany unintelligible, not to say meaningless." Richmond, *Ritschl*, 172 (emphasis original).

65. The consequences are still palpable today, as Christoph Schwöbel argues. "Modern Christology seems to be increasingly unable to conceive and to conceptualize the unity of the person of Christ and seems to be left with the fragments of the 'historical Jesus,' the 'Christ of faith' and the 'Son of God' of christological Dogma.

still relevant in his role as a Prophet, by educating us in moral principles, his roles as Priest and as King were now obscured since redemption from sin was questioned and his authoritative call into follow-ship was weakened. According to this line of thought, what matters more is what *we* think about Jesus and perhaps not so much about what *he* thinks of us and demands of us.⁶⁶ Yet this lopsided version of Christ is not one that could call us authoritatively into radical discipleship. Caricatures of Jesus Christ are rampant though, and closely connected to the caricature of a simply human Jesus is the one of an emptied Jesus Christ.

Today we still feel the aftershock of modern attempts that try to account for the self-emptying of the Son of God. The question revolves around the following conundrum: What did St. Paul mean when he wrote to the Philippians that Jesus Christ "emptied himself" (Phil 2:7)? The Greek word here for "emptied" is *ekenosen*, and theologians, therefore, speak of kenotic Christology in this context.⁶⁷ Over the last years, I have witnessed with growing unease rather crude views regarding *kenosis* in church services and even academic settings.⁶⁸ In his incarnation, so goes the common reductionist teaching, the Son of God laid aside his divinity and performed miracles as a mere human being through the power of the Holy Spirit. At his resurrection or ascension, he again took on his divine attributes in full. According to a quick system one judgment, it seems that the christological conundrum has been solved. And there is also the temptation that one could now conclude, "Look, if Jesus performed so many miracles as a mere

---

Therefore modern christological reflection seems mainly concerned with finding ways of integrating the fragments in a new synthesis, of joining together what has been put asunder." Schwöbel, "Christology and Trinitarian Thought," 119.

66. Jesus was still unique to Ritschl, to whom we do not intend to do any injustice at all. The person of Christ was still the focal point of where he believed God made himself known. However, Jesus's uniqueness was no longer grounded in the special tension of humanity and divinity according to orthodox teaching. Now it was about how Jesus fulfilled his extraordinary role given to him by the Father. Ritschl, *Christian Doctrine*, 589. "His vocation, however," writes Ritschl, "is unique in its kind; for its special character is directed to the general moral task [*allgemeine sittliche Aufgabe*] as such, in other words to the founding of the Kingdom of God and the community destined for this task . . . Therefore nobody can directly imitate Him; and an imitation which selects particular visible aspects of His life-course would still be no imitation of Christ." Ritschl, *Christian Doctrine*, 589 (emphasis mine). Other scholars followed in Ritschl's wake, most notably Wilhelm Herrmann and Adolf von Harnack, further developing and refining his ideas, but the general thrust remained the same. Weinhardt, *Wilhelm Herrmanns Stellung*.

67. We make, what Ritschl called, subjective value judgments about Jesus Christ. It is now about the worth the disciple attributes to Jesus Christ that is paramount. For an overview see Law, "Kenotic Christology"; Evans, *Exploring Kenotic Christology*.

68. Melbourne pastor Murray Campbell notices that too; see Campbell, "Did Jesus Empty Himself."

human, I could do the same—or even greater things, as Jesus himself had promised (John 14:12)."[69] There are considerable problems, however.

First, this idea is irreconcilable with key Scripture passages (as we will see in a minute), and it presents a considerable clash with the cornerstone of orthodoxy—namely, the Symbol of Chalcedon: Jesus was, is, and remains truly divine and truly human, neither his divinity nor humanity was diminished in his earthly life. Second, and this applies to kenotic theories in general, there are some misunderstandings as to what *emptying* actually means.

For Jesus to empty himself does *not* primarily refer to what he let go of, such as some or all of his divine attributes. Rather, it is more about what he took on and assumed that impoverished and emptied him: namely, assuming humanity in its fullness and adopting the low status of a slave and servant of God.[70] "The pouring out or emptying," writes Richard Bauckham, "is the self-renunciation in service and obedience, which begins with incarnation and leads inexorably to death."[71] The passage in Philippians is therefore to be interpreted "as his voluntary descent from the highest status, 'equality with God,' to the lowest, that of a slave, giving up all his rights and privileges in order to serve," Markus Bockmuehl notes.[72] If God decides to clothe himself in humanity, it means addition of limitation, and thus humiliation—although, paradoxically, this very step into humiliation is simultaneously glorious (more on this later in chapter 10). In other words,

---

69. One of the most popular contemporary teachers of this idea is Bill Johnson of Bethel Church, who has consistently through his works claimed that Jesus "*performed miracles, wonders and, signs*, as a man in right relationship to God . . . not as God. If He performed miracles because He was God, then they would be unattainable for us. But if He did them as a man, I am responsible to pursue His lifestyle." Johnson, *When Heaven Invades Earth*, 29 (emphasis original). Later in the book, he asserts that Jesus "laid his divinity aside as He sought to fulfil the assignments given to Him by the Father." Johnson, *When Heaven Invades Earth*, 79. Based on this premise, he writes elsewhere, "When I realize that He [Jesus] did what He did as a man yielded to God, then I am compelled to follow, discovering that is my real assignment!" Johnson, *Experience the Impossible*, 37.

70. "This interpretation," Markus Bockmuehl writes, "once popular in the so-called 'kenotic' Christology of the late nineteenth and early twentieth centuries, is now on the whole discredited. It presumes a literalistic reading of Christ's 'self-emptying' and fails to recognize that the 'emptying' is in fact explicated by the participles of 'taking' and 'becoming,' rather than by cancelling who and what he was, viz. 'in the form of God' and 'equal to God.'" Bockmuehl, *Philippians*, 134. See also Adolf Schlatter's interpretation of *kenosis* along these lines, in Bräutigam, *Union with Christ*, 139–41.

71. Bauckham, *Jesus*, 44.

72. Bockmuehl, *Philippians*, 136.

while in his incarnation the Son of God intentionally limits himself, it never involved the loss of divinity.[73]

Radical discipleship is about following a divine person who became (and remained) incarnate. The consequences, of course, are perplexing. The idea that baby Jesus could uphold "the universe by the word of his power" (Heb 1:3) is difficult to comprehend, not to say utterly puzzling.[74] Paul's phrase, "And he is before all things, and in him all things hold together" (Col 1:17) applies to the whole range of Jesus's life, yesterday, today, and forever. In Jesus, "the whole fullness of deity dwells bodily" (Col 2:9). "I and the Father are one," says Jesus of himself (John 10:30). This is staggering, yet rather than trying to resolve the tension, disciples are called to embrace the wonder that in Jesus Christ, God's transcendence and immanence meet in the most harmonious (yet mysterious) way. God, unfathomably great in wisdom and power, comes near to us and even becomes like us in the person of Jesus Christ, the great Immanuel, God with us: "And the Word became flesh and dwelt among us" (John 1:14). There lies the fragile and vulnerable baby in the manger, and then he suffers at our hands and dies a cruel death on the cross for our sake. Having saved us for himself, he is now even living in his disciples through his Spirit (2 Cor 13:5). Rather than artificially reducing their view of Christ, radical disciples seek to broaden their ever-expanding vista of the glorious One whom they follow.

GOSPEL DISTORTIONS

One-sided views of the person of Jesus Christ obviously lead to distorted ideas about his work. Theologians usually consider Jesus's person and work to be harmoniously united. According to Adolf Schlatter, for instance, Jesus's person and work "penetrate each other completely."[75] If we lose the balance on one side, we will struggle on the other. Nothing less than the core of the gospel is at stake. This is where we touch on the uncomfortable doctrine of sin. Sin is not much talked about these days. Both in our theology and in our lives, laments Thomas McCall, "we commonly find ways to downplay, deny, or ignore the reality of sin."[76] I suspect it has to do with the

---

73. At the end of the day, we need to hold fast to the truth that whatever happened in the *kenosis*, there was "no change in God," as Bruce L. McCormack states. McCormack, "Kenoticism," 455–56.

74. Macleod, *Person of Christ*, 209–10.

75. Schlatter, *Der Glaube*, 232. "In Christ," notes Schlatter, "office and person are one; as the office is given to him by God so also is the person made by God." Schlatter, *Das christliche Dogma*, 332.

76. McCall, *God and Nature*, 21.

current tendencies toward the taming of God we mentioned earlier. When our view of God's transcendence, his holiness, anger, and wrath is clouded, it naturally leads to an attenuated view of sin. The lower our regard for the offended party, the easier it is to downplay our offense. God is so nice, surely he wants my "best life now."[77]

Yes, of course, God wants our "best life now," even more than that: life of eternal quality here and now that spills over into eternity. Yet this life we receive only in counterintuitive ways: namely, by dying to self, taking up the cross, and following the One through whose death we have life. Sin, originally considered a serious offense against a holy God, is now reduced to an inconvenience. "If 'people today' find the preaching and teaching of sin and the cross irrelevant," writes Michael Horton, "it is only because we, like Israel, have dulled their sense of God's holiness and righteousness."[78] Today sin is more likely to be found on dessert menus. "'Peanut Butter Binge' and 'Chocolate Challenge' are sinful; lying is not. The new measure of sin is caloric," sociologist James Davison Hunter argues.[79] When I try to type "sinner" into my mobile smartphone, it automatically corrects to "dinner"—that says it all.

A reduced understanding of sin raises some questions about the necessity of the atonement. Or, when our view of the divinity of Christ is clouded, as highlighted in the previous section on the reduced Christ, questions arise as to whether his death on the cross was really necessary. "Where God's wrath is no longer a problem," writes Michael Horton, "Christ's cross is no longer the solution."[80] Why then did Jesus have to die if all I did was to take a cookie from the jar? What is happening here? Why is the Father punishing his innocent Son? Is this not an overreaction, bordering on "cosmic child abuse"?[81] Was the cross just a big mistake, a colossal tragedy? This is not the place to offer a theological defense of the penal substitution model—it has been done successfully elsewhere.[82] Instead, I would like to

77. Osteen, *Your Best Life Now*.
78. Horton, *Gospel-Driven Life*, 51.
79. Quoted in Plantinga, *Not the Way*, x.
80. Horton, *Gospel-Driven Life*, 52.

81. This charge against the traditional penal substitution model was made by Brock, "Little Child," 52. She incorrectly uses the adjective "cosmic" to describe the "child abuse," which does not actually reflect her position on the matter, for it is God the Father, and not the cosmos, who is the alleged criminal. Elsewhere, the adjective is changed to "divine." See, for example, Carlson Brown and Parker, "God So Loved," 2. Here, the authors suggest that Jesus's death on the cross is "divine child abuse paraded as salvific." For a response to this charge, see Macleod, *Christ Crucified*, 63–64.

82. Jeffery et al., *Pierced*; Gathercole, *Defending Substitution*.

drill down to the core of the problem. We meet again our usual suspect, the old reluctance to use system two, to think hard, and to embrace tensions and complexities. Of course, we are faced with a massive cognitive dissonance as we look at the cross and wonder, "Really? Is *this* what my sin required? Am I *that* bad?" And, "Really? God loves me *this much* that he would give his only Son to save me from his wrath? Am I at the same time that sinful and that immensely loved?" The answer the Scriptures offer us again and again is a firm: yes, yes, and yes! It leaves us with a tension, but it is an attractive tension. Once we begin to embrace this magnificent truth, we have made a substantial step toward understanding the nature of costly grace, and, with that, our journey as radical disciples has begun.

This is the heart of the costly gospel, the "mystery of Christ," as Paul called it (Eph 2:4): Christ has atoned for our sin and thereby removed the barrier that stood between us and God. God has truly forgiven us, restored us, and has reconciled us to himself through his Son Jesus Christ. He has begun the project of renewal within us through his Holy Spirit to conform us into the image of his Son. In all of this, we have neither contributed in any way nor have we made amends for our sins; we are always on the receiving end, and we will always remain entirely undeserving. Radical disciples master the art of embracing the tension when the New Testament gospel message continues to surprise them again and again—when they are overwhelmed by grace and the beauty of this counterintuitive gospel.

It is easy to imagine how one-sided approaches toward understanding this costly grace can result in contortions of discipleship. Some disciples might have first enjoyed the sweet taste of grace but then assumed that they would have to continue the good work that God has begun in them in their own strength—loosely based on the view that as long as we do our best, God will do the rest.[83] "God helps those who help themselves" is the age-old heresy that still blinds the mind even of believers. Having lost sight of the good news that God moves in them "both to will and to work for his good pleasure" (Phil 2:13), they are worn out and consider throwing in the towel. They clearly meant well, but their constant focus on the question, "What would Jesus do?" has clouded their view of what Jesus has already done for them and is accomplishing in and through them in their own life.[84] Crushed

---

83. On this see McGrath, *Iustitia Dei*, 83–90.

84. This is the point that Michael Horton makes in *Christless Christianity*. Horton writes: "The effects of confusing law and gospel in *content* has wide-ranging effects in church *practice* as well. If the message is *deeds, not creeds*, focusing on 'What would Jesus do?' while assuming that everybody already knows what Jesus has done (and is doing and will do), it only stands to reason that the flow of gifts from Christ to us will be reversed in the way we live out our personal and corporate life as God's people." Horton,

with a burden too heavy to bear, they feel like failures and are either fading out or dropping out. A balanced view of Christian discipleship, therefore, requires a recovery of the gospel and the dynamic nature of God's work in us through his Spirit. It is all about growing in our relationship with Jesus Christ through his Spirit.

Encountering Christ is a life-changing event in the disciple's life. "Christian discipleship," writes Lucy Peppiatt, "is not about a set of rules and propositions, but is about *being captivated by a person*."[85] Jesus is the "unknown plane" (*unbekannte Ebene*), as Karl Barth put it, "that cuts vertically from above through the plane that is familiar to us."[86] As they fix their eyes on Jesus, the author and perfecter of their faith (Heb 12:2), radical disciples are ready to embrace the tensions they meet on their journey of discipleship. It means living and even thriving in what Dietrich Bonhoeffer called the "this-worldliness of life" (*Diesseitigkeit des Lebens*).[87] In a letter written from his Berlin-Tegel prison cell to his friend Eberhard Bethge, Bonhoeffer explains his own approach toward embracing the tension of discipleship (writing a day after the failed attempt to assassinate Adolf Hitler):

> Later on I discovered, and am still discovering to this day, that one only learns to have faith by living in the full this-worldliness of life [*in der vollen Diesseitigkeit des Lebens*]. If one has completely renounced making something of oneself—whether it be a saint or a converted sinner or a church leader (a so-called priestly figure!), a just or an unjust person, a sick or a healthy person—then one throws oneself completely into the arms of God, and this is what I call this-worldliness: living fully in the midst of life's tasks, questions, successes and failures, experiences, and perplexities—then one takes seriously no longer one's own sufferings but rather the suffering of God in the world. Then one stays awake with Christ in Gethsemane. And I think this is faith; this is μετάνοια. And this is how one becomes a human being, a Christian (cf. Jer 45).[88]

Living in the this-worldliness of life is the mark of radical disciples of Jesus Christ. This is where faith grows and our perception of the Master gains clarity with each step we take.

Christless Christianity, 250 (emphasis original).

85. Peppiatt, *Disciple*, xiv (emphasis original).

86. "Jesus als der Christus ist die uns unbekannte Ebene, die die uns bekannte senkrecht von oben durchschneidet." Barth, *Der Römerbrief (Zweite Fassung, 1922)*, 51.

87. DBWE 8:486. For a recent argument for the lasting relevance of Bonhoeffer's idea of this-worldliness for church and society today, see Welker, "Tambacher Vortrag."

88. Bonhoeffer to Bethge, July 21, 1944. DBWE 8:486 [DBW 8:542].

CONCLUSION

Our journey of discipleship begins by getting a clear picture of who it is who calls us into discipleship. As we have seen in this first chapter, though, getting a comprehensive picture is easier said than done, since our default tendency as human beings is to avoid strenuous thinking. Yet thinking carefully about God the Father, Jesus Christ, and the gospel is a vital prerequisite for our understanding of radical discipleship. Quick system one judgments only lead to distorted views. At worst, God is tamed, Jesus Christ is reduced to a human teacher, and the gospel is trivialized by being turned into cheap grace. Radical disciples are challenged to engage in serious system two activity as they approach God's transcendence, the person and work of the divine-human Jesus Christ, and the magnificent gospel with openness and a sense of awe. They are invited to embrace a complex vision of God, of Jesus, and of the gospel that moves them into worship and reverence. When Jesus calls his first disciples, he repeatedly invites them with the words, "Come and see" (John 1:46, 39). Yet what they are supposed to see is not immediately visible to their physical eyes. On the contrary, they are promised a rather strange sight: "Truly, truly, I say to you, you will see heaven opened, and the angels of God ascending and descending on the Son of Man" (John 1:51). This is certainly a vista that requires serious system two involvement as one is required to make the connection with the ladder that appeared in Jacob's dream (Gen 28:10–15).

Of course, cognitive effort does not guarantee that we will fully understand the mystery of this christological ladder and the presence of the angels, but it may pave the way as we approach it in prayer and admiration. This, in fact, is the posture of the radical disciple: prayerful admiration. They are not hyperactive disciples who frantically seek to emulate a merely human teacher; nor are they deluded as they hope they can be little Christs, performing miracles and wonders wherever they go. No, theirs is an attitude of confident expectancy. Like the Bereans, they are open-minded, seriously searching the Scriptures (Acts 17:11), hoping to learn more about Jesus who is the Christ, who is God with a capital G. Jesus is not simply the Prophet who gives us helpful advice on our walk through life, but he is the incarnate Christ, who lived a perfect human life in our place, who is One with God and thus authoritatively calls us to deny ourselves, bear our crosses and let everything go and follow him alone. Having outlined some of the foundational challenges (and promises!) of Christian discipleship, we turn our attention in the next chapter to the first item of Jesus's call to discipleship: deny yourself.

PERSONAL REFLECTION

What forms of domesticating God, or reduced views of Jesus Christ or the gospel, do you observe in your own context? Think about a conversation you had recently in which you were talking about God. Can you detect any ways in which God was "domesticated"?

In your own view, which theological tensions have perhaps not received the attention that they deserve—in church, in the academy, and in your own spiritual life?

Where do you think a more intentional system two use could help you form a more adequate understanding of key theological themes, such as the doctrine of God, the person and work of Jesus Christ, and the gospel? How could a more rounded view of these themes also draw you near to God in worship and empower you in your walk with God?

What could be attractive about the idea of embracing tensions by faith as we follow Jesus Christ?

In which ways do you expect your faith to grow as you seek to live in what Bonhoeffer calls the "this-worldliness of life"? What could this look like for you, personally?

I
Deny Yourself

2

Understanding the Self

"This is a hard saying; who can listen to it?" (John 6:60). That is the response of the people who tuned in on Jesus's sermon in the synagogue of Capernaum. Indeed, the message was hard to digest, since Jesus expected his followers to feed on his flesh and drink his blood (John 6:53). Jesus was clearly not interested in attracting followers at any price.[1] Nothing less than costly discipleship is advertised here. Only the one who pursues *this* form of discipleship "will live" and Jesus will "raise him up on the last day" (John 6:54–57). "Deny yourself!" is the antipode of what every clever marketing strategist would suggest to anyone who seeks to attract a considerable following.[2] The audience wonders, "Why would I want to deny my self?" Does this not run counter to psychologists' and counselors' sound advice, namely, that we are to accept ourself and practice self-compassion?[3] Even Jesus's closest disciples seem somewhat skeptical as to whether they ought to continue with this experiment in discipleship. Sensing their reluctance, Jesus challenges them: "Do you want to go away as well?" (John 6:67).

---

1. His goal was not to gather "fans," as Kyle Idleman put it, but "completely committed" followers. Idleman, *Not a Fan*.

2. The call to self-denial is not made explicit in John 6; however, it is implicitly present in the way Jesus stipulates that discipleship depends entirely on divine initiative and any self-related ideas are excluded (John 6:65).

3. See, for instance Bernard, *Strength of Self-Acceptance*.

Jesus's call to self-denial is challenging and it requires serious system two use as we seek to figure out its meaning. It is a call that clashes with our innate desire for self-reliance, self-preservation, and self-actualization. In other words, it is the opposite of what we *want* to hear. Our ears itch for something else and we quickly tune in to far more attractive offers out there. A quick browse through my local Christian bookstore offers me far more alluring invitations as I note titles such as *Amazing You*, *Irreplaceable You*, *Perfectly You*, *Exceptional You*, or *Successfully You*.[4] Add to this list books designed to draw you in with the promise of self-development: *Become a Better You*, or *You Can, You Will*, or *You Can If You Think You Can*, or *You Can*, or *You Have It In You*.[5] Yes, that sounds more like it—this is music to our ears! I rather fancy books that promise to help me improve myself, find and develop my hidden potential, and discover God's blessings for myself. Definitely *not* on top of my shopping list—and thus not on the shelves—are books with rather unpleasant titles, such as *Ten Steps Toward Radical Self-Denial*. At the end of the day, Christian self-help books by and large shy away from approaching the tension that "deny yourself" inevitably creates. Yet it is exactly this tension that radical disciples seek to explore from all angles, and ultimately embrace. The disciple who investigates and practices self-denial is promised to find true, abundant life here and now, life that has purpose and meaning (Matt 16:25; John 10:10). The road toward finding this kind of life leads through the valley of self-denial. That is the only route available and there are no shortcuts. First of all, though, before we can even talk about self-denial, the more pressing question is this: What is our self anyway? Only with a refined self-understanding will we be in the position to determine what and which part to deny, and how we are to deny our self.

IDENTITY CONFUSION

We all struggle to come up with straightforward responses regarding the question of identity. Figuring out who we are is a perplexing task, especially in our digital age, where an online identity has been added to our off-line identity, and sometimes, one wonders whether the latter is overshadowed by the former. It is then not surprising that theologians and psychologists write about identity confusion, perhaps more so today than in previous decades. Whereas in the last centuries biographies were still more or less mapped out

---

4. Hanna, *Amazing You*; Olson, *Irreplaceable You*; Kai, *Perfectly You*; Osteen, *Exceptional You!*; Valentine, *Successfully You*.

5. Osteen, *Become a Better You*; *You Can, You Will*; Peale, *You Can*; Brady, *You Have It In You!*

and stable, today the development of careers and prospects is more fluid and complex. Our society is growing more diverse, social roles are becoming more multifaceted and we are moving with an accelerated pace. We used to own our landline telephone for ten or more years, but now our smartphone needs to be replaced every two to three years. Developmental psychologist Jochen Brandtstädter labels this phenomenon "cultural acceleration."[6]

Of course, I react with confusion when a major search engine today is suggesting personal memories for me, and a popular app is constantly asking me whether I am hungry (conveniently recommending the restaurant at the next corner). Rapid progress and immense changes in technology accompany a complex mix of novel trends and worldviews.[7]

Confusion prevails as a rich kaleidoscope of identity markers compete for our attention. Gender is nowadays considered to be fluid, and sexual orientation—surely one of the strongest identity markers today—is thought to be malleable. One also has the option to identify oneself based on diet (vegan, vegetarian, carnivore, etc.), cultural belonging, physical appearance, or environmental concern. We are exposed to an array of options to (re)invent ourselves.[8] There are even options for various forms of virtual identity. We truly live in the "age of the chameleon," as Eric Lippmann put it.[9] Modern pop culture mirrors this trend well. One thinks of Lady Gaga's regular changing personas, styles, and outfits—from her meat dress (yes, made of real raw flank steak) to that time she walked the streets of Paris dressed as a giant sea urchin.[10] Nowadays, as we live in what David Brooks calls the age of "I'm Free to Be Myself," we have to make our own informed choices in the jungle called opportunity, and yet we realize that this freedom comes with its own challenges.[11]

A constant felt need for reinvention and self-improvement adds to our stress levels and it is no wonder psychological unrest is the malaise of our times. I assume there is a correlation, perhaps even a causal connection,

---

6. See Brandtstädter and Lerner, *Action and Self-Development*, xiii.

7. Above all a growing postmodern relativism, where "[r]eality is fluid, changing, and always open," as David Wells put it. Wells, *Earthly Pow'rs*, 85. Regarding terminology, I share David F. Ford's confusion, "How do we describe the epoch we are now living in? Is it modern, late modern, 'chastened modern,' postmodern, 'a secular age,' post-secular, religious and secular, or none of these?" Ford, *Future*, 43.

8. Webber, "Reinvent Yourself."

9. Lippmann, *Identität*.

10. A creative versatility she has probably adopted from Madonna, the "queen of reinvention." Although I would rather leave this particular question open for debate amongst the specialists in pop culture and pop music. Sweeney, "Happy 60th."

11. Brooks, *Second Mountain*, 7.

between the prevailing unease regarding identity formation and rising stress and anxiety levels in the Western world (including the increasing abuse of tranquilizers and anti-depressants).[12] Ironically, in our search for a lasting, stable identity, we have become unstable and restless. In his book, *The World's Unrest* (*Die Unruhe der Welt*), German philosopher Ralf Konersmann, writes, "[It is] not this moment that counts, not the here and now, but only the next. This unrest does not know any results, but only loose ends, which are new beginnings, transitions, and connections."[13]

If unrest and identity confusion characterize the (post)modern person, the message of Jesus Christ offers stability and hope. For disciples of Christ are being promised peace. "Peace I leave with you; my peace I give to you. Not as the world gives do I give to you. Let not your hearts be troubled, neither let them be afraid" (John 14:27). Following Christ means an end to restless pursuits of identify formation as the Master speaks his shalom into the core of our being. Keeping this promise in mind, we move on with our diagnosis. Again, our task is to familiarize ourselves with our self so that we would be able to deny our self and in this way find true life. Having identified our underlying problem of identity confusion, we now dig a little deeper, trying to figure out the exact reasons for our confusion. In what follows, we explore our inherent problems of inconsistency and self-centeredness. The diagnosis might be unpleasant, yet admitting our flawed identity will open up for us the opportunity to receive the gift of a new identity in Christ that is marked by the divine shalom.

THE INCONSISTENT SELF

Generally, we do consider ourselves to be fairly consistent and coherent—although the previous section might perhaps have put a slight dent into our self-image already. Overall, though, we believe our views, attitudes, and values do not shift greatly but remain rather stable over time, various contexts, and situations. Plus, of course, we expect that our attitudes are usually matched by our actions. We expect ourselves to practice what we preach. Psychologist Prescott Lecky described this tendency as early as the 1940s

---

12. The Western world, in particular North America, is experiencing an opioid crisis of epidemic proportions. Every day, more than "130 people die after overdosing on prescription pain relievers, heroin, and synthetic opioids such as fentanyl." National Institutes of Health, "Opioid Overdose Crisis."

13. "[N]icht dieser Augenblick zählt, das Hier und Jetzt, sondern immer nur der nächste. Die Unruhe kennt keine Resultate, sondern nur lose Enden, die neue Anfänge, Übergänge und Anschlüsse sind." Konersmann, *Die Unruhe der Welt*, 9.

with his theory of "self-consistency,"[14] and, a decade later, Fritz Heider developed a model in which he showed that we all seek psychological balance.[15] This all sounds plausible since I want to make sense as a human being. I want to remain and act in a manner true to myself, as Shakespeare put it (through Polonius's mouth), in Hamlet.[16] Yet can I really be true to my self? We have all said it or heard it being said, "You are not being true to yourself." "Oh, right, I was acting out of character." But then again, what is my true self, or true character? A brief survey of biblical-theological, philosophical, and psychological evidence suggests that we are far less consistent than we might have assumed.

Some fellow pilgrim disciples were brave enough to venture into the abyss of our human self-understanding and reported frankly what they discovered. Already in the Old Testament the prophet Jeremiah confesses his perplexity when it comes to understanding the self: "The heart is deceitful above all things," he laments, "and desperately sick; who can understand it?" (Jer 17:9). St. Augustine exhibits, similarly, an astute sense for the intricacies of our self-knowledge.[17] "What then, am I, my God?" he prays in his *Confessions*, "What kind of being am I? A confusing and multifaceted life, frighteningly vast."[18]

Both the philosophers of the Enlightenment and the early psychoanalysts and psychologists have exposed our limited abilities to arrive at an adequate self-assessment.[19] Immanuel Kant, for instance, was quite skeptical here (but then again, he was skeptical about many things). "I have no knowledge of myself as I am," he writes, "but merely as I appear to myself."[20]

14. Lecky and Taylor, *Self-Consistency*.

15. Heider, *Psychology*.

16. "This above all—to thine own self be true,
And it must follow, as the night the day,
Thou canst not then be false to any man.
Farewell. My blessing season this in thee!"
Shakespeare, *Hamlet*, 22 (act 1, scene 3, lines 77–80).

17. For a recent evaluation of Augustine's view of the self from a Christian perspective, see Burns, "Augustine of Hippo." On Augustine's understanding of the self, see Otten, *Augustine our Contemporary*; Dixon, *Augustine*.

18. "Quid ergo sum, deus meus? Quae natura sum? Varia, multimoda vita et immensa vehementer." "Was also bin ich, mein Gott? Was bin ich für ein Wesen? Ein unübersichtliches und vielgestaltiges Leben, zum Erschrecken unermesslich!" Augustinus, *Confessiones*, 498–99 (*Confessiones*, 10.17.26).

19. In this section I have drawn on the following resources: Grenz, *Social God*, 58–97; Mummendey, *Psychologie des "Selbst"*, 25–36; Baressi and Martin, "History as Prologue."

20. Kant, *Pure Reason*, 113 (B158). "Da nun zur Erkenntnis unserer selbst außer der Handlung des Denkens, die das Mannigfaltige einer jeden möglichen Anschauung zur

We simply do not have access to the core of our identity, Kant argued. This skepticism was taken even further by his Scottish contemporary, the philosopher David Hume, who claimed in his *Treatise of Human Nature* that a "substantial, persisting self is an illusion."[21] Sigmund Freud, the father of psychoanalysis, came up with some creative insights regarding the human endeavor of self-exploration, and he offered a sophisticated explanation as to why we at times seem to act out of character. Freud highlighted the importance of the unconscious and exposed the significant influence of drives that motivate our behavior—often hovering under the radar of our conscious experience. In his view, there is a hidden force acting within us, called the "Id" (*Es*). We might think we are in charge, but actually, we are not, the "Id" is.[22] "I have no idea why I had that second portion of ice-cream, this is so out of character, I guess my 'Id' made me do it," goes our jaded psychological excuse for gluttony. Freud's speculations stimulated considerable research in subsequent generations of analysts and psychologists. Over the past few decades, there have been published a whole range of findings that shed more light on our own attempts at making sense of our self, which have only proved, again and again, its inconsistencies.

With her groundbreaking research, Hazel Markus paved the way in the 1980s for a renewed effort to explore the self from a social psychological perspective.[23] Rather than understanding our self as a stable and fixed entity, Markus and her colleagues suggested that our self is in fact quite fluid and flexible. They coined the term "dynamic self-concept" to describe how certain aspects of our self are accessed and activated in certain situations.[24] Put me in the lecture theater and I will wear my teacher's hat, and immediately, various aspects of my professional self will be activated. I will

---

Einheit der Apperzeption bringt, noch eine bestimmte Art der Anschauung, dadurch dieses Mannigfaltige gegeben wird, erforderlich ist, so ist zwar mein eigenes Dasein nicht Erscheinung (viel weniger bloßer Schein), aber die Bestimmung meines Daseins kann nur der Form des inneren Sinnes gemäß nach der besonderen Art, wie das Mannigfaltige, das ich verbinde, in der inneren Anschauung gegeben wird, geschehen, und ich habe also demnach keine Erkenntnis von mir wie ich bin, sondern bloß wie ich mir selbst erscheine." Kant, *Kritik*, 174b–76b.

21. This is how Barresi and Martin capture Hume's position. Baressi and Martin, "History as Prologue," 43.

22. "Das Ich nicht Herr sei in seinem eigenen Haus." Freud, *Schwierigkeit der Psychoanalyse*, 8.

23. I am grateful to my psychology professor, Sigrun-Heide Filipp, who introduced me to Markus's important work and, in general, self-concept research—much of what I am sharing here is inspired and informed by her lectures delivered at the University of Trier, Germany.

24. Markus and Wurf, "Dynamic Self-Concept"; Markus and Kunda, "Stability."

act and speak very differently, though, when playing table tennis with my friends. Here, aspects of my leisure self are in the limelight. We do seem to have a whole set of selves that are being activated in different situations and contexts. Researchers thus suggest that we have a "diffuse self," "public self," "private self," and "collective self."[25] "Identities," write Oyserman and Smith, "are not the fixed markers people assume them to be but are instead dynamically constructed in the moment."[26] In his book, *Selfie*, Will Storr puts it poignantly: "We have a self for work and a self for home, a self for lovely restaurants and a self for roadside diners; a self for Twitter and a self for Facebook; a self for the plumber and a self for the mayor; a morning self and an evening self."[27] These various selves also play an important role when it comes to motivating our actions. Markus and Nurius argued in this context for a whole set of possible selves.[28] "Possible selves," they write, "represent individuals' ideas of what they might become, what they would like to become, and what they are afraid of becoming, and thus provide a conceptual link between cognition and motivation."[29] So I could say: "I am now a lecturer, but I could also become a famous graffiti artist" (highly unlikely, though). Or, more realistically (and much more desirably): "I am at present a lukewarm disciple, but I could become a more committed follower of Christ."

Rather than having simply one steady and stable self, we might want to think of ourselves as possessing various selves that motivate our behavior and inspire our visions and goals. Of course, this presents a challenge, and we experience frustration when our selves are perceived to be incompatible with each other. Edward Tory Higgins developed what is now known as self-discrepancy theory. Higgins distinguished between an "actual self," an "ideal self," and an "ought self," which often operate in competition with each other.[30] Social media might be the platform where one advertises how one would like to be perceived, the ideal self, and yet the perceived contrast to the actual self might render the person frustrated and unhappy.[31] All too often, we seem to be occupied with curating our self rather than seeking the cure for our fragmented and fluid selves.

25. Breckler and Greenwald, "Motivational Facets."
26. Oyserman et al., "Self," 70.
27. Will Storr, *Selfie*, 144.
28. Markus and Nurius, "Possible Selves."
29. Markus and Nurius, "Possible Selves," 954.
30. Higgins, "Self-Discrepancy."
31. Detweiler, *Selfies*.

Theologians, by the way, arrive at similar conclusions via a different route.[32] In his *Social God and the Relational Self*, Stanley Grenz argues that one of the key markers of the modern self is its diversity and instability.[33] He speaks of a "splintering of the self into multiple subjectivities."[34] David Wells writes, along similar lines: "The modern self . . . has grown very thin, insubstantial, and distracted. It lives in a world of fleeting experiences and constantly shifting images, images which we create and by which we sometimes even pass ourselves off as something we are not."[35] Our self has moved, Wells continues, "away from what is eternal, unchanging, and enduring, and into what is shifting, faddish, fleeting, and ephemeral."[36] Dietrich Bonhoeffer expresses his own struggles with the question, "Who am I?" in a poem composed in his Berlin-Tegel prison cell in 1944. Bonhoeffer here describes the discrepancy of feeling torn between how others perceive him, apparently bearing "days of calamity serenely, smiling and proud like one accustomed to victory," and the way he sees himself, "[r]estless, yearning, sick, like a caged bird."[37] Finally, and this is how he ends the poem, what counts for Bonhoeffer is that he is known by God and that his identity is safe in God's hands: "Whoever I am, thou knowest me; O God, I am thine."[38] We will return to this important insight of being known by God at a later stage.

Who, then, am I? Or, to ask with the title of Richard David Precht's best seller, *Who Am I, and If So, How Many*?[39] To sum up the lessons drawn from evidence past and present, we note that our self is less stable and coherent than we might have expected and more inconsistent than we might have feared. German psychologist Hans D. Mummendey suggests that the "self" in fact belongs in parentheses since there is no such thing as a (stable) self.[40] David Dunning and colleagues come to the conclusion that their research "calls into question whether people are, or ever can be, in a position to form accurate self-impressions."[41] It seems that, at the end of the day,

---

32. Léon Turner offers an illuminating comparison between psychological/philosophical and theological approaches to understanding the self. Turner, *Theology*.

33. Grenz, *Social God*, 136.

34. Grenz, *Social God*, 136.

35. Wells, *Earthly Pow'rs*, 45.

36. Wells, *Earthly Pow'rs*, 43.

37. DBWE 8:459.

38. DBWE 8:460.

39. Precht, *Who Am I?*

40. Mummendey, *Psychologie des "Selbst,"* 13–24.

41. Dunning et al., "Why People Fail," 86. Dunning and Suls, "Flawed Self-Assessment."

we remain "strangers to ourselves."[42] At the famous ancient Greek dictum, "Know thyself," we simply shrug our shoulders and reply, "I wish I could know who I was."[43]

All is not lost though. As we shall see in due course, radical disciples are being offered a new self that is governed by God's Spirit and that brings stability, wholeness, and coherence to our self-experience. Before we turn to the cure though, we continue with our diagnosis. Having questioned the myth of a stable and consistent self, we turn next to our tendency to think too highly of ourselves. Evidence gathered by social psychologists and a close reading of the New Testament suggest that we all tend to construct a more positive image of ourselves than might be justifiable. Whether one wants to call it illusional or delusional, we are all to some extent little narcissists.

THE SELF-CENTERED SELF

Psychological research, largely conducted in the West, shows that Westerners tend to overestimate the positive aspects of their selves.[44] John Tierney and Roy Baumeister write: "We typically exaggerate our virtues, and our capacity for self-delusion can be astonishing . . . We're all prone to overestimate our abilities as well as our power to control our destiny."[45] David G. Myers refers in this context to the "inflated self."[46] Shelley Taylor and colleagues point out that we all harbor, to some degree positive self-illusions, both consciously and subconsciously.[47] Of course, this is not necessarily detrimental, on the contrary, the illusion of control over one's self and destiny can protect us from anxious and depressing thoughts.[48] Still, it remains

42. Wilson, *Strangers to Ourselves*.

43. See Moore, *Socrates and Self-Knowledge*.

44. Dunning, *Self-Insight*. Will Storr argues that this looks different in the Asian context, where the individual is more oriented toward the community. In Chinese language, one looks in vain for a word for individualism, Storr claims, and one also does not come across the genre of autobiography. Whereas in Western societies the individual is the hero of his or her own story, in Asian cultures it is generally the other way around: "[T]hose who neglect their duty to bring harmony to the group," writes Storr, ". . . are more likely to be considered failures." Storr, *Selfie*, 80.

45. Tierney and Baumeister, *Power of Bad*, 13.

46. Myers actually offers one of the first interdisciplinary approaches to the self—engaging both theology and psychology in a competent discussion. See Myers, *Inflated Self*.

47. Taylor and Brown, "Illusion"; Taylor et al., "Psychological Resources"; Taylor, *Positive Illusions*.

48. Taylor and colleagues focus predominantly on the positive effects of illusions on well-being. See Tierney and Baumeister, *Power of Bad*, 78–79.

what it is, an illusion. Based on our quick system one judgments, we tend to radiate the air of "unrealistic optimism" regarding our own destiny.[49] While I might be able to imagine the tragedy that one of my friends could potentially die in a car accident, I categorically underestimate the probability that this could happen to me, too. In this context, the perceived locus of control is a decisive factor. When I think of myself as a good driver, I will consider the risk of suffering an accident lower when I am behind the wheel than, say, my partner.[50] This optimistic bias, paired with an unrealistic expectation regarding control, by the way, is the secret of the gambling industry's success—but that is another story.[51]

It is ironic that most people consider themselves to be more attractive than others; psychologists call this the "better-than-average effect."[52] We tend to regard ourselves as superior to others, and we have mechanisms in place that boost our self-esteem—psychologists refer to these as self-serving biases. If I feel down, for instance, one way to make me feel better about myself is to compare myself with someone who is less successful or fortunate than I am, a tendency known as the "downward social comparison."[53] Another quite common self-boosting strategy is this: if my football team wins, I shout, "*We* won!" and I feel good about myself (although, to be honest, of course, I contributed zero to the result; I simply watched the game). However, if it loses, I shrug my shoulders and mumble, "*They* lost," thereby distancing myself from them, protecting my fragile self from the shame of loss. Robert Cialdini and colleagues have arrived at these conclusions based on their "football studies" and dubbed this phenomenon "basking in self-reflected glory" (BIRGing).[54] The chances are that this applies to other sports and contexts, too.

We also tend to be rather selective in how we process information about ourselves.[55] Information that relates to our self and that we perceive to be congruent with our self is being processed and remembered more efficiently (this is referred to as the self-reference effect[56] and self-congruence

---

49. See Weinstein, "Unrealistic Optimism."

50. Harris, "Sufficient Grounds?"

51. Langer, "Illusion of Control"; Langer and Roth, "Heads I Win." See also Rothbaum et al., "Changing the World."

52. Alicke and Govorun, "Better-Than-Average."

53. Wills, "Downward Comparison"; Taylor and Lobel, "Social Comparison."

54. Cialdini et al., "Basking."

55. Hewstone et al., *Social Psychology*, 129–30.

56. Hewstone and colleagues describe the self-reference effect as "the tendency to process and remember self-related information better than other information." Hewstone et al., *Social Psychology*, 133.

effect[57]). In general, we favor information that corresponds with our preconceived notions about the world and our self and we thus commit what is known as the confirmation bias.[58] Negative feedback about ourselves, though, is being ignored or quickly discarded—Anthony Greenwald called this the "junk mail theory of self-deception."[59] If I consider myself to be an effective communicator, I will gratefully remember the elderly gentleman who shook my hand after the service saying, "Good sermon today, pastor, it really connected with my life." But I will ignore and quickly forget the young adult with the quizzical look on his face and the lady who fell asleep halfway through my address. Another common strategy is to rewrite one's personal history nonchalantly to make it fit with one's positive view of self.[60] Self-deception even works on a subconscious level. Jozef M. Nuttin conducted an experiment where he showed that we subconsciously tend to prefer letters of our own name among randomly assorted letters.[61] While some psychologists argue that this effect points—positively speaking—to our implicit self-esteem, Nuttin was less convinced here. He in fact published his findings in a paper entitled, "Narcissism beyond Gestalt and Awareness: The Name Letter Effect." Narcissism, however, needs to be clearly distinguished from self-esteem. Narcissism, as recent research suggests, is a form of unleashed, or oversaturated self-esteem. At least this is the straightforward conclusion drawn by the world-leading self-esteem expert Roy F. Baumeister.

In the 1970s, Baumeister implemented a program in California to boost self-esteem.[62] He assumed that self-confident citizens would be healthier and more successful, and of course, the government was happy to fund any program that promised such positive results. Baumeister writes: "Psychologists everywhere were persuaded that if only we could help people to accept and love themselves more, their problems would gradually vanish and their lives would flourish. They would even treat each other better."[63] About thirty years later, in the early 2000s, Baumeister and colleagues evaluated the effects of their generously funded self-esteem programs. Surprisingly, the results were quite mixed. In 2005, Baumeister reviewed his findings in the *Los Angeles Time*s with refreshing honesty:

57. See, for instance, Mueller, "Self-Awareness."
58. Nickerson, "Confirmation Bias."
59. Greenwald, "Self-Knowledge." See also Greenwald, "Further Consideration."
60. Ross and Conway, "Remembering."
61. Nuttin, "Narcissism."
62. An insightful account of Baumeister's story is found in Storr, *Selfie*, 221–27.
63. Baumeister, "Lowdown."

> Here are some of our disappointing findings. High self-esteem in schoolchildren does not produce better grades . . . Self-esteem doesn't make adults perform better at their jobs either . . . Likewise, people with high self-esteem think they make better impressions, have stronger friendships and have better romantic lives than other people, but the data don't support their self-flattering views. If anything, people who love themselves too much sometimes annoy other people by their defensive or know-it-all attitudes. Self-esteem doesn't predict who will make a good leader, and some work . . . has found *humility rather than self-esteem to be a key trait of successful leaders.*[64]

While it is insightful to read about the unfulfilled expectations regarding self-esteem, one is particularly intrigued to hear that Baumeister identifies humility as a "key trait of successful leaders." This fits well with the picture presented in the biblical witness (e.g., Luke 18:14) and the Christian tradition.[65] Baumeister also highlights, toward the conclusion of his article, some important Christian virtues. "After all these years," Baumeister states, "I'm sorry to say, my recommendation is this: Forget about self-esteem and concentrate more on self-control and self-discipline."[66] This profound conclusion by the psychologist Baumeister offers an opportunity for the theologian to step in and pose the teleological question: Perhaps we were never created to esteem ourselves but someone else instead? Clearly, our purpose is not to worship ourselves, but to "glorify God and enjoy him forever," as the framers of the Westminster Shorter Catechism put it. We will return to these significant insights later. For now, we note that the unlimited pursuit of self-esteem is not as unproblematic as is generally assumed. Baumeister's message, though, does not yet seem to have penetrated the public mind. The push to promote self-esteem, as Baumeister observes, has morphed into a self-obsession. What we witness today, he notes, is "narcissism as a kind of addiction to self-esteem."[67]

Craig Detweiler draws a parallel between the movement of Narcissus, who, according to Greek mythology, as he reached into the water, was "seeking to hug his own neck," and the way we take selfies today.[68] The physical resemblance is indeed striking—as is the risk involved. Narcissus in the

---

64. Baumeister, "Lowdown" (emphasis added).

65. According to the desert fathers, for instance, "The elders used to say that the crown of the monk is humble-mindedness." Wortley, *"Anonymous" Sayings*, 75.

66. Baumeister, "Lowdown."

67. Baumeister, "Narcissism as Addiction," 227.

68. Detweiler, *Selfies*, 36.

story, of course, died, and nowadays, apparently, more people die taking selfies than from shark attacks.[69] Narcissism comes with its own risks.

Will Storr, who recounts Baumeister's story in his book, *Selfie*, concludes that "the self-esteem generation has become the selfie generation."[70] "We're all, to some degree, anxious and hyperactive PR agents for ourselves," he writes.[71] Psychiatrist Hans-Joachim Maaz speaks of a "narcissistic society,"[72] and Jean Twenge and Keith Campbell refer to a "narcissism epidemic" that plagues our current culture.[73] "For six decades," writes New York Times columnist David Brooks, "the worship of self has been the central preoccupation of our culture—molding the self, investing in the self, expressing the self."[74] "The great sins," he notes, "come from excessive worship of self and callousness about others: covetousness, injustice, prejudice, greed, dishonesty, arrogance, and cruelty."[75] It is interesting to note that Brooks here uses the theological concept of "sin" to describe his observations. It is an appropriate reference to these excesses we observe today. At the root of it, though, has always been the default tendency toward self-centeredness.[76] Martin Luther referred to human beings as bent in on themselves,[77] and John Calvin wrote about the "blind self love" that stands in our way as a massive obstacle.[78] Pronounced self-centeredness bordering on narcissism is the key problem of the modern self. "The modern culture of subjectivity," Jürgen Moltmann wrote forty years ago, "has long since been

---

69. Detweiler, *Selfies*, 7.

70. Storr, *Selfie*, 240.

71. Storr, *Selfie*, 33. Sociologists of religion refer to today's "I-Society" (*Ich-Gesellschaft*). See Stolz et al., *Religion und Spiritualität*.

72. Maaz, *Die narzisstische Gesellschaft*.

73. Twenge and Campbell, *Narcissism Epidemic*.

74. Brooks, *Second Mountain*, xxii.

75. Brooks, *Second Mountain*, 254.

76. One thinks here of the sons of Zebedee, James and John, who demanded from Jesus to sit at his right and left in his glory (Mark 10:37). The bold request is met by the sobering question whether they are able to follow Jesus into death: "You do not know what you are asking. Are you able to drink the cup that I drink, or to be baptized with the baptism with which I am baptized?" (Mark 10:38). Full of self-confidence, they answer boldly: "We are able" (Mark 10:39).

77. *WA* 56:304.25–29 (Scholion zu Röm 5,4). "Ratio est, Quia Natura nostra vitio primi peccati tam profunda est in seipsam incurua, vt non solum optima dona Dei sibi inflectat ipsisque fruatur (vt patet in Iustitiariis et hipocritis), immo et opso Deo vtatur ad illa consequenda, Verum etiam hoc ipsum ignoret, Quod tam inique, curue et praue omnia, etiam Deum, propter seipsam querat." For an examination of Luther's view, see Jenson, *Gravity of Sin*, 47–97.

78. *Inst.* 2.1.2:243. On Calvin's view of Jesus's call to discipleship, see Zachman, "Deny Yourself."

in danger of turning into a 'culture of narcissism,' which makes the self its own prisoner."[79] And, more recently, John Webster claimed that we are living in "a culture which values self-fulfilment and self-preservation above all things."[80] The key problem of our human tendency toward self-centeredness is its exclusive focus on the self at the expense of the broader perspective that includes God and neighbor. "Who is the greatest?" was the question on the disciples' mind (e.g., Luke 22:24–30); yet Jesus aimed at directing their attention toward God and others in faithful service. Our way to our neighbor, however, is "blocked by one's own ego [das eigene Ich]," Bonhoeffer argues.[81] By our exclusive focus on self we are being pulled away from what would be a healthy orientation toward God and others.[82] And as long as we commit what Matt Jenson calls the "relational sin" of looking inward, self-ward instead of focusing God-ward and neighbor-ward, our identity will rest on shaky legs, since occupation with self, independent of God, will always imply instability.

Our obsession with self, it seems, is the symptom of a pointless attempt to fill the void within. Every selfie communicates the desire to be valued and appreciated, as Craig Detweiler points out. In his view, the current phenomena of selfies and social media activities are expressions of our "search for authenticity: real love, genuine connection."[83] We seek what Erich Fromm has termed an "authentic life."[84] We want to pursue a life that makes sense; that has purpose and meaning. The question is, how do we do that?[85] While our own, self-made attempts at arriving at meaning and authenticity have been shown to be unsuccessful or even damaging due to our exclusive focus on the self,[86] the good news is this: disciples of Jesus Christ do not need to

---

79. Moltmann, *Trinity*, 5.
80. Webster, "Discipleship and Obedience," 17.
81. DBWE 5:33.
82. As Matt Jenson argues, in Jenson, *Gravity of Sin*.
83. Detweiler, *Selfies*, 38.
84. Fromm, *Authentisch Leben*.

85. Following Heidegger, it is about "knowing how to pursue a purpose for the sake of which we live and in light of which certain features of this world become salient and solicit us." Käufer, "Jaspers," 108.

86. While various suggestions have been put forward in recent psychological research, it seems that approaches toward measuring authenticity are fraught with difficulties. Sanaz Talaifar and William Swann list the following attempts: "authentic self" (Johnson and Boyd, 1995), the "true self" (Newman et al., 2014), "real self" (Rogers, 1961), "intrinsic self" (Schimel et al., 2001), "essential self" (Strohminger and Nichols, 2014), or "deep self" (Sripada, 2010). The key problem, according to Talaifar and Swann is that all these measurements rely on self-assessment; the self-referential nature of the experimental design is therefore problematic (i.e., how authentic can our own

engage in frantically constructing their own identity, polish their battered self-image, or pretend to be someone they are not. They are aware that God knows their frame and remembers that they are dust (Ps 103:14), and yet they also know that meaning, fulfillment, and purpose is promised in close union with Jesus Christ, who authenticates their selves. They therefore admit, freely and humbly, that their self is a broken, fallen self, suffering from the diseases of inconsistency and egocentrism. Confessing their inherent self-centeredness, they are happy to bid farewell to what St. Paul calls the old self (Rom 6:6; Eph 4:22; Col 3:9), and they are open and ready to embrace the new self that is offered in union with Christ. The road to recovery, then, to true contentment and fulfillment, leads through the valley of honest self-assessment and contrition. The path toward true authentic living leads through the admission of our own self-confusion, inconsistency, and hypocrisy (e.g., Mark 7:6–8).[87]

CONCLUSION

When enjoying a concert of the Leipzig Gewandhaus Orchestra a few years ago, I noticed the orchestra's motto displayed in big letters above the organist's seat for everyone to see: *res severa verum gaudium* (true joy is serious business). While this is certainly true for musical performance—to produce proper joy for the audience requires serious practice—it is equally applicable to discipleship. A breakthrough to true joy in God requires deliberate system two use. In this chapter, we have devoted some significant mental energy on the diagnosis which ought to serve as a catalyst for proper joy in the chapter to follow. We have done some honest self-assessment, as we acknowledged and digested the sobering condition of our fallen human nature. Regardless of whether one identifies primarily as Australian or French, flexitarian or teetotaler, there are two inclinations about the way we think about our self that we all share in common: as both psychologists and theologians suggest, we are inconsistent beings that are biased toward ourselves.

---

disclosure about our own, as we have seen, multifaceted and discrepant self be?). Talaifar and Swann, "Self and Identity."

87. Writing from prison to his friend Eberhard Bethge, Bonhoeffer admitted: "I often wonder who I really am: this one always cringing in disgust, going to pieces at the hideous experiences here, or the one who whips himself into shape, who on the outside (and even to himself) appears calm, cheerful, serene, superior, and lets himself be applauded for this charade—or is it real? What does 'poise' [Haltung] mean, actually? In short, one knows less about oneself than ever and is no longer interested in it, weary with psychology and thoroughly averse to any analysis of the soul." Bonhoeffer to Bethge, December 15, 1943, in DWBE 8:221.

We all seek affirmation, we want to be loved and affirmed, yet through our various inconsistencies and biases, this valid desire has morphed into an obsession with self that ignores God and neighbor. Worshipping self instead of our Maker, we have built our identity on shaky ground. We are busy curating ourselves, when in fact, our selves need to be cured. A healthy identity, as we will see in the following chapters, is not constructed by us, but received from God as we follow Christ, our Prophet, Priest, and King. So far, we have done our fair share of psychology and analysis of the soul, which, however, can only lead so far. It is about time that we move from diagnosis to cure. In the next chapter we explore how disciples of Jesus Christ experience transformation as they are endowed with a new self in union with him.

PERSONAL REFLECTION

How does it make you feel to read about our flawed self? What sort of responses and reactions does it trigger in you?

In which areas of your own life do inconsistency and self-centeredness express themselves?

Do you sense a longing for coherence, meaning, and purpose—an authentic existence? Why could such a life be attractive or desirable?

How do you want to pray for yourself right now?

3

Embracing Newness

We are still on the quest of finding out what Jesus means when he calls us to self-denial—the first requirement of his call to discipleship. Our reflections so far have been quite sobering as we ascertained that our default self that comes by the sheer virtue of being a fallen human is a distorted self. Marked by inner inconsistencies and self-centeredness, it is a caricature of what God intended us to be. Right into the confusion and calamity of our old mode of existence, though, breaks the liberating message that God offers us a new self through Jesus Christ. This is a restored self, a "new self, created after the likeness of God in true righteousness and holiness" (Eph 4:24; see also Col 3:10). By being placed into Christ, the disciple becomes alive in her new self, finds wholeness, purpose, and a new direction as she is now oriented toward God and neighbor. In what follows, we inspect the elements of this new mode of being and living in Christ, discover the mysterious nature of our new identity in Christ, and explore how radical disciples thrive in the dissonance of old and new self.

ELEMENTS OF THE NEW SELF

Five aspects of our new self stand out: we receive it as a gift from God (1), and enjoy a completely new mode of existence as we are united with Christ in his dying and rising (2), which is illustrated in baptism (3), goes hand in hand with the granting of forgiveness and bestowal of righteousness (4), and results in an entirely new outlook as we are now directing our attention away from self toward God and neighbor (5).

First, we note that the disciple receives the new self as a "gift of God" (Eph 2:8). Freed from the frantic attempts at fabricating their own identity, followers of Christ gladly receive their new identity from God. It is certainly no coincidence that Jesus's call to discipleship was, in some cases, followed by a renaming of his disciples. Simon, for instance, was renamed Peter, and the brothers James and John were named Sons of Thunder (Mark 3:17). The step into discipleship comes with the embrace of a new identity in Christ by faith. Recent works on theological anthropology, such as Klyne Snodgrass's *Who God Says You Are*,[1] or Brian Rosner's *Known by God*,[2] capture well the direction here: the disciple is being named and known by God. It is not so much about arbitrary identity formation, but active reception of a new identity bestowed by God.[3] Jesus Christ defines the new identity of the disciple, and we respond by embracing the grace of being known and named by God, and by seeking to grow up in it.

Second, the disciple who is united with Jesus Christ by faith enjoys a new form of existence. St. Paul tells his readers that God "made us alive together with Christ" (Eph 2:1). Our new life is now "hidden with Christ in God" (Col 3:3). The disciple, who is "in Christ," is now a "new creation" (2 Cor 5:17; Gal 6:15), a regenerated being that has been "born of the Spirit" (John 3:8).[4] The disciple here acknowledges the somewhat mysterious agency of the Holy Spirit in the generation of this new form of existence. The disciple does not know *how* the new birth happened, for "the wind blows where it wishes" (John 3:8), and is told that "the Son gives life to whom he will" (John 5:21).[5] The activity of the Holy Spirit might be mysterious, but

1. Snodgrass, *Who God Says*.
2. Rosner and Lunde, *Known by God*.
3. Michael Horton writes: "We all want to be and to do something rather than to be made and to receive our identity from above. It is a blow to our spiritual ego to be told that everything has already been done. Yet that is the glory of the gospel! That is why it is Good News." Horton, *Gospel-Driven Life*, 93.
4. In the words of John Webster, "Regeneration is the entire conversion of the fallen creature away from self-will and self-direction towards glad embrace of the divine will and direction which is set forth in Christ. The beginning of discipleship is, as it were, the most concentrated moment of regeneration; it is the abandonment of a ruined way of life and setting out on a new way." Webster, "Discipleship and Obedience," 9. For an in-depth treatment of the doctrine of regeneration, see, for instance, Bavinck, *Reformed Dogmatics*, 29–95. See also Frame, *Systematic Theology*, 944–58.
5. Adolf Schlatter argues that to insist on getting an answer to the question of how we were born again is futile. We are not to question the intricacies of the new birth but what matters is "whether we are alive with the life that is of God the Father." Schlatter, *Das christliche Dogma*, 463.

it is certainly effective. Not knowing how exactly it happens, we observe in the biographies of self and others that renewal in fact does happen. And when it happens, the radical newness of being and living in Christ is utterly life-transforming. Endless is the list of believers' biographies who experienced as a result of their new life radical turns of direction. The apostle Paul himself, of course, is a classic example here who performed the most spectacular U-turn from self-righteous persecutor of Christians to a vulnerable and yet courageous ambassador for the gospel. Intimately united with Jesus Christ, the disciple experiences profound newness of being and living. Something entirely new has begun in the disciple in a comprehensive and astonishing way. The inward change finds expression in a new perspective and an entirely new focus. Only with regenerated eyes can the disciple "see the kingdom of God" (John 3:3), see God at work, and recognize God's purposes in this world. Most importantly, perhaps, the disciple is now equipped with a new desire—a new love for God and a longing to see him glorified in their life (an important point to which we shall return again later).

Third, the sacrament of baptism illustrates well the new mode of existence of the radical disciple. "What the Synoptics describe as hearing and following the call to discipleship," Bonhoeffer notes, "Paul expresses with the concept of baptism."[6] Immersed into the water of baptism, we are reminded of our union with Christ as we are buried with him "by baptism into death" (Rom 6:4). Our old mode of existence, the old inconsistent and self-centered ego of "being in Adam," died; it has been "crucified with Christ" (Rom 6:6). Disciples of Christ, then, Bonhoeffer writes, "know themselves only as those who have already died."[7] What has died here, in fact, was already dead—useless in its inconsistency and inauthenticity.[8] Yet there is a real break involved here: the dead old self has gone and something entirely new has begun.[9] Emerging from the waters, radical disciples now

---

6. DBWE 4:207.

7. DBWE 4:211.

8. Wolfhart Pannenberg states that "the human being before the redemption through Christ did not possess a true identity, since he lived in contradiction to himself," and, of course, in contradiction to God, one might add. "Dieses neue Leben begründet nicht eine gänzlich neue Identität des Menschen gegenüber seinem alten Leben ohne Christus. Vielmehr stellt sich aus christlicher Perspektive der Sachverhalt so dar, daß der Mensch vor seiner Erlösung durch Christus gar keine wahre Identität besaß, da er vielmehr im Widerspruch gegen sich selber lebte . . ." Pannenberg, "Identität und Wiedergeburt," 611.

9. John Webster writes: "There is no significant continuity with the old; that which has gone before is not the basis for what lies ahead nor the power in virtue of which the one called is able to make the turn which is required by Jesus. The old has, indeed, been set aside as hopelessly compromised, as flight from God, as death."

enjoy "newness of life" (Rom 6:4; cf. Col 2:12). The term "newness" here "connotates startling freshness, a quality in something that makes it unlike anything else of its type."[10] Of course, baptism is not a solitary endeavor—no one baptizes himself or herself. Baptism, which symbolizes our intimate union with Jesus Christ, always happens in the context of the church. The believing disciple is, through baptism, incorporated into the community of faith. (We focus in more detail on the important notion of the disciple's new life in the context of the community in chapter 9.)

Fourth, an important mark of newness is that disciples enjoy forgiveness of sins and the gift of righteousness that inspires them to love their neighbor in word and deed.[11] Having put their faith in Christ, they are cleansed from sin through the sacrifice of God's own Son (1 John 1:7; cf. Ezek 36:25–26; Titus 3:5), and they hear the divine verdict "not guilty" pronounced over them. Even more than that, they receive the "the righteousness of God" (Rom 3:22). The apostle Paul explains that disciples come to enjoy this privilege through a kind of transaction: "For our sake he made him to be sin who knew no sin, so that in him we might become the righteousness of God" (2 Cor 5:21). This is the astonishing, tension-creating wonder of costly grace: God considers our sins on Jesus's shoulders, entirely dealt with on the cross, and Jesus's righteousness is credited to our account. Based on this verse, Luther spoke of the "joyful exchange" (*froelich wechsel*) between the believer and Christ.[12] Jesus fully identified with our sins and we become the "righteousness of God" through him.[13] While this declaration of righteousness applies to the disciple in a very personal way, Bonhoeffer is keen to point out the implications of justification by faith for our new mode of existence in the community of faith.[14] Those who have been declared righteous in God's sight are at the same time members of the new community of Christ.[15] This important communal trajectory, some argue, has not been sufficiently emphasized in Reformation and post-Reformation

---

Webster, "Discipleship and Obedience," 10.

10. Thielman, *Romans*, 305.

11. Althaus, *Die christliche Wahrheit*, 402.

12. WA 7:25.34.

13. Bonhoeffer follows the Reformer here as he notes: "The innocent one is killed because he bears our sinful flesh; he is being hated and cursed by God and the world; he is made sinful for the sake of our flesh. But in his death we find God's righteousness." DBWE 4:257.

14. DBWE 4:181, 278–80.

15. Michael F. Bird offers a middle way between the classic Reformed emphasis on forensic declaration and the insights from proponents of the New Perspective on Paul and their focus on the covenant community. See Bird, "Justification."

orthodoxy.[16] However, one wonders whether this aspect perhaps was not highlighted as much in early modern theology because it was simply too obvious.[17] Church was front and center in believers' lives back in those days and there was no way they could have imagined themselves in isolation, as single individuals. Only in our late modern times today, where many are oblivious to the communal context of our faith, is it vital to put into relief again the fact that Christian disciples are not isolated hermits who twiddle their thumbs and meditate on God's gracious gift of righteousness. No, disciples who are intimately united with Christ are at the same time joined with their brothers and sisters. They flourish in fellowship and serve one another in humility and docility (Heb 10:19–25; we return to this important aspect in section three).

Fifth, and following on from this, united with Christ by faith, the disciple is now distinctly oriented toward God and neighbor. Whereas the old mode of "being in Adam" was characterized by inconsistency and self-centeredness, the disciple by "being in Christ" is freed for an entirely new, meaningful existence.[18] The mark of this new existence is that we live in a dual relation to God and neighbor, and as we do so, Bonhoeffer argues, we become true human beings.[19] This is a very Lutheran idea, according to Robert Kolb. "Being 'bound' to the neighbour's need is, in fact," writes Kolb, "being free to be human according to God's design."[20] A whole new perspective opens up for the disciple as she becomes alive in close communion with Jesus Christ and thrives by relating to God and neighbor in love.

CHRISTOTHENTIC IDENTITY

Taking a step back and considering our new existence as disciples of Christ, we realize that everything about our new life is defined and shaped by Jesus

---

16. See Wright, *Pauline Perspectives*, 397–406, 410–14.

17. I am grateful to Bruce Pass for pointing this out to me.

18. According to Bonhoeffer, being "'in Adam' means to be in untruth, in culpable perversion of the will, that is, of human essence. It means to be turned inward into one's self, *cor curvum in se*." DBWE 2:137. For a helpful analysis of Bonhoeffer's view of "being in Adam," see Elliston, *Dietrich Bonhoeffer*, 55–62.

19. This is Dietrich Bonhoeffer's key argument put forward both in his *Act and Being* and *Sanctorum Communio*. Christiane Tietz summarizes Bonhoeffer's thought as follows: "[W]e human beings recognize who we are only in the encounter with another person, when we are confronted with a concrete You who demands our help and attention. In this moment the human being becomes a person." Tietz, *Theologian of Resistance*, 10.

20. Kolb, "Christ and Culture," 267.

Christ. "The incarnate, crucified, and transfigured one has entered into me and lives my life," Bonhoeffer writes.[21] That is certainly true and yet there is much about the ways in which Christ shapes our identity that we might find perplexing. The apostle Paul has intriguing ways of describing his Christ-shaped new self. In his letter to the Galatians, he writes:

> I have been crucified with Christ. It is no longer I who live, but Christ who lives in me. And the life I now live in the flesh I live by faith in the Son of God, who loved me and gave himself for me. (Gal 2:20)

And to the Colossians, he writes that their new life is now "hidden with Christ in God" (Col 3:3). How are we to understand this? Does this not sound as if Paul is almost losing his self here? It is easy to misunderstand the hiddenness, and the "It is no longer I who live" here. It is important to clarify at this stage that Paul's emphasis is far removed from any aspirations of self-eradication, which one finds in some Eastern religions. For the contemporary, this sounds a bit like Buddhism where the self dissolves as it moves into a desired higher state of consciousness or karma.[22]

At least two aspects deserve closer attention as we try to make sense of Paul's argument.

First, Paul reminds his readers of the deep intimacy that exists between the believer and Christ, and it is this intimacy that now defines this new way of living. "'I no longer live' means that the 'old I,' the 'I' enslaved to sin and the law," Douglas Moo notes, "has been done away with, to be replaced by a new 'I' whose existence is determined by the indwelling Christ."[23] Martin Luther used analogies from the trades to explain the conundrum here: the disciple is firmly "welded" (*zusammengeschweißt*) to Christ.[24] Welded to Christ the two become one. The connection is like that of "whitewash sticking to a wall."[25] Yet the intimate togetherness highlighted here does not equate to a canceling out of our self. Paul's "I," his character, whatever makes Paul *Paul*, does not vanish. Rather, Jesus Christ moves in through his Spirit and transforms what is there, shapes it, makes it whole, and forms it more and more into his image. "The Spirit transforms and empowers the

---

21. DBWE 4:287.
22. Coogan and Narayanan, *Eastern Religions*.
23. Moo, *Galatians*, 171.
24. Luther, *Der Galaterbrief*, 111.
25. "So muß man ganz im Rohen die Sache veranschaulichen; denn wir könnens geistlich nicht begreifen, daß Christus so ganz nah und innerlich in uns hänge und bleibe, wie Licht oder weiße Farbe an der Wand haftet." Luther, *Der Galaterbrief*, 110.

self rather than obliterates it," Craig Keener explains, "divine activity shapes human agency rather than replaces it."[26]

Second, the renewal that happens in us, in our faculties of willing and thinking, is therefore an organic, harmonious renewal.[27] Adolf Schlatter summarizes it as follows:

> We think, feel and want formally in the same manner as in every other aspect of life. Through the Holy Spirit's activity does not arise a special psychology, but with the same cognitive and volitional capacities do we now think and will another content; now, we think of God and desire not egoistically, but love him.[28]

Based on these insights, I suggest that we speak of the disciple's new existence as a *Christothentic* mode of being. It is an existence that derives authenticity and integrity not from the self, but from Christ.[29] The disciple's self is being authenticated by Jesus Christ himself; it is a Christothentic identity. As we have seen earlier, our attempts to discover or construct an authentic self within us are doomed to failure since we never arrive at adequate identity formation without Jesus Christ. Again, this does not mean a negation or eradication of our personality, but in fact a flourishing of the person God intends us to become.[30]

Based on our reflections so far, one could get the impression that the disciple is being rendered rather passive and one wonders about the disciple's active involvement in living out this newness of life. However, God's grace, Adolf Schlatter is convinced, has both a "calming" and "activating" effect on us.[31] Radical disciples, therefore, arrive at the complex self-understanding of being passively active—another paradox to embrace.

---

26. Keener, *Galatians*, 113.

27. See my essay, Bräutigam, "Good Will Hunting."

28. Schlatter, "Noch ein Wort," 80. Elsewhere, Schlatter notes: "The use of the name 'disciple' for their communion with him does not prove that he intended to give them nothing but instruction. Of course, they should learn from him, but not merely insights; they rather were to learn how to obey God. His influence on them was directed toward the entire person, not merely toward their cognition but also toward their will." Schlatter, *History*, 240.

29. Andrew Purves writes, "[O]ur deepest identity as human beings is found in union with Christ, who is the truly human one, the core of who we are is defined not by our achievements, possessions, personalities, natural endowments, or even our religious associations and experiences. We find and claim our own authentic personal humanity in the fact that God has been gracious to us and become one with us in Jesus Christ, and by the Holy Spirit made us one with him." Purves, *Reconstructing*, 25.

30. Radical disciples therefore gladly adopt Søren Kierkegaard's maxim, "Now, with God's help, I shall become myself." Kierkegaard, *Papers and Journals*, 295.

31. Schlatter, "Der Dienst des Christen," 4.

Having been renewed through the spirit of God, we continue to grow up as disciples by intentionally appropriating this newness (and denying oldness)—through the Holy Spirit.

We focus next on how disciples flourish as they actively embrace the tension of oldness and newness in themselves, and we are, in this sense, moving closer to the exploration of the nature of self-denial—which is the primary focus of our undertaking.

OLD AND NEW SELF TENSION

The New Testament documents speak of a continuous renewal of the new self. The apostle Paul, for instance, writes about the "new self, which is being renewed" (Col 3:10), and he explains that "our inner self is being renewed day by day" (2 Cor 4:16). The present indicative here conveys an ongoing action. At first this sounds like a contradiction in terms: Why would a new self require continuous renewal?[32] Unusual as it may sound, it seems as though this is indeed a viable option. We remember the occasion where Jesus explained to his disciples that they were all clean (expect for one, of course), but they still needed to have their feet washed (John 13:10). Newness, it seems, does not imply completeness—at least not at this side of the eschaton. In this life, the newness that has been granted to the disciples is still in need of daily renewal and appropriation. "Costly grace is the gospel which must be sought again and again," writes Bonhoeffer, "the gift which has to be asked for, the door at which one has to knock."[33] On this basis then, disciples are called to live out their new self, not just occasionally, but continuously, every day. "The disciple," Webster writes, "is always a beginner, always starting out afresh, always the *new* creation."[34] Paul Althaus puts it similarly when he writes that "[t]he new human being is not simply there, once and for all, rather it must be recreated daily."[35] Constant renewal is enabled by the Holy Spirit as the disciple is being led and keeps in step with the Spirit (Rom 8:14; Gal 5:18; 5:25).

This constant dynamic of renewal is mirrored by constant demolition—and this is where the tension comes in that radical disciples experience and embrace by faith. Disciples are faced with the dilemma that their

---

32. Willem van Vlastuin explores the notion of personal renewal in, Vlastuin, *Be Renewed*.

33. DBWE 4:45.

34. Webster, "Discipleship and Obedience," 12 (emphasis original).

35. "Der neue Mensch ist nicht ein für allemal da, er muß täglich neu geschaffen werden." Althaus, *Die christliche Wahrheit*, 455.

old self—thought to be dead (Col 3:3)—keeps cropping up. It seems that deadness does not imply complete elimination. Or, more poetically, or rather crudely, as Karl Barth put it, the old Adam, "the slut" (*das Luder*), which we thought drowned, is in fact a formidable swimmer.[36] The disciple's old mode of being in Adam, then, needs to be renounced day after day. "I die every day!" Paul exclaims (1 Cor 15:31).[37] This constant renewal and demolition process is usually referred to as the disciple's (progressive) sanctification. Adolf Schlatter writes in this context:

> Not this or that expression of evil, but "the old human being" is being killed; not this or that exercise in goodness, but "the new human being" is being raised. Accordingly, the result of sanctification is entirely positive: the old human being is not simply weakened or diminished, but dies "with all sins and evil lusts," and the new [one] emerges in eternal righteousness and purity. This is not merely a future, hoped-for goal but the [present] possession of the believer: today the old human being is given over to death, today the new [one] is raised to life, and that day after day.[38]

The idea of constant renewal and mortification pervades the New Testament witness, and it is vital for radical disciples to figure out ways in which they not only survive but thrive as they embrace the tension of constant renewal and demolition (we discuss some central suggestions in the next chapter when we look at specific practices of self-denial).

---

36. "Against the old Adam having drowned is just this, namely that the slut (*Luder*) in fact knows only too well how to swim." ["Gegen die Ersäufung des alten Adam nur eben dies, daß das Luder sich leider nur zu gut aufs Schwimmen versteht!"] KD IV/3:291.

37. Oswald Bayer argues: "[F]irst, the baptized are wholly righteous through justification, and second, they are in the process of becoming righteous through the constant drowning of the old Adam in a life of daily repentance. Decisive is the difference in perspective: insofar as the baptized are still sinners, they look only to themselves, are captive to sin, and are totally self-absorbed. But insofar as they are righteous, they look to Christ alone, are free from captivity to sin, and are no longer curved in on themselves." Bayer, "Iustus et Peccator," 264.

38. "Nicht diese oder jene Äußerungen des Bösen, sondern 'der alte Mensch' wird getötet, nicht diese oder jene Bethätigungen des Guten, sondern 'der neue Mensch' wird erweckt. Demgemäß ist das Resultat der Heiligung ein vollständig positives: der alte Mensch wird nicht nur geschwächt oder gemindert, sondern stirbt 'mit allen Sünden und bösen Lüsten,' und der neue kommt hervor in ewiger Gerechtigkeit und Reinigkeit. Dies stellt sich nicht nur als ein künftiges und gehofftes Ziel dar, sondern als der Besitz des Glaubenden: heute wird der alte Mensch in den Tod, heute der neue ins Leben versetzt, und so Tag um Tag." Schlatter, "Der Dienst des Christen," 37.

While the event of baptism and the spiritual realities of dying and rising with Christ are "unrepeatable events in the strictest sense," as Dietrich Bonhoeffer put it, they still need to be appropriated again and again—they are "in need of daily repetition."[39] Radical disciples die and rise with Christ on a daily basis, as John Webster points out: "Both in its beginning and in its continuation, discipleship involves dying and coming to new life."[40] This is, in fact, a key element of Luther's theology.[41] Luther writes, "The Christian life does not consist of being but of becoming, not of victory but of battle, not of being just but of being justified, not of having taken possession but of striving [as in Philippians 2:12], not of purity but of purification."[42] This is clearly a challenging endeavor. The task at hand is not only that we are to acquire a complex and dynamic, self-understanding of dying deadness and renewing newness, but we are to engage actively and courageously in what is a formidable in-house struggle.[43] In the remainder of this section we

---

39. DBWE 4:258. Of course, we cannot repeat our baptism (and neither our justification). However, "[w]hat can be repeated is only the recollection of what happened to us once and for all; it is, in fact, not only capable of, but in need of, daily repetition." DBWE 4:258. Paul Althaus notes, along similar lines, "We essentially experience and achieve conversion (and the new birth—for both are one and the same event) as a continuous, ever-new event. Even though conversion defines the starting point of the Christian life and emerges as such biographically, it must always be reappropriated and specifically repeated." [". . . Bekehrung (und die Wiedergeburt—denn beide sind ein und dasselbe Geschehen) wird von uns wesentlich als ein fortdauerndes, immer neues Geschehen erfahren und verwirklicht. Auch wo die Bekehrung den zeitlichen Anfang des Christenlebens bildet und als solcher biographisch hervortritt, muß sie doch immer aufs neue angeeignet und konkret wiederholt werden."] Althaus, *Die christliche Wahrheit*, 455.

40. Webster, "Discipleship and Obedience," 12.

41. As Karl Holl observes, "'Being a Christian is not a matter of being, but rather of becoming' is an ever-recurring refrain in Luther's writings." Holl, "Was verstand Luther?," 69.

42. "Das christliche Leben besteht nicht im Sein, sondern im Werden, nicht im Sieg, sondern im Kampf, nicht in der Gerechtigkeit, sondern in der Rechtfertigung, nicht im 'Ergriffenhaben,' sondern im 'Streben' [nach Phil 2,12], nicht in Reinheit, sondern in der Reinigung." Luther in Danz and Tuck, *Martin Luther*, 203. The quote is found in his lecture on Galatians, "Ex quibus patet, quomodo vita christiana non stet in esse, sed in fieri, non in victoria, sed in pugna, non in iusticia, sed in iustificatione, non in 'comprehendisse,' sed in 'extendere,' non in puritate, sed in purificatione etc." (Scholion regarding Gal 5:16; WA 57/2:102.15–18.)

43. Paul Althaus explains that "the shape [*Gestalt*] of new life that is gifted and opened up to us by faith can be nothing else but struggle, the battle of the new human against the old." ["Also kann die Gestalt des neuen Lebens, das uns im Glauben geschenkt und aufgetan ist, keine andere sein als Kampf, der Widerstreit des neuen gegen den alten Menschen."] Althaus, *Die christliche Wahrheit*, 456.

explore some features of this tension more carefully, before we turn in the next chapter to some more practical aspects of self-denial.

THRIVING IN DISSONANCE

Radical disciples are determined to live and even flourish in the tension between the old and new self. They seek to thrive in what Peter K. Nelson calls "discipleship dissonance."[44] Right in the friction between old and new self the disciple is provided with the opportunity for self-denial. What exactly is the nature of this friction? On the one hand, the disciple welcomes God's guidance; the good shepherd is nudging her through his Spirit to will the right thing and to do the good deed. She rests assured that he works in her "both to will and to work for his good pleasure" (Phil 2:13). These valuable promptings, however, are set in competition with and even sabotaged by inklings of the old Adam, the dead man walking. The apostle Paul knew this tension well and he describes it midway through his letter to the Romans: "For I do not understand my own actions. For I do not do what I want, but I do the very thing I hate" (Rom 7:15).[45] "The self is split," Charles Talbert observes regarding Paul's statement, "and the will is pulled in two directions."[46] Martin Luther describes with refreshing honesty how this might play out in the disciple's life:

> I now want to address pious husbands and wives: whoever examines himself carefully will undoubtedly find that he likes the looks and mannerisms of his neighbor's wife better than those of his own wife. He disdains the woman to whom he has a right and he loves the one to whom one has no right . . . We are always striving for what is forbidden.[47]

---

44. Nelson, "Discipleship Dissonance."

45. There is disagreement amongst interpreters whether the "I" here (and in the whole passage in Romans 7:7–25) refers to Paul's pre- or post-conversion experience. For a summary see Schreiner, *Romans*, 379–90. Some commentators suggest a middle way, emphasizing our dependency upon God's grace in our lives. As John D. Harvey put it, "The passage corrects the belief that we are able to serve God using our own resources. It commends total dependence on Christ in order to serve God." Harvey, *Commentary*, 199.

46. Talbert, *Romans*, 196.

47. "Ich will jetzt mit den frommen Ehegatten beiderlei Geschlechts reden: Wer sich hier selbst sorgfältig erforscht, wird ohne Zweifel finden, daß ihm mehr gefallen Gestalt und Lebensart der Ehegattin des anderen als die der eigenen. Die Frau, zu der man Recht hat, verachtet man, zu der man kein Recht hat, die liebt man . . . Wir streben immer nach dem Verbotenen." Luther, *Der Galaterbrief*, 315 (commentary on Gal 5:16).

This striving toward what is forbidden should not happen. How could this be? "How can we who died to sin still live in it?" (Rom 6:2). Luther spoke of the divided disciple who is both righteous and sinner at the same time (*simul iustus et peccator*).[48] Some believers past and present felt, and still feel, an urgency to avoid this inconvenient duality, however. Seeking to reduce the obvious tension, they downplay the label "sinner" and wish to come up with less offensive designations instead. In some movements of the Christian tradition (one thinks of the Wesleyan perfectionist stream, for instance), one finds a particular renitence towards embracing the term "sinner."[49] This hesitation is somewhat justified, since in the New Testament, believers are not referred to as sinners, but commonly are called "saints."[50] Our identity derives from what God in Christ has done for us rather than what we do: we are saints that sin. As we have noted so far, when referring to themselves, radical disciples are encouraged to think primarily about their newness of life, about constant renewal and maturation into the image of Christ. That is the first thing that comes to mind when the disciple is asked: "Who are you?" It is particularly important to call to mind for disciples who struggle with a distorted view of self, perhaps due to an underlying mental health condition, such as depression, for instance, that is often associated with a very low view of self. It is especially these vulnerable disciples who are called to focus more intentionally on the definitive characteristic of their identity: newness—sainthood. Insofar, some of the criticism that has been brought forward, is justified.

However, there is still a real tension. Newness and sainthood do not entirely describe the disciple's condition. Peter Stuhlmacher has offered a

---

48. On Luther's distinction, see Bayer, "Iustus et Peccator." Paul Althaus notes: "The Christian remains until death not merely tempted but a sinner . . . Despite all Pietistic protest, Luther's formula must stand: the Christian is at once justified and a sinner, no different on the last day from when he first believed." ["Der Christ bleibt bis zum Tode nicht nur ein Versuchter, sondern ein Sünder . . . Allem pietistischen Widerspruch zum Trotze muß es bei Luthers Formel bleiben: der Christenmensch ist gerecht und Sünder zugleich, am letzten Tage nicht anders als am ersten, da er glauben lernte."] Althaus, *Die christliche Wahrheit*, 456. To Luther's mind, God's justification renders us truly human, as Marc Cortez observes. Cortez, *Christological Anthropology*, 83–110. "And since our standing *coram Deo* is always an act of grace, a relationship gifted to us by our maker," Cortez writes, "then human persons receive their essence, their very being, as a gift." Cortez, *Christological Anthropology*, 96.

49. There have been a number of studies on the Wesleyan Perfectionist influence behind such renitence. See, for example, Dieter, *Holiness Revival*, 15–78; McLoughlin, *Modern Revivalism*, 122–65; Warfield, *Perfectionism*, 166–215.

50. Michael Kruger, quoted in Pennington, *Sermon on the Mount*, 292n6. See, for instance, Acts 9:13; 9:32; 9:41; 26:10; Rom 1:7; 8:27; 1 Cor 1:2; 2 Cor 1:1; Eph 1:15; Phil 4:22; Col 1:2; Heb 13:24.

slightly attenuated version of Luther's dogma as he speaks of the believer as being "both righteous and susceptible to temptation" (*gerecht und versuchlich zugleich*).[51] Perhaps, then, the formula could reach consensus where disciples understand themselves to live (and, ideally, thrive) in the tension of being susceptible saints. The aspect of oldness is here downgraded to an adjective and the noun, "saint," stands as the definitive characterization of the disciple. Susceptible saints seek to thrive in the dissonance of shedding their old, inauthentic, and susceptible self-existence and grow up as saints who rejoice in their new life through Christ. Disciples then approach the task of self-denial with a clear awareness and sensitivity for the dissonance that they experience within themselves. Only from this vantage point is self-denial thinkable and possible—even if it means, as Bonhoeffer put it, to live right in "*unresolved contradictions*":

> This new life does not disintegrate into a parallel Yes and No . . . Instead, this new life, which is *one* in Jesus Christ, is held between the Yes and the No so that in each Yes already the No is perceived, and in each No also the Yes. Both the flourishing of life's strength and self-denial, growth and death, health and suffering, happiness and renunciation, achievement and humility, honor and self-deprecation belong inextricably together in *a living unity full of unresolved contradictions.*[52]

Through the Spirit, disciples do not recoil from these contradictions, but they expect that their faith and they themselves will grow as they experience dynamic renewal. On the one hand, they rejoice in the certain definitiveness of their newness of existence—as St. Paul implies with his passionate use of the past tense: "But you *were* washed, you *were* sanctified, you *were* justified in the name of the Lord Jesus Christ and by the Spirit of our God" (1 Cor 6:11; cf. Heb 10:10). Yet on the other hand, they know that they have this "treasure" of newness "in jars of clay," and they are thus always reminded that "the surpassing power belongs to God" and not to them (2 Cor 4:7). And so they continue to struggle under a cloud of not-yet-ness, unfinished-ness, and not-yet-consummated-ness. Part and parcel of our pilgrimage as disciples is that we live, and, ideally, flourish amid provisionality and contradictions.

---

51. Stuhlmacher, *Der Brief an die Römer*, 107.
52. DBWE 6:252 (emphasis added).

CONCLUSION

Giving heed to Jesus's call to self-denial, we continued our exploration of the self in this chapter. We noted that any self-engineered attempts at identity formation will remain futile and end in frustration and failure. An authentic, healthy self-concept with integrity comes only as a gift from God. Stepping into discipleship, we are being turned from our old mode of existence, which was intrinsically inconsistent and self-focused, to our new self-existence as we are united with Jesus Christ by faith. Our new self is the Christothentic self that derives authenticity from Christ alone. It is equipped with a redeemed self-esteem that is informed by who Christ is for us and in us. We no longer seek meaning, purpose, and validation through what we do, but receive all this and more through what Christ has done for us. We are saints who in this life remain, paradoxically, susceptible to sin. Yet our sinful actions do not define us anymore. As we are being changed in our focus, through the Holy Spirit, from self toward God and neighbor, we become truly human and gain true life. Having set the stage for a dynamic understanding of our self that thrives in the dissonance of old and new, we are finally in the position to focus more carefully on the aspect of *denial* in Jesus's call to self-denial.

PERSONAL REFLECTION

Which aspects of your new mode of existence do you enjoy most right now as you live in union with Jesus Christ? Which traits of the new self would you like to see growing stronger in your life?

Can you find words to express your gratitude to God that he "began a good work in you" and that he will also "bring it to completion at the day of Jesus Christ" (Phil 1:6)?

How does it make you feel to think about yourself as saint?

How does the struggle of living in "*unresolved contradictions*," as Bonhoeffer put it, express itself in your own life? Do you feel that your faith is growing as you seek to thrive as a susceptible saint?

How do you want to pray for yourself right now?

4

Practicing Self-Denial

WHEN SPEAKING OF PRACTICING self-denial, we enter treacherous territory. Taking just one wrong turn can lead down the slippery slope of self-sufficiency and leaves the disciple frustrated in the cul-de-sac of spiritual burnout. According to a common misconception, it falls to the disciple to discipline the self, like a rider of a disobedient horse. In this picture, it is the disciple herself who is supposed to come up with strategies and tactics of self-denial.[1] However, to speak of strategies, tactics, and even spiritual disciplines is risky business in discipleship.[2] These terms all carry the connotation of self-mastery and self-efficacy, hence, implicitly feeding our old tendency that focuses exclusively on the self and expects compensation: if *I* try very hard to implement a new discipleship strategy, I expect progress in spiritual maturity—and perhaps I even deserve a reward from God if I do particularly well. This human-centered way of thinking avoids the

---

1. Lucy Peppiatt highlights some of these misunderstandings in Peppiatt, *Disciple*, 27.

2. Discipline is a central aspect of discipleship, Bonhoeffer argues, but it needs to be defined carefully: "So a disciple's life requires strict external discipline. This is not to suggest that the will of the flesh can be broken by discipline. The daily death of the old self cannot be achieved by anything other than faith in Jesus. But persons of faith, disciples whose will is already broken, whose old selves have died to Jesus Christ, know precisely the rebellion and daily pride of their flesh. They know their lethargy and lack of discipline and know that to be the source of arrogance which must be conquered. This takes place in daily and extraordinary practice of discipline." DBWE 4:159.

complexities of Christian discipleship we have touched on so far and it obscures the activity of the Holy Spirit in the disciple's life. At the outset, we have introduced discipleship as an artform that we seek to appropriate through the Holy Spirit. And in the previous chapter we have explored how we are placed in the strange condition of passive activity: passively receiving our identity through Christ and actively living out our newness of life through the Holy Spirit. While it is, of course, helpful to develop spiritual disciplines, skills, and strategies, it is vital to make room for faith and, most importantly, for the divine agency in the process. Perhaps instead of disciplines, it is more adequate to speak of virtues or "holy habits" of self-denial.[3] Understood in this sense, it is about developing a new sense of being, of living actively as radical disciples. Oliver O'Donovan's definition of virtue is insightful in this regard.[4] "[B]y stressing the intuitive and habituated nature of virtue," O'Donovan argues, "it offers a way of talking about excellence not simply as *acting* in a certain way, but *being* in a certain way."[5] Rowan Williams puts it similarly when he speaks of discipleship as "a state of being," and a condition of "awareness."[6] From this perspective then, we understand discipleship not in terms of performance or frantic implementation of rules and rituals, but as an invitation to grow up in a new mode of existence, a rather participatory mode, as the Spirit brings about transformation in us. Self-denial correctly understood, then, is pursued from a posture of relaxed attentiveness to the Spirit who is alive and active in the disciple. Still, this does not take away anything from the disciple's agency and resolve. Since radical disciples understand themselves placed into the serious challenge of constant demolition and renewal, they approach self-denial with sincerity. Recognizing the urgency, they are intentional about rejecting impulses from their old mode of existence. Yet they always do so from a posture of serenity, attentive to the ways in which the Holy Spirit moves in them and enables them to deny their selves.

In this chapter we first explore these theological foundations of self-denial more carefully. This will lead us to a discussion of the more practical aspects of self-denial in close fellowship with the Holy Spirit. Three key virtues of self-denial deserve closer inspection: the idea of putting off the old self and putting on the new, considering newness, and adopting an attitude of quiet self-awareness.

---

3. Peppiatt, *Disciple*, 27.

4. For a helpful introduction to the concept of "virtue," see O'Donovan, *Finding and Seeking*, 88–95.

5. O'Donovan, *Finding and Seeking*, 93–94 (emphasis original).

6. Williams, *Being Disciples*, 1–4.

OBEDIENCE

When it comes to self-denial, radical disciples are poised since the imperative of "Deny yourself" is based on the solid indicative of their close union with Christ. Built on this precious cornerstone, the disciples' identity, status, and destiny are secure. Having been "sealed with the promised Holy Spirit" (Eph 1:13), their bond with Christ is unbreakable and all the promises that come with it (2 Cor 1:20). From this perspective, self-denial is always exercised from the position of grace, as German mystic John Tauler insists: "Whoever seeks to have the virtue of true self-denial, acquires it only through grace and not by nature."[7] The disciples' connection with Jesus Christ is the source from which the virtues of self-denial flow. Radical disciples are "rooted and built up in him" (Col 2:7), and they receive "power from on high" (Luke 24:49) as they grow new habits and new ways of living as sons and daughters of their heavenly Father. One thinks of the Johannine picture of the vine and the branches, where the latter are organically connected with the former. The disciples' branches humbly acknowledge and subscribe to Jesus's statement, "apart from me you can do nothing" (John 15:5). The stipulation of self-denial thus cannot be isolated from our close fellowship with Christ. "Deny yourself" remains unthinkable and impossible without the subsequent invitation, "Follow me."[8] Disciples, therefore, approach self-denial in a relaxed posture, knowing that the dynamics of self-denial are rooted in their union with Christ.

Yet at the same time they seek to take this endeavor seriously, for the call to discipleship still contains the imperative: "Deny yourself."[9] And this call involves active obedience; it demands to be obeyed. A few words about the unpopular term of obedience are in order. Obedience, and what it stands for, is increasingly met with a degree of resistance. Decades of antiauthoritarian dogma and *laissez-faire* pedagogy have raised a generation of skeptics who react with suspicion when hearing the word "obedience."

---

7. "Wer aber die Tugend in rechter Verläugnung seiner selbst haben will, der erlangt sie nur von der Gnade und nicht von der Natur" (no. 60); Tauler, *Nachfolge Jesu Christi*, 76.

8. Medi Ann Volpe describes well the significance of the disciple's intimate relationship with Christ through the Spirit: "We 'put on Christ' not by our own doing, but by the work of the Holy Spirit. The disciple's task is to allow that identity, her being in Christ, to orient and to define her . . . Our identity in Christ is secured by relationship, not by virtue. Disciples are marked by the relationship to the Master first of all, and develop in accordance with their own gifts and capabilities." Volpe, *Rethinking Christian Identity*, 229.

9. Webster speaks of "an eternal indicative which is itself also an imperative." Webster, "Discipleship and Obedience," 8.

Some theologians apparently even want to get rid of it altogether, as Mathias Wirth, in his recent "Distance of Obedience" (*Distanz des Gehorsams*), for instance, advocates. The idea behind this sounds plausible at first, although a closer look reveals that one is encountering here another attempt to reduce a tension in the call to radical discipleship. Wirth suggests that we need to bid farewell to the "untenable" (*unhaltbar*) concept of "obedience" in theology, anthropology, and ethics.[10] Instead, he claims, we ought to substitute obedience with the concept of friendship.[11] In other words, our attitude as disciples of Christ should be: "I *want* to keep God's commands as his friend," and not, "I *have* to be obedient." Yet this means setting up a false dichotomy. Of course, friendship is certainly a vital aspect of Christian discipleship—Jesus is the great friend of the disciples, and we turn to this important theme in a separate chapter. However, one wonders whether it is an adequate move to juxtapose God's role as lawgiver and his role as friend. Our friendship with God does not excuse us from our obligation to obedience. Disciples are Jesus's friends, but they are also his servants who obey his commands. Reducing the tension between our roles as friend and servant puts us again down the risky path of cheap grace.

What we could say, though, is that our friendship with God—having been turned from enemy into friend through our great friend Jesus Christ—we now will and want (!) to become obedient. Essentially, only the friend is able to obey in the first place. In this sense, our friendship with God is the basis for our obedience. It does not abolish but empowers obedience. "If you love me," Jesus tells his disciples, "you will keep my commandments" (John 14:15). Yes, God is our friend, but Jesus is still God, as we have stressed in the first chapter, and any attempt to soften the fact that we enjoy an unequal relationship with him is again a sign of a domestication of God.[12] We do not forget, too, our dilemma that in this life we still drag after us the remnants of a dead body of rebellion that simply does not want to be Jesus's friend, let alone keep any of his commandments. Our obedience remains a fragile one.

Disciples, although friends, are not in the position to negotiate with Jesus the terms of discipleship. In his *Discipleship*, Bonhoeffer examines the example of the rich young man who was told that for him, the opportunity for discipleship would present itself only if he were to give away his possessions (Matt 19:16–30). This, however, he did not do, and Bonhoeffer insists in this context that discipleship entails the "demand to stop discussing and

10. Wirth, *Distanz des Gehorsams*, 344.

11. Wirth, *Distanz des Gehorsams*, 342–88.

12. John Webster explains that Jesus's call into discipleship is "not an invitation but a command. In this call, there does not take place a meeting between equal partners." John Webster, "Discipleship and Calling," 143.

start obeying."[13] He thus calls for "personal obedient discipleship"[14] and for "simple obedience."[15] Again, this simple obedience is always grace-enabled obedience. Radical disciples thrive in the tension that while obedience is commanded, they know it is both God almighty and intimate friend Jesus who issues the demand, and in that tension, they thrive as they respond with faith and anticipation, relying on the Holy Spirit's work in them.[16] Radical disciples realize that their own obedience is based on Christ's perfect obedience. Jesus Christ, as their representative, was passively obedient, giving his life as a sacrifice for them and obtaining a perfect righteousness for them; and he lived a perfect human life in their place, always actively obedient to the Father and in intimate fellowship with the Holy Spirit, now enabling them to follow him on the path of obedience by virtue of their union with him. Grant Macaskill summarizes it well: "Jesus Christ is not represented simply as the one *through* whom we have forgiveness, or even as the one *by* whom the moral life is exemplified, but as the one *in* whom the life of discipleship takes place. Christ himself is present *in* the life of the disciple as the principal moral agent."[17]

With this in mind, we examine more closely what obedience looks like in real-life situations. Having touched on the constant need for demolition and renewal of the self in the previous chapter, we now apply our insights to the actual habits of putting off oldness and putting on newness as we seek to arrive at quiet self-awareness.

PUTTING OFF OLDNESS

The apostle Paul encourages his readers in several places to "put off" the old self and to "put on" the new self that is being renewed in Christ. Both activities are closely linked, and we deal with each one in turn, first with the "putting off" imperative. Paul reminds the believers in Colossae that they have "*put off* the old self with its practices" (Col 3:9), and he instructs the disciples in Ephesus to "*put off* your old self, which belongs to your former

---

13. DBWE 4:72.
14. DBWE 4:59.
15. Title of chapter 3 in his work, DBWE 4:77–83.
16. Jens Zimmermann interprets Bonhoeffer's view of the disciple's obedience in the following words: "The obedience Bonhoeffer envisions is not that of one who fulfills a duty but of one who has entered into an enterprise, carrying out his mission intelligently with passionate conviction. Participation in Christ thus draws the follower into the Christ-reality of 'vicarious representative responsibility.'" Zimmermann, "Dietrich Bonhoeffer," 645.
17. Macaskill, *Union with Christ*, 2 (emphasis original).

manner of life and is corrupt through deceitful desires" (Eph 4:22). The Christians in Rome are told that their "old self was crucified" (Rom 6:6; cf. Gal 5:24), and that they thus ought to consider themselves "dead to sin" (Rom 6:11).[18] The message conveyed in these passages is clear: only because the old self is the dead, inauthentic self that has already lost its power over the disciples, are they actually in the position to deny, day after day, its inconsistent and self-centered impulses.[19]

By actively pursuing self-denial, then, radical disciples assume the role of a pathologist and they expose the corrupt parts of their old self. They seek to identify what Dorotheus of Gaza calls the "chronic illnesses of the soul."[20] Illnesses not only call for diagnoses but require also subsequent treatments. Having identified the selfish "desires of the flesh" (Gal 5:16–17) they can be put to death by the Spirit (Rom 8:13). John Owen spoke about the "mortification of indwelling sin" through the Holy Spirit in this context, which was, in his view, "the constant duty of believers."[21]

Radical disciples, therefore, are keen to pursue an honest self-assessment: "Pay attention to yourselves!" (Luke 17:3). This is the first, practical, step of self-denial, where disciples carefully examine the inauthentic tendencies of their old self. Part and parcel of this dismantling process is to inquire in the light of Scripture which relics of the old self need particular attention.[22] In his letter to the Galatian disciples, the apostle Paul

---

18. Peter Stuhlmacher explains that as the disciple now lives in newness of being, they are to act with "acts of obedience" according to this newness: "Therefore it is now her task to become true to her new self through acts of obedience." ["Ihre Aufgabe ist es deshalb, ihrem neuen Sein durch Taten des Gehorsams nun auch gerechtzuwerden."] Stuhlmacher, *Der Brief an die Römer*, 87.

19. Peter Dschulnigg notes, "The first imperative speaks of self-denial . . . by which is probably meant the gainsaying of one's own interests and the rejection of the self that is addicted to sin and death." ["Der erste Imperativ spricht von der Selbstverleugnung . . . womit wohl der Widerspruch gegen die eigenen Interessen und die Absage an das der Sünde und dem Tod verfallene Selbst gemeint ist."] Dschulnigg, *Das Markusevangelium*, 238.

20. Quoted in Ruppert, *Geistlich Kämpfen lernen*, 39.

21. "The mortification of indwelling sin remaining in our mortal bodies, that it may not have life and power to bring forth the works or deeds of the flesh, is the constant duty of believers." Owen et al., *Overcoming Sin*, 49.

22. I have borrowed this language from François Bovon, who writes: "To 'deny oneself' does not mean to hate oneself . . . but, expressed in modern terms, to negate one's non-authentic existence, to dismantle the proud façade of one's identity, and to bring out, in relationship with Christ, one's actual, plain and fragile I." ["'Sich selbst verneinen' bedeutet nicht, sich selbst hassen . . . sondern, modern ausgedrückt, seine nichtauthentische Existenzweise verneinen, die stolze Fassade seiner Identität abbauen, sein eigentliches, nüchternes, fragiles Ich in der Beziehung zu Christus zum Vorschein bringen."] Bovon, *Das Evangelium nach Lukas* (1. Teilband), 483.

lists some traits of the old self, which are supposed to help them in their self-assessment. I am using Eugene Peterson's paraphrase here, since it very lucidly brings Paul's point to life:

> It is obvious what kind of life develops out of trying to get your own way all the time: repetitive, loveless, cheap sex; a stinking accumulation of mental and emotional garbage; frenzied and joyless grabs for happiness; trinket gods; magic-show religion; paranoid loneliness; cutthroat competition; all-consuming-yet-never-satisfied wants; a brutal temper; an impotence to love or be loved; divided homes and divided lives; small-minded and lopsided pursuits; the vicious habit of depersonalizing everyone into a rival; uncontrolled and uncontrollable addictions; ugly parodies of community. I could go on. (Gal 5:19–21, MSG)

Putting off the old self, Paul insists, works through the Spirit (Rom 8:13). Mortification of sin, therefore, is *not* an arbitrary human performance. In keeping with our initial remarks, Dallas Willard issues the warning that mortification, falsely understood, will deteriorate into just "one more technique to be mastered by people who want to save their life."[23] Self-denial can become a source of self-infatuation, and in this way defies its purpose. "Practices of mortification can become exercises in self-righteousness," Willard points out. "This dreary and deadly self-denial is all too commonly associated with religion."[24] Hans Bayer argues, similarly, that the "problem with pathological interpretations of self-denial and cross-bearing is that they by no means vanquish egotism and autonomous self-determination, but merely conceal them with pseudo spirituality."[25] The old self's bias toward religious-legalistic tendencies, what Bonhoeffer called the "pious self," calls for constant and careful monitoring.[26] Radical disciples do not put off their old self on their own. Only by remaining in Christ can the disciple, through the Holy Spirit, engage in putting to death the deeds of the old self (John 15:4). As noted earlier, the command to self-denial comes only in combination with the invitation to walk closely with Christ: "Follow me." As the disciple matures in her relationship with Christ, through prayer,

---

23. Willard, *Renovation*, 52.

24. Willard, *Renovation*, 52.

25. "Das Problem bei pathologischen Interpretationen von Selbstverleugnung und Kreuztragen ist gerade, dass sie Egoismus und autonome Selbstbestimmung in keiner Weise überwinden, sondern diese lediglich pseudo-geistlich verschleiern." Bayer, *Das Evangelium des Markus*, 320.

26. DBWE 4:48.

reading, meditating, and contemplating—as we observe more carefully in chapter 10—she will be conformed to the image of Christ (2 Cor 3:18).[27]

Putting off our old self is positively a function of our relationship with Jesus Christ. Oldness is curtailed by newness through him and intimacy with him. The newness of our union with Christ exposes the decay and distortion of our old self and brings to light our new self. By focusing on the new and by abiding in Christ, the old suffocates, and here, we truly "overcome evil with good" (Rom 12:21). As the disciple becomes increasingly captivated with her vision of Christ who defines her new mode of existence, the old self withers and her new self grows and matures. Putting off oldness, then, works principally by putting on newness, and to this important idea we turn next.

PUTTING ON NEWNESS

Paul encourages the believers to "*put on* the new self, created after the likeness of God in true righteousness and holiness" (Eph 4:24). Disciples who put on this new self put on Christ himself: "But *put on* the Lord Jesus Christ" (Rom 13:14). And the disciple wonders: "How does this putting on work in real life?" Paul has something to say about this, too. He sends the disciples in Rome this advice: "So you also must *consider yourselves* [*logizesthe*] dead to sin and alive to God in Christ Jesus" (Rom 6:11). The imperative "consider" implies a sense of urgency.[28] Two aspects are noteworthy.

First, in a very basic sense, Paul wants his readers to remember that their old self has died and that their new self is now "alive to God in Christ Jesus." Karl Barth argues that, strictly speaking, the disciple in her new self does not pursue self-knowledge (*Selbsterkenntnis*) anymore; instead, she seeks to grow up, knowing herself to be placed in Christ.[29] It is not about

---

27. "The great change takes place," writes Bonhoeffer, "as we now come to understand, the moment the unity of human existence no longer consists in its own autonomy, but, by the miracle of faith, is found in Jesus Christ, beyond one's ego and its law." DBWE 6:278.

28. "As the context makes clear," writes James Dunn, "it is a strong word, a firm conviction (present tense) expressed in daily conduct." Dunn, *Romans 1–8*, 323–24.

29. Barth writes: "Es geht dabei wohl um Selbsterkenntnis, aber um die Erkenntnis unserer Selbst in Christus und also nicht hier, nicht in uns, sondern außer uns, dort, in diesem Anderen, der mit mir nicht identisch ist und mit dem ich nicht identisch bin noch werde, in dessen Menschlichkeit mir ja auch Gott selbst ein Anderer, ein konkretes Gegenüber wird, ist und bleibt. Uns selbst als das zu erkennen, was wir in ihm sind, kann also mit Selbstbetrachtung, Selbsterforschung, Selbstschau, Selbsteinschätzung, mit Introspektion in allen ihren bekannten und denkbaren Formen solchen Unternehmens gerade nichts zu tun haben . . ." *KD* IV/2:313–14.

introspection anymore, but about Christospection. It sounds obvious, but so often in the Christian life, the most difficult things to remember are the obvious ones.[30] All too often we forget. We forget many things, and, of course, forgetting is a healthy cognitive process, for it protects us from becoming mentally overwhelmed.[31] However, forgetting becomes a problem when we not only forget irrelevant information (such as what I had for dinner last Saturday), but when we are oblivious to critical data, like our best friend's birthday, where we parked the car, or what it means to be alive in Jesus Christ.[32] "The root of all evils is forgetfulness," says the wisdom of the desert fathers.[33] Radical disciples, then, seek to remember the most foundational facts about their new identity in Christ. They remember, on a daily basis, that they are indeed radical disciples, transformed in their being and transplanted into the kingdom of God.

Second, Paul's use of "consider" also carries the notion of rigorous reflection by faith.[34] On the one hand, by faith we are to reckon ourselves dead to sin when we are prone to sin. And on the other hand, we discover by faith what it means to be alive in Christ, intentionally appropriating newness. Again and again, we put on the specific grace presented to us in the gospel. Disciples are to live "worthy of their calling," notes Bonhoeffer, and "the only way they will be worthy is by daily reminding themselves of the gospel from which they live."[35] We, therefore, dwell with gratitude on the call into discipleship issued to us; we treasure God's forgiveness in Christ and our being made right with him; we enjoy the privilege of living as beloved members of God's household; we marvel at the wonder of our new self, fashioned in likeness with Christ; and we treasure the prospect of seeing him one day face-to-face. Paul's encouragement to the Colossians, "Set your minds on things that are above" (Col 3:2), though, is not an invitation to escapism, that is, he does not recommend that the disciple daydreams about the bliss of heavenly paradise and forgets her earthly calling. Rather, he presents a summons to explore the marvelous facets of one's new identity

---

30. This is a point my teacher Donald Macleod reiterated in his theology lectures. "Remember to restate the obvious," he constantly encouraged his students.

31. Richards and Frankland, "Persistence and Transience."

32. Jean Bethke Elshtain addresses this particular problem of forgetfulness in chapters 2 (Forgetting That We Are Fallen: The Prideful Self) and 3 (Forgetting That We Are Fallen: The Slothful Self) in her work, Elshtain, *Who Are We?*

33. Wortley, *"Anonymous" Sayings*, 55n65.

34. "Consider" (*logizomai*) refers to a conviction one has reached through a careful assessment ("auf Grund e. Berechnung bewerten, taxieren, erachten, ansehen als"). Bauer et al., *Griechisch-Deutsches Wörterbuch*, 965–66.

35. DBWE 4:262–63.

in Christ here and now. By constantly looking at him, the disciple discovers who she truly is, as she is being fashioned and shaped into the image of the Master. We return to the important transformative effects of contemplating Christ's face at a later stage (see chapter 10).

A vital habit of the radical disciple, then, is to find ways of reminding herself of the newness she enjoys through her union with Christ. With a view to some practical aids regarding the consideration of newness there is room for creativity. Disciples today, at the outset of a new millennium, have all the modern means of technology at their disposal. Smartphones can be programmed to remind them daily about precious details of their newness of being in Christ. A daily, brief invitation to stop and remember who they are as they "walk in newness of life" (Rom 6:4) may become a healthy habit, especially during a busy day. Benedictine monk Fidelis Ruppert (OSB) recommends his workshop participants in Münsterschwarzach Abbey to wear a scarf that reminds them of their baptism.[36] The very tangible action of putting on the scarf in the morning is a valuable reminder of our putting on Christ. Another strategy is creative self-talk. "Have you realized," asks D. Martyn Lloyd-Jones of his readers, "that most of your unhappiness in life is due to the fact that you are listening to yourself instead of talking to yourself?"[37] Lloyd-Jones sees precedence for encouraging soliloquy in Psalm 42 where the psalmist indeed talks to his self: "Why are you cast down, O my soul, and why are you in turmoil within me? Hope in God; for I shall again praise him, my salvation and my God" (Ps 42:5–6). Listening to one's old self-talk might lead the disciple into the depths of despair, guilt, and self-condemnation. Instead, the radical disciple deliberately shifts her focus onto her new mode of existence through Christ-centered soliloquy.

While acknowledging the value of Lloyd-Jones's self-talk approach, Kelly Kapic argues that it does not go far enough as it tends to overlook the communal aspect of discipleship.[38] The limits of self-talk lie in the fact that "we don't always know how to handle ourselves, nor can we be trusted to handle ourselves," Kapic writes—"We need others."[39] Martin Luther, in fact, made a similar observation. In a letter to the depressed musician and organist Matthias Weller, Luther counsels him to listen to others through whom God speaks. "Dear Matthias," Luther writes, "do not dwell on your own thoughts, but listen to what other people have to say to you." He continues:

---

36. Ruppert, *Geistlich Kämpfen lernen*, 118.
37. Lloyd-Jones, *Spiritual Depression*, 20.
38. Kapic, *Embodied Hope*, 138–40.
39. Kapic, *Embodied Hope*, 139.

> For God has commanded men to comfort their brethren, and it is his will that the afflicted should receive such consolation as God's very own . . . And when good people comfort you, my dear Matthias, learn to believe that God is speaking to you through them. Pay heed to them and have no doubt that it is most certainly God's word, coming to you according to God's command through men, that comforts you.[40]

This is a compelling reminder that developing skills and habits of self-denial is a communal activity.[41] Radical disciples flourish in the tension of old self-denial and new self-embrace by relying on their brothers and sisters who walk with them. Having highlighted the positive effect of intentionally remembering and considering the new self's mode of existence on a regular basis, it is important to keep the balance. Too strong a focus on oneself, even the new self, might have an unintended harmful effect on the disciple's spiritual health and formation. Radical disciples therefore seek to rest in a quiet yet confident new self-focus.

QUIET SELF-AWARENESS

In Thomas Mann's famous novel about the decline of a family dynasty, *The Buddenbrooks*, protagonist Thomas Buddenbrook warns his sister Tony against too much attention to the self: "I have thought a great deal about this curious and useless self-preoccupation, because I had once an inclination to it myself. But I observed that it made me unsteady, hare-brained, and incapable—and control, equilibrium, is, at least for me, the important thing."[42] Equilibrium is indeed the pivotal point. Radical disciples balance

---

40. Luther to Matthias Weller, October 7, 1534, in Luther, *Letters of Spiritual Counsel*. ["Aber, lieber Matthia, folget hierin nicht Euren Gedanken, sondern höret, was Euch ander Leute sagen! Denn Gott hat's befohlen, daß ein Mensch das ander trösten soll, und will auch, daß der Betrübte solle gläuben solchem Trost, als seiner eigen Stimm . . . Und wenn Euch gute Leute trösten, mein lieber Matthia, so lernet ja gläuben, daß Gott solchs zu Euch saget; folget und zweifelt nicht, es sei Gottes Wort gewißlich, der Euch, seinem Gebot nach, durch Menschen tröstet."] WA Br 7:104.4–5; 105.45–48.

41. Dietrich Bonhoeffer observes in this context: "Christians need other Christians who speak God's word to them. They need them again and again when they become uncertain and disheartened because, living by their own resources, they cannot help themselves without cheating themselves out of the truth." DBWE 5:32.

42. Mann, *Buddenbrooks*, 218–19. "Ich selbst habe manchmal über diese ängstliche, eitle und neugierige Beschäftigung mit sich selbst nachgedacht, denn ich habe früher ebenfalls dazu geneigt. Aber ich habe gemerkt, dass sie zerfahren, untüchtig und haltlos macht . . . und die Haltung, das Gleichgewicht ist für mich meinerseits die Hauptsache." Mann, *Die Buddenbrooks*, 264–65.

their deliberate self-examination regarding old habits with a quiet, yet confident, new focus that rests on Jesus Christ and is mindful of the present. Failure to seek the balance here may lead to serious difficulties. It can result in caricatures of discipleship, such as the *pretentious*, the *legalistic*, or the *depressed* disciple.

An exclusive focus on the new self, for instance, increases the risk of a licentious tendency, which is the hallmark of the *pretentious disciple*. Overjoyed by the prospect of living in her new self through Jesus Christ, the disciple marvels—and rightly so—at the qualities of this new life. Yet the exaggerated focus on the new self distracts from the discipleship dissonance of constantly renouncing oldness and ever emerging in newness. The disciple here is tragically oblivious to "old Adam" and his obnoxiously persistent ability to swim. Since grace has been showered on her, she even wonders—at worst—whether to continue in sin so "that grace may abound" (Rom 6:1). Licentiousness and antinomianism are the defining markers of disciples who have lost their balance here. Pride and self-admiration, ironically traits of the old self, begin to emerge in the disciple, which puts them back on the slippery path of cheap grace.

There is, secondly, the tendency of paying pathological attention to the dead, old self at the expense of one's new mode of existence. This leads either to the depressed or the legalistic disciple. The *legalistic disciple* struggles with the judgment that the old self is truly part of the disciple's complex existence and that it is indeed in constant need of being put to death. In this rather religious, legalistic occupation with oneself, the busy person pursues the futile agenda of trying to polish the old self, without realizing that it is a Sisyphean task. In the end, the cup might be shiny on the outside, but inside it remains "full of greed and self-indulgence" (Matt 23:25). The constant attempt to resuscitate what is already dead can only lead to disappointment and frustration. According to Adolf Schlatter, the Pharisees are a case in point here. They were, in fact, unable to practice self-denial, he argues, since "pharisaical piety constantly occupied the human being with himself," namely, with one's old nature.[43] This pseudo-disciple deals with the old self *not* in order to put to death its negative impulses through the Spirit, but to conceal and obscure them. No visible appropriation of newness has been welcomed—the person remains blind to the newness that Jesus Christ offers.

The *depressed disciple* also focuses predominantly on the old self, but this happens in more subtle ways. Here the disciple exhibits an almost

---

43. According to Schlatter (commentary on Matt 16:24): ". . . die Forderung, 'sich selbst verleugnen' innerhalb des Pharisäismus unmöglich ist, da die pharisäische Frömmigkeit den Menschen beständig mit sich selbst beschäftigte." Schlatter, *Der Evangelist Matthäus*, 519.

morbid fascination with the dead old self. The disciple's own sin, past and present, is always on his mind and there is a difficulty in accepting God's forgiveness and embracing the newness offered in the gospel. In this case, the disciple follows with good intentions the imperative to mortification, and the old self is indeed the correct target of the attack. Yet self-examination is taken to an extreme—so much so that the dead relic of the old self overshadows the disciple's new mode of existence and he sinks into despondency and depression. The disciple constantly broods over already confessed and forgiven sin, mourns over his sinful past, or laments what is a perceived lack of progress in sanctification. Psychologists label this constant introspection "rumination," and it clearly has a detrimental effect on the disciple's mental health.[44]

In rumination we are fixing our attention on our old self, on our self-centered actions, mistakes, and problems, and we turn round and round in circles. Rumination's mischievous catch, of course, is that we are not solving the problem by thinking about it. Rumination is only for rumination's sake, and one frantically treads around in the hamster wheel of despondency. It is not surprising to note that rumination correlates with hopelessness and anxiety, with pessimism and depression.[45] Ruminative self-absorption is thus labeled by some as the "root of all (psychological) evil."[46] Rumination is a trait of the old self-centered self that existed in unfreedom. Hence, throughout the centuries, pastors and theologians have recognized this risk and warned fellow disciples of the dangers of excessive self-examination, recommending instead a good portion of self-forgetfulness. Charles Spurgeon, for instance, names self-forgetfulness as a virtue of every Christian,[47] and Martin Lloyd-Jones distinguishes between healthy, regular self-examination and unhealthy introspection which might lead to morbidity.[48] John

---

44. Mor and Winquist, "Self-Focused Attention."

45. Nolen-Hoeksema, "Role of Rumination"; Roelofs et al., "Effects of Neuroticism"; Watkins and Teasdale, "Adaptive and Maladaptive"; Vassilopoulos, "Social Anxiety."

46. Seltzer, "Self-Absorption."

47. "We are to stand equipped with the whole armour of God, ready for feats of valour, not expected of others: to us *self-denial, self-forgetfulness*, patience, perseverance, longsuffering, must be every-day virtues." Spurgeon, *Lectures*, 14 (emphasis original).

48. "We all agree, that we should examine ourselves, but we also agree that introspection and morbidity are bad. But what is the difference between examining oneself and becoming introspective? I suggest that we cross the line from self-examination to introspection when, in a sense, we do nothing but examine ourselves, and when such self-examination becomes the main and chief end in our life. We are meant to examine ourselves periodically, but if we are always doing it, always, as it were, putting our soul on a plate and dissecting it, that is introspection . . . and that in turn leads to the condition known as morbidity." Lloyd-Jones, *Spiritual Depression*, 17.

Piper comes to similar conclusions,[49] and Timothy Keller recommends "Blessed Self-Forgetfulness" to his congregation.[50] Psychologists, too, highlight the positive effects of self-forgetfulness. German psychologist Peter Becker, for instance, regards self-forgetfulness as a main contributor to mental well-being.[51] In his research, Becker was able to show that subjects with high scores in self-forgetfulness brood less and are less anxious. Self-forgetfulness, he reports, is highly correlated with emotional stability and psychological well-being.[52]

While this sounds all very plausible, one wonders, though, whether the antidote to this particular form of negative old self-absorption is indeed self-*forgetfulness*. I tend to side with Oliver O'Donovan who expresses some doubt in response to "the advocates of 'self-forgetfulness.'"[53] "We cannot overlook where we stand," he writes, "love of God and of neighbour must not be absent-minded, but self-aware."[54] O'Donovan, in my view, shows the way forward here. Instead of completely forgetting about themselves, radical disciples assume a posture of quiet self-awareness that keeps a healthy balance between rejection of the old self and flourishing of the new self. Only loosely attached to self-related thoughts, the disciple is therefore able to take seriously the things of God and the needs of neighbors, as O'Donovan points out.[55] Wayment and Bauer speak of a "quiet ego" in this context.[56] The goal, then, is not self-forgetfulness in and of itself. Instead, radical disciples pursue a quiet self-focus, where they are keenly aware of the kingdom of God and the present concerns and needs of the community. Self-denial then is not about basking excessively in one's new qualities or

---

49. "Mental health is, in great measure, the gift of self-forgetfulness. The reason is that introspection destroys what matters most to us—the authentic experience of great things outside ourselves." Piper, *Hidden Smile*, 112.

50. Keller, *Blessed Self-Forgetfulness*. See also the booklet, Keller, *Freedom*.

51. Becker, *Seelische Gesundheit*, 35.

52. Becker, *Seelische Gesundheit*, 34–38; 45.

53. O'Donovan, *Finding and Seeking*, 53.

54. O'Donovan, *Finding and Seeking*, 53.

55. John Calvin, likewise, achieves a balance here when he notes, "almost forgetful of ourselves, surely subordinating our self-concern, we try faithfully to devote our zeal to God and his commandments." *Inst.* 3.8.2:691.

56. Bauer and Wayment, "Quiet Ego." Matt Bloom explains in this context: "People with a quiet ego spend most of their time thinking of others and very little time thinking of themselves. Because they experience self-transcending humility, people with a quiet ego have an open, teachable mind-set and have a high willingness to admit mistakes. They report having many more deeply spiritual experiences. And yet they also seem to pay enough attention to themselves to engage in appropriate self-care." Bloom, *Flourishing in Ministry*, 35.

trying to polish or repair the broken old self. It is about striking a healthy balance between relaxed, but serious rejection of the old self and appropriation of the new self. It is about developing a new posture and attitude of "having an unpretentious sense of self and low self-focus," as Matt Bloom argues.[57] Walking the tightrope by God's grace, one is concerned not about the old self's past, or the new self's future, but about the concrete acts of love toward God and neighbor in the present moment. In Dietrich Bonhoeffer's words: "Love as the deed of simple obedience is death to the old self and the self's discovery of existing now in the righteousness of Christ and in one's brothers and sisters. Then the old self is no longer alive, but Christ is alive in the person."[58]

CONCLUSION

In this chapter we looked at the comprehensive newness of life that radical disciples enjoy. They have been moved out "from the domain of darkness" and relocated to the "kingdom of [God's] beloved Son" (Col 1:13). United with Christ by faith, they are clothed with his righteousness and they now have access to God the Father (Eph 2:18), enjoying their adoption as the children of God (Gal 4:5; Eph 1:5; Rom 8:14–17). In their new mode of existence, they are promised joy (Phil 4:4) and contentment in every situation (Phil 4:11–13). Less preoccupied with their own self they become alive in their new focus on God and neighbor. And it is right at this point where a creative implementation of discipleship skills by faith and through the Holy Spirit enables them to grow up and to mature. Granted, the progress that radical disciples make often seems marginal and appears not to be easily discernible. Breakthroughs might seem modest but are, in fact, momentous. Progress in self-denial depends on small steps. The transformative questions below are designed to assist us as we seek to implement new strategies in our lives (always, of course, in dependence on the Holy Spirit). Drawing to a close our reflections on self-denial, then, we conclude how self-denial, appropriately understood and pursued, in fact leads to authenticity, coherence, and fulfillment. Thriving in our internal tension of constant demolition of the old self and formation of the new self, we focus, in quiet self-awareness, outward, toward the concerns of our fellow disciples and the suffering in this world. In so doing we experience a true sense of purpose and discover how Jesus's words are being fulfilled, namely that "whoever loses his life for my sake will find it" (Matt 10:39).

57. Bloom, *Flourishing in Ministry*, 35.
58. DBWE 4:152.

PERSONAL REFLECTION

What do you find attractive about the work of the Holy Spirit in you that prompts you to become obedient to the call to self-denial?

What does putting off the old self and putting on the new self look like for you in everyday life?

What could help you to achieve a posture of quiet self-awareness as discussed in this chapter?

Do you notice moments when you thrive in the tension of old and new self?

What distracts you from focusing on God and the needs of your neighbor at the present moment?

Where are you perhaps at risk of turning into one of the caricatures of a radical disciple (the pretentious, legalistic, or depressed disciple), and what can you do to avoid it?

Can you remember a situation where you experienced a sense of purpose and fulfillment as a follower of Christ by loving God and neighbor?

What do you think God appreciates about you as he looks at you?

How do you want to pray for yourself right now?

II

Take Up Your Cross

5

Cross-Bearing and Christ's Suffering

ARRIVING AT THE NEXT stage of discipleship, Jesus's followers are called to take up their crosses. "Anyone who wants to come after me," Jesus says, needs to "*take up his cross* and follow me" (Matt 16:24; Mark 8:34).[1] Luke renders the rather unpleasant summons even more unattractive by adding the word "daily" (Luke 9:23). What sort of invitation is this?[2] This is a strange charge, indeed. We associate with the cross excruciating (hence the word) pain and suffering, and ultimately, agonizing death. The cross is one of the most horrific torture instruments ever devised.[3] The call to take it up, therefore, sounds preposterous. It is a fool who picks up a brown snake, touches a box jellyfish, or the high-voltage line. Every fiber of our human nature resists what seems to be an absurd call. Does Jesus invite his disciples on a suicide mission? It seems that one is faced again with a considerable tension. The wish to avoid this tension is a plausible one and presents a serious temptation to the disciple. The disciple's ears are itching for something

---

1. While in Luke the call to cross-bearing is issued to "all" or "many crowds" (Luke 9:23; 14:27), in Matthew it is only directed at the disciples. Bøe, *Cross-Bearing*, 88–91; 221–22.

2. "Jesus' exhortation would not be seen as an appealing call to discipleship in its original setting," notes Ben Witherington. "The exhortation means the disciple in principle gives up his right to his own life up front. He or she would be affirming a willingness to give all, even his or her very life, in order to follow Jesus." Witherington, *Matthew*, 322.

3. Hengel, *Crucifixion*.

else altogether (2 Tim 4:3). We would rather listen to more attractive invitations, which are legion. Following our hedonistic instincts, we pursue pleasure and avoid anything that is remotely associated with pain and suffering.[4] The slogan YOLO, "You Only Live Once," certainly trumps "Take up your cross" in terms of attractiveness. And it seems that our tendency to avoid anything that is slightly uncomfortable or inconvenient is relatively stable. Almost five-hundred years ago, Martin Luther referred to himself and his generation as "weaklings" (*zertlinge*) in that respect: "For we are so soft—such weak martyrs—that if only a leg aches or a small pock-mark erupts, then we can scream until heaven and earth are full of complaints and howls, grumbles and curses, and we do not see what an utterly trivial evil such a pock-mark is compared with God's other countless blessings, which remain fully and entirely ours."[5]

Today, whenever we feel down, challenged, or threatened, we are quick to dampen any potentially painful effects. In Australia, opioid prescriptions have increased by 40 percent over the past eight years.[6] According to pain specialist, Jennifer Stevens, Australia is on the verge of a painkiller epidemic.[7] The effects of the COVID-19 pandemic with its various lockdowns and levels of restrictions will most likely accelerate this trend. Now painkillers are, of course, a great blessing. Like all good things, though, too much of them can quickly turn into a very unpleasant thing. If I were to start taking an aspirin every time one of my students confidently (and quite vocally!) mistook a major heresy for orthodoxy in the classroom, I would be in big trouble.

In his book, *The Other Side of Happiness*, Melbourne-based psychologist and pain researcher Brock Bastian critically examines our tendency to avoid painful experiences in life. He observes an increasing readiness in our society to alleviate pain by taking all sorts of drugs. Bastian claims that

---

4. Hedonism is the view that the human being is motivated only by pleasure and pain—more specifically, by seeking out pleasure and by avoiding pain. As a school of thought, hedonism can be traced back to the classical Greek philosophers (e.g., Plato, Epicurus). Two recent works that discuss its history are Lampe, *Birth of Hedonism* and Arenson, *Health and Hedonism*. Later, English philosopher Jeremy Bentham took hedonism further and developed a system of ethics (utilitarianism) based on its premises. "Nature has placed mankind under the governance of two sovereign masters, pain, and pleasure," Bentham writes. "It is for them alone to point out what we ought to do, as well as to determine what we shall do." Bentham, *Introduction*, 1.

5. "Denn wir sind solche zertlinge und so weiche merterer, wenn uns nur ein bein wehe thut odder ein klein blatterlin auff feret, so konnen wir himel und erden vol schreien mit klagen und heulen, murren und fluchen, und nicht sehen, wie gar ein geringes ubel, ein solchs blatterlin ist, gegen die andern unzeligen guter Gottes, die wir noch vol und gantz haben . . ." WA 31/1:73.8–12.

6. Reddie, "Australia on Brink."

7. Reddie, "Australia on Brink."

"[w]e have come to treat even commonplace experiences of pain and sadness as pathological, as things that need to be medicated and eradicated."[8] An army of helicopter parents has raised what is sometimes called the "cotton-wool" or "snowflake generation."[9] Young students today have often been shielded from any potentially painful experiences. Parents considered playgrounds unsafe, and their children are now far less resilient than earlier generations.[10] Understandably, they now feel they need "safe spaces" and "trigger warnings" wherever they go.[11]

Bastian's key argument is important for our purposes. By taking the edge off, he argues, we might miss out on the potentially positive effects of our afflictions and challenges. "[W]e have come to believe our lives are *supposed* to be pain free," he writes, and we falsely assume that all pain is "counterproductive to life."[12] Yet not all pain proves to be detrimental. Everyone, presumably, has his or her own story to tell where a painful experience led to personal growth and maturation. We came out at the other end, and that even more refined and rounded. Psychologists Richard Tedeschi and colleagues showed in their research that even people who suffered traumatic events, still experienced what they called "post-traumatic growth." They grew in their resilience, their capacity to cope with painful situations, and even became more compassionate and altruistic.[13] These insights confirm what Austrian psychiatrist Victor Frankl intuitively observed as he suffered in the National Socialists' concentration camps during the Second World War. In his *Man's Search for Meaning*, he notes how some fellow prisoners were able to change their attitude toward a situation that they could not change; this helped them even to find meaning in suffering and to transform their apparent defeat into victory.[14]

Positive growth, even flourishing, is promised to radical disciples who take up their crosses. Following Jesus is intrinsically unsafe as one might lose one's life (Matt 16:25). But as we have already established, this is ironically—and rather paradoxically—the only way to gain real life of fruitfulness, purpose, and meaning. When Jesus invites his disciples to take up their

8. Bastian, *Other Side of Happiness*, vii.

9. Bastian, *Other Side of Happiness*, 43–44.

10. Bastian, *Other Side of Happiness*, 30–46.

11. See, for example, Wiener, *Microaggressions*; Campbell and Manning, *Victimhood Culture*.

12. Bastian, *Other Side of Happiness*, viii (emphasis original).

13. Calhoun and Tedeschi, *Posttraumatic Growth*; Tedeschi and Moore, *Posttraumatic Growth Workbook*. I am grateful to Lisa Miller for pointing out these resources to me.

14. Frankl, *Man's Search*, 86, 116–17.

cross, he does not want to see them harmed. On the contrary, he makes sure that his disciples ultimately grow up and mature as *radical* disciples. As the disciple sets out on the journey by faith, she is not given any trigger warnings or promised safe spaces. Rather, she is invited to walk by faith and to trust that the Master will use her cross to shape her into his image to the glory of God.

In this section, we first take a closer look at Christ's suffering, his cross, so to speak, since it is to be assumed that his cross in many ways defines our own cross. We remind ourselves that Jesus in his role as Priest took up his own cross and gave himself as a sacrifice to the Father.[15] In a second step, we compare Jesus's cross and ours more carefully, examining parallels and differences, moving, thirdly, and more practically, to the question of what it means for us to pick up our cross (daily).

What is this cross that we are called to take up?[16] Some commentators find Jesus's demand so ambiguous that they see no way that he could actually have said it. Originally, they argue, Jesus probably taught the crowd something about "carrying his yoke," as he did elsewhere (Matt 11:29). After Jesus's crucifixion, they argue, the cross was associated with new meaning, such as self-sacrificial love and self-denial, and therefore, the early Christians put this saying about taking up one's cross in his mouth.[17] While this sounds certainly plausible, I wonder whether this is not another attempt at reducing the tension in discipleship. What if there is more to it and that this is indeed a hard saying that requires serious system two use? It is worthwhile to embrace the tension here and engage in a more serious quest for the underlying meaning. Assuming that Jesus indeed called his disciples to take up the cross, what then are some potential interpretations? How can we possibly understand this difficult command?

WHAT IS THIS CROSS?

First, and this is the most obvious route to take, there is the attempt to interpret the command literally. The disciples and the crowd who listened—note, by the way, that Jesus includes the crowd here in his call to

---

15. Adolf Schlatter describes Jesus's priestly self-giving on the cross in Schlatter, "Jesu Gottheit."

16. For an overview of interpretations of this call, see Bøe, *Cross-Bearing*, 28–48.

17. Fitzmyer, for instance, offers the following comments on Luke 9:23: "Consequently, the reformulation of an original saying of Jesus about carrying his yoke stands the best chance of surviving as the explanation of this enigmatic demand for discipleship." Fitzmyer, *Gospel*, 786.

discipleship[18]—clearly knew what a crucifixion looked like.[19] How would the original listeners have understood the call to take up the cross? It is highly unlikely that they thought they were being called into immediate martyrdom or some kind of suicide mission. "If Jesus had wanted to invite his disciples to martyrdom," writes Camille Focant, "he would have talked about 'the cross' to indicate the form of torture, and not about 'his or her cross.'"[20] Of course, many of Jesus's followers would die a martyr's death; but this would not be of their own, active initiative, but simply because of their allegiance to Christ. Still, even today believers take the command (somewhat too) literally.[21] Each year, some very devout Filipino believers carry their crosses through town, have themselves whipped, and are finally crucified during holy week.[22] After a few minutes, though, they are taken down and receive medical treatment. It is highly unlikely that Jesus expects us to perform this kind of cruel cross reenactment. Taking up one's cross is not about "self-destruction or pathological self-accusation or, worse, a martyr complex," writes Hans F. Bayer.[23] Sverre Bøe observes that Luke's inclusion of "daily" in the call to cross-bearing excludes a literal understanding of martyrdom here.[24] One needs to come up with a more refined interpretation. Yes, Jesus calls us to take up our cross—but this call does not necessarily include crucifixion.[25]

---

18. "And he said to *all* . . ." (Luke 9:23). "Luke's 'all' . . . assures the reader that this is a general call for discipleship and not one that should be restricted to leaders or any group of special Christians." Nolland, *Luke 9:21—18:34*, 482.

19. Hengel, *Crucifixion*. On crucifixion and cross-bearing in the Greco-Roman world, see Bøe, *Cross-Bearing*, 52–74.

20. "Si Jésus avait voulu inviter ses disciples au martyre, il aurait parlé de 'la croix' pour désigner le supplice et non de 'sa croix.'" Focant, *L'évangile selon Marc*, 327.

21. Vandermeersch, "Self-Flagellation."

22. McKirdy, "Crux of the Matter; Bautista, "Filipino Devotees."

23. ". . . Selbstzerstörung oder pathologische Selbstanklage oder gar einem Märytererkomplex gleichgesetzt werden." Bayer, *Das Evangelium des Markus*, 320. Similarly, Bøe writes that cross-bearing does not mean "self-crucifixion." Bøe, *Cross-Bearing*, 224.

24. "Luke does not intimate a martyrological understanding of cross-bearing, since he explicitly speaks of taking up one's cross 'daily,' 9.23. The idea of martyrdom is not evoked in the context of the cross-bearing saying either, at least not directly." Bøe, *Cross-Bearing*, 222.

25. Bøe, *Cross-Bearing*, 50–78. Based on his exploration of the idea of cross-bearing in the Greco-Roman world, Bøe notes that there is no "indication that cross-bearing was used as independent punishment; cross-bearing would always lead up to actual crucifixion, unless something extra-ordinary happened." On this basis, he writes, "We may therefore safely conclude that a reference to cross-bearing would be understood to be closely associated with death." Bøe, *Cross-Bearing*, 78.

Second, there are those who argue that the call to take up one's cross is simply a reaffirmation of the call to self-denial, albeit a radical one.[26] What is involved here, they claim, is an extreme form of the call to deny ourselves that implies the readiness to face serious inconvenience.[27] Leon Morris, for instance, suggests that the intended meaning here is "a very death to selfishness and all forms of self-seeking."[28] Hans Klein notes that as we take up our cross, we "accept the daily hassles of this world."[29] These are important points and they are surely all included in the cross we are to carry. However, I still wonder: is that all? Does the cross not stand for something even more radical? Dietrich Bonhoeffer, for example, clearly distinguished between self-denial and the call to take up the cross. One is the prerequisite for the other, but they refer to different things. Only when self-denial is being put into practice, only "when we really no longer know ourselves," Bonhoeffer writes, "only then are we ready to take up the cross for his sake."[30]

Third, the most widespread interpretation I came across as I rummaged through a whole stack of commentaries is this one: Taking up one's cross means enduring opposition, affliction, persecution, and even death for the sake of Jesus Christ and the gospel. Since the beginning of the early church, believers have experienced opposition and persecution, simply because they self-identified as followers of Christ.[31] For many of our brothers and sisters around the globe today, taking up one's cross is a very tangible, even life-threatening endeavor. But what about our own situation as we sit comfortably in our study in the suburb of a Western metropolis? Compared to many other Christians, we do lead a rather sheltered life, and the only opposition we might experience is being sidelined in the office in a discussion due to what some secular colleagues consider our allegedly bigoted Christian views. The worst-case scenario is that we risk our reputation or even our job. But that is of course a piece of cake compared to what others have to face in the majority world. Are we therefore excluded from the cross-bearing experience simply because we live in the "wrong" place? I suggest that we are to

---

26. Bøe, *Cross-Bearing*, 41–45. At least, in Luke, cross-bearing is closely paired with self-denial, as Bøe shows. Bøe, *Cross-Bearing*, 98–110. "Cross-bearing," he writes, "is rather an expression of the basic idea of putting oneself aside in order to make room for Jesus." Bøe, *Cross-Bearing*, 225.

27. According to Heinz Schürmann, taking up the cross is a renewed "actualization" of self-denial. Schürmann, *Das Lukasevangelium*, 541.

28. Morris, *Gospel*, 431 (commentary on Matt 16:24).

29. Klein speaks of "die täglichen Widrigkeiten dieser Welt annehmen." Klein, *Das Lukasevangelium*, 341 (commentary on Luke 9:23).

30. DBWE 4:86.

31. See Plasger and Stobbe, *Gewalt gegen Christen*.

understand the idea of cross-bearing in a much more comprehensive way. It is highly promising to compare the Synoptics' reference to the cross with the apostle Paul's statements about *sharing in Christ's sufferings*.

We will make significant progress in our quest when examining the vital link between the Synoptics' presentation of Jesus's call to take up one's cross and the apostle Paul's notion of sharing in Christ's sufferings.[32] According to Paul, believers "suffer with [Jesus]" (Rom 8:17), they "share his sufferings" and become "like him in his death" (Phil 3:11). David Oliver Smith examined the influence of Matthew, Mark, and Luke on Paul, and he comes to the conclusion that the command in the Synoptics to take up the cross is in fact *identical* with Paul's emphasis on sharing in Christ's sufferings.[33] Our suffering, then, in cross-bearing is not about a literal imitation of Christ's own sufferings, or about a serious exercise in self-denial, but a *participation in his own suffering*.[34] This is an important step in a promising direction. The challenge now is to figure out what it means to share in Christ's sufferings, and it is a formidable one. Taking the route of interpreting the Synoptics' expression of cross-bearing via Paul's sharing in Christ's sufferings is both viable and illuminating. We isolate first the question of Christ's sufferings, and then move, in a second step, to the aspect of sharing in Christ's sufferings.

CHRIST'S SUFFERINGS

When we think of Jesus's sufferings, our mind immediately turns, of course, to the cross.[35] We might also think about his struggle in Gethsemane or the flagellation under Pilate's henchmen. These are the vivid images that appear before our eyes, and art galleries around the globe are replete with paintings depicting these scenes. They are burned into the collective memory of

---

32. Ulrich Luz points to the "surprising . . . factual convergence" between Paul's notion of sharing in Christ's suffering and Mark's emphasis on taking up the cross." ["Die sachliche Konvergenz zwischen der paulinischen Betonung der Konformität mit dem Gekreuzigten und der markinischen Kreuzesnachfolge bleibt m.E. erstaunlich. Und schließlich wird man immerhin fragen müssen, wodurch denn die paulinische Aufnahme nicht nur des Leidens und Sterbens Jesu, sondern insbesondere seines Kreuzes angestoßen sein könnte, wenn nicht durch Jesu Logion vom Kreuz-Aufnehmen (Mt 10,38)."] Luz, "Nachfolge Jesu," 685.

33. Smith writes: "While Paul does not specifically say he has 'taken up the cross,' he does say he is willing to 'share his [Christ's] sufferings.' Christ's sufferings were on the cross, so if Paul shared his sufferings, he took up his cross." Smith, *Influence of the Epistles*, 140.

34. Bultmann, *Der zweite Brief*, 29.

35. I am deeply indebted to Donald Macleod here. Much of what I am sharing here is influenced by my reading of his work. See Macleod, *Christ Crucified*.

our culture.³⁶ However, these scenes do not tell the whole story. We might want to take a step back and look at the bigger picture of Jesus's earthly life and work, from beginning to end. Doing so, we notice straightaway that his whole earthly biography, in fact, was a kaleidoscope of suffering. "His whole life," writes Donald Macleod, "from the cradle to the tomb, was suffering."³⁷ In what follows we seek to get a clearer picture of what cross-bearing and thus sharing in Christ's sufferings means. We pursue a (more or less) chronological approach, moving from the incarnation to the cross.

Incarnation and Identification

It is not only on the cross where Jesus suffered and atoned for our sin, but already in his incarnation and his life do we encounter suffering and note redemptive value. Christ redeemed us, argues John Calvin, "by the whole course of his obedience," not just his death. "In short," Calvin continues, "from the time he took on the form of a servant, he began to pay the price of liberation in order to redeem us."³⁸ In the incarnation, the Son of God, the eternal Word of God, assumed human nature on account of God's grand project of renewing the created order in Christ. By assuming humanity, Jesus Christ became a perfect representative for us, the perfect human being without sin (Heb 4:15).³⁹ His incarnation and his life lived for us are central parts of Jesus's messianic mission. And on both accounts, by clothing himself with humanity and by representing us in his own life before God, he suffered.

We have already touched on the question whether the Logos suffered the loss of some (or even all) of his divine attributes (see chapter 1). We arrived at the conclusion that the Logos's self-emptying, to which Paul refers in Philippians 2:7, is not about what he laid aside, but what he *took on* for

---

36. Harries, *Passion in Art*.

37. Macleod, *Christ Crucified*, 16. Macleod vividly summarizes the kind of suffering Jesus endured and that we often overlook as follows: "He was poor beyond our imagining, owning only the clothes he stood in; homeless, without a pillow for his head; oppressed by crowds demanding a sign and plying him with endless questions; often exhausted, as when he lay dead to the world in the stern of a tiny fishing boat caught in the eye of a fearful storm (Mark 4:38). Ulrich Luz, similarly, observes that "suffering and persecution are the master's way of life . . . This is expressed in persecutions, trials, family disputes, and finally, martyrdom." ["Leiden und Verfolgung sind die Lebensform des Meisters . . . Sie zeigt sich in Verfolgungen, Prozessen, Familienspaltungen und schließlich im Martyrium."] Luz, *Das Evangelium nach Matthäus*, 144.

38. *Inst.* 2.16.5:507.

39. There is some discussion as to whether Jesus adopted a fallen or an unfallen human nature. For an introduction to the debate see Crisp, "Vicarious Humanity"; McKinley, *Tempted For Us*.

our sake. "It is what Christ *assumes* that impoverishes him," Donald Macleod insists.[40] As Christ took the role of a servant, or more precisely, the role of the "suffering servant" (Isa 53), he suffers "condescension . . . beyond imagining."[41] One observes a radical inversion of responsibility here. Deserving our service, he serves the undeserving. Instead of being served, it is he who washes the dirty feet of his disciples (John 13:1–17). And even more than that, he ultimately serves and suffers as the great shepherd who lays down his life for the sheep (John 10:11).

We touch here on the substitutionary nature of Jesus's suffering as the perfect and sinless One who took on our sins. Jesus was identified as closely as possible with our sin, as the apostle Paul explains to the Corinthians: "For our sake he made him to be sin who knew no sin, so that in him we might become the righteousness of God" (2 Cor 5:21). As Jesus was charged with the particular mission "to redeem those who were under the law" (Gal 4:5), the Logos voluntarily subjected himself to a significant demotion for our sake. For himself, this meant that his presence as the God-human was concealed, notes Bonhoeffer, his presence was "veiled."[42] In his very act of assuming humanity and carrying our sin, Christ suffers humiliation.[43]

It is appropriate to pause here for a minute and remind ourselves of the utterly astonishing nature of the incarnation and Jesus's identification with us and our sins in order to understand the nature of Christ's suffering here. For it was not an ordinary human who took on the status of a slave, but the one who was "in the form of God," who was and is the "the radiance of the glory of God and the exact imprint of his nature" (Heb 1:3). In the words of an early Christian hymn,

> He is the image of the invisible God, the firstborn of all creation.
> For by him all things were created, in heaven and on earth, visible and invisible, whether thrones or dominions or rulers or

---

40. Macleod, *Person of Christ*, 216 (emphasis original).

41. Macleod, *Person of Christ*, 218.

42. "In his death, Jesus does not reveal any of his divine attributes. To the contrary, he is a dying human being, despairing of God. And of this one we say, this is God. God is not concealed in Christ as a human being but rather is revealed as God-human. But this God-human is veiled in his existence as the Humiliated One." DBWE 12:355–56.

43. Bonhoeffer notes: "How is Jesus's particular way of existing as the Humiliated One expressed? In that he has taken on sinful flesh. The conditions for his humiliation are set by the curse, the fall of Adam. In being humiliated, Christ, the God-human, enters of his own free will into the world of sin and death. He enters there in such a way as to conceal himself [there], so that he is no longer recognizable visibly as the God-human. He comes among us humans not in μορφῇ Θεοῦ but rather incognito, as a beggar among beggars, and outcast among outcasts; he comes among sinners as the one without sin, but also as a sinner among sinners." DBWE 12:356.

authorities—all things were created through him and for him. And he is before all things, and in him all things hold together. (Col 1:15–17)

This is the One whose whole life was marked by the way he lived a perfect human life in our place and carried our sin. "[F]rom the moment of his birth," notes Donald Macleod, "Jesus was identified with sinful humanity, and all the circumstances of his life reflected the fact that he was bearing the sin of the world (John 1:29)."[44] We lack the words and the imagination to fathom what it must have been like for an immaculate being to be intimately identified with what is most repulsive and repugnant to perfect divinity. The complexities and conundrums associated with his assumption of humanity are therefore inaccessible to us and remain a mystery. In the words of Bonhoeffer,

> "God revealed in the flesh," the God-human Jesus Christ, is the holy mystery which theology is appointed to guard. What a mistake to think that it is the task of theology to unravel God's mystery, to bring it down to the flat, ordinary human wisdom of experience and reason! It is the task of theology solely to preserve God's wonder as wonder, to understand, to defend, to glorify God's mystery as mystery.[45]

It is important to underline that from the very beginning, Jesus Christ lived and suffered *for us*. Dietrich Bonhoeffer adopted Luther's emphasis that in Christ, God is always acting for us (*pro nobis*).[46] Right from the outset, in his very nature, and in his life lived on earth, Christ is totally and faithfully for us.

In his life he demonstrated what it means to be truly human. Very much unlike us, he lived in perfect obedience toward the Father, completely dependent upon him, seeking his will and glory alone and not his own, always acting in and through the Holy Spirit. As the incarnate One, Jesus Christ fulfilled the law in our place,[47] Bonhoeffer notes, and in so doing, he "is the one who acts [as the new] humanity."[48] By becoming like us, living a perfect life in our place, he enables us to be transformed and to become

---

44. Macleod, *Christ Crucified*, 16.

45. Letter to the young brothers of the church in Pomerania, Christmas 1939. Bonhoeffer et al., *Testament to Freedom*, 448.

46. "With Luther, Bonhoeffer maintains that God is always *pro me* and *pro nobis*, God *for* us," notes John de Gruchy in his introduction to Dietrich Bonhoeffer, *Dietrich Bonhoeffer*, 9 (emphasis original).

47. DBWE 11:297–98.

48. DBWE 11:298.

more like him as we follow in his footsteps. Michael Gorman writes that "to become like Christ is to become reshaped into the image of God that God originally intended for humans to embody."[49] As we follow Christ on the way of discipleship, we are being changed into his image. "He became like us so that we could become like him," Lucy Peppiatt notes.[50]

Physical and Spiritual Suffering

Jesus Christ assumed a true human nature. As it is expressed in the Symbol of Chalcedon, Jesus is "consubstantial with us" according to humanity.[51] This involves Jesus sharing with us our physiological condition and psychological experience in the context of a fallen world.[52] Immersing himself fully in everyday life in first-century Palestine, he enjoyed the taste of juicy figs on a hot day, and he also might have suffered a headache due to the hot sun. From our perspective today, where most of us enjoy the modern conveniences of air-conditioning, health care, and transport, it is difficult to imagine what life was like back then. Jesus traveled long distances on foot, down to Jerusalem and back up to Galilee (if you have ever been foolish enough to visit Israel in summer, as I once did, you will know that this climate does not lend itself to a comfortable walking experience). Understandably, Jesus was at times tired and weary of his journey, well acquainted with physical and mental exhaustion (e.g., John 4:6). It is reasonable to assume that Jesus probably suffered from a fever at some point, and since he was trained as a carpenter (Mark 6:3), we easily imagine nasty blisters and injuries on his hands. Life at the workplace in a pre-health and safety era was no picnic at all.

Jesus was also intimately familiar with the whole spectrum of human sinless emotions.[53] He experienced everything from exuberant joy to crushing sorrow (for our purposes we focus here on the negative emotions). Jesus, we are told, was "a man of sorrows and acquainted with grief" (Isa 53:3; Acts 8:35). The New Testament authors report that Jesus "sighed deeply in his spirit" in face of human unbelief (Mark 8:12); he "wept over" Jerusalem (Luke 19:41), and also on the occasion of the death of Lazarus (John 11:35);

---

49. Gorman, "Missional Theosis," 198.

50. Peppiatt, *Disciple*, 31.

51. Schaff, *Greek and Latin*, 62.

52. In regard to Jesus's full experience of humanity, my thinking has been shaped considerably by my teacher Donald Macleod and I refer to him here throughout this section.

53. Stephen Voorwinde has written an excellent study of Jesus's emotions in the Gospels. Voorwinde, *Jesus' Emotions*. Note also the classic study by Warfield, "Emotional Life." See also Elliott, *Faithful Feelings*, 249–50.

he expressed righteous anger at the money changers in the temple (Matt 21:12), and vis-à-vis the self-righteous religious leaders (Matt 12:34). In the garden of Gethsemane, Jesus suffered utterly crushing depression and emotional exhaustion. Here, he tells his friends: "My soul is very sorrowful, even to death" (Matt 26:38). "The burden of grief was life-threatening," writes Donald Macleod, "and associated with it were distress and agitation."[54] As he was in agony, praying for the cup to be removed, "his sweat became like great drops of blood falling down to the ground" (Luke 22:44). Here, he suffered the gaze into the most horrific abyss that before or after him no other pair of human eyes would have to behold. Proceeding on his way to the cross, Jesus suffered relational pain as he was betrayed, humiliated, falsely accused, degraded, and even denied by one of his closest friends (e.g., Luke 22:54–62). These episodes evoke a whole range of emotions, such as shame, disappointment, hurt, and grief. In terms of physical suffering, we could obviously add the torture: the crown of thorns, the beatings, and the brutal flagellation (John 19:1–3). Jesus suffered the ridicule and the scorn of soldiers, and, ultimately, he died an agonizing death on the cross.[55] The physical exhaustion is accompanied by the crushing weight of carrying the burden of humanity's sin. This moves Jesus's experience completely beyond the limits of our apprehension and ability to empathize even remotely. Jesus clearly suffered the extremes of what is possible to suffer as a psychosomatic being. We have simply no idea what it was like phenomenologically and experientially for Jesus to suffer in our place.[56]

Opposition and Persecution

Jesus's life was marked by opposition and persecution from the very beginning. Right after what was a rather uncomfortable birth in the stable (Luke 2:7), Jesus's life was at risk, since King Herod was out to kill him (Matt 2:13). A young refugee, he and his parents had to flee to Egypt until the threat was over and the king was dead (Matt 2:19–20). As he grew up and eventually began his ministry, Jesus constantly suffered misunderstanding and rejection, even by those closest to him. Donald Macleod puts it like this:

> He was misunderstood by his family, who feared for his sanity; pursued by the sick and their desperate relatives; stalked by the Pharisees with their undisguised hostility and their sly

---

54. Macleod, *Christ Crucified*, 27.
55. See Chapman, *Ancient Jewish*.
56. Bonhoeffer speaks of Christ's "vicarious representative act for the new humanity." DBWE 11:297–98.

coadjutors with their entrapping conundrums (Mark 12:13). His whole life followed a pattern of rejection: rejection in "his own country," Nazareth; rejection by the religious establishment; rejection by public opinion, always fickle; and rejection, at last, by his disciples, who all forsook him and fled.[57]

All this left a visible mark in Jesus's appearance, quite naturally so, with the effect that, when he was still in his early thirties, he had the appearance of a man in his late forties: "So the Jews said to him, 'You are not yet fifty years old, and have you seen Abraham?'" (John 8:57).[58] Throughout his public ministry, Jesus suffered open rejection and latent persecution by the religious elite and their constant attempts to "to trap him in his talk" (Mark 12:13). Jesus Christ, the Son of God, here is present "incognito," Bonhoeffer notes, "as a beggar among beggars, an outcast among outcasts; he comes among sinners as the one without sin, but also as a sinner among sinners."[59]

Testing and Temptation

Throughout his life, Jesus was exposed to testing, trials, and temptations.[60] "Jesus was dogged and harassed by the Prince of Darkness throughout his life," notes Donald Macleod.[61] Right at the outset of his ministry he was "led up by the Spirit into the wilderness to be tempted by the devil" (Matt 4:1). Having fasted for forty days, Jesus was weak and vulnerable, and the tempter aimed right at the heart of Jesus's self-understanding as the Son of God. "*If* you are the Son of God . . ." (Matt 4:3, 6), the enemy taunts him, sowing seeds of doubt regarding his own identity. Jesus is here tempted to rely on self instead on God, as Hans Weder observes. His self-understanding as the One who lives in dependent and intimate fellowship with the Father is being targeted.[62] Weder writes: "The three temptations reveal wherein the substance of the real trial [*Anfechtung*] lies: The Son of God is tempted with

---

57. Macleod, *Christ Crucified*, 17.
58. Macleod, *Christ Crucified*, 17.
59. DBWE 12:356.
60. Theologians discuss whether Jesus was, theoretically, able to succumb to temptation. That is, does Jesus's humanity require the capacity to succumb to temptation. For an in-depth discussion see Crisp, "Was Christ Sinless?"
61. Macleod, *Christ Crucified*, 17.
62. Jesus has, "als Gottessohn die tiefste Beziehung, nämlich ein Lebensverhältnis zu Gott." Weder, "Der Lebensraum des Zweifels," 27.

a view to power, domination, irresistibility. The Son of God is tempted not to live out of [his relationship with] God, but out of himself."[63]

This subtle, yet powerful temptation to self-reliance was part of the evil one's arsenal through to the very end. Of course, with one snap of the finger, Jesus could have changed everything and managed an easy escape. At his arrest, he assures the combative Peter that his Father could immediately send him "more than twelve legions of angels" (Matt 25:53). This makes the mocking voices surrounding him later on the cross so much harder to endure: "[S]ave yourself, and come down from the cross!" (Mark 15:30).[64] Yet Jesus did not give in, he carried on as our great high priest, who "in every respect has been tempted as we are, yet without sin" (Heb 4:15).

Sacrifice and Forsakenness

This great high priest gave himself as the perfect sacrifice to God. As the spotless lamb of God, he took our sins on himself and covered them with his blood (John 1:29). He came "to give his life as a ransom for many" (Matt 20:28), so that we would be reconciled to God and receive the adoption as sons and daughters of God (Gal 4:5). He faithfully and patiently carried our sins, made them his own, nailed them to the cross (Col 2:14), and accomplished his mission of reconciliation: "It is finished" (John 19:30).

This mission, however, involved that Jesus would have to pass through the valley of godforsakenness, which was the apex of his suffering. When surrounded by darkness, "Jesus cried with a loud voice, 'Eloi, Eloi, lema sabachthani?' which means, 'My God, my God, why have you forsaken me?'" (Mark 15:34). Using the psalmist's words (Ps 22:1), Jesus agonized over the godforsakenness he suffered at the very end. "There is now no sense of his own divine sonship," writes Donald Macleod, "no sense of God's love and no sense of his Father's approval. God is not hearing him. He cries, but there is no answer, and God even seems to mock his trust (Ps 22:8)."[65] Our finite human minds lack insight into this conundrum of forsakenness, and we are well advised to tread carefully here. "In its very nature," Macleod adds, "the spiritual content of this climax of his suffering is inaccessible to us."[66] There

---

63. "Die drei Versuchungen lassen erkennen, worin die eigentliche Anfechtung besteht: Es ist die Versuchung des Gottessohns, zur Stärke, zur Übermacht, zur Unwiderstehlichkeit. Es ist die Versuchung des Gottessohnes, gerade nicht aus Gott zu leben sondern aus sich selbst." Weder, "Der Lebensraum des Zweifels," 32.

64. Macleod, *Christ Crucified*, 39–40.

65. Macleod, *Christ Crucified*, 48.

66. Macleod, *Christ Crucified*, 48.

comes the point when the theologian puts her hand on the mouth and simply stands in awe of the mystery. The mystery grows even deeper when one considers, as Bonhoeffer insists again and again, that Jesus "is there for others"—especially right there in the midst of godforsakenness. "'[T]he human being for others'! therefore the Crucified One."[67] Jesus's self-sacrificial love for sinners (and God!) is sustained even in and through godforsakenness.[68]

JESUS'S UNIQUE CROSS

Before we move on and examine more closely our own crosses in light of Jesus's cross, it is appropriate to pause for a moment and to ponder the uniqueness of his cross. Based on our considerations so far, we note that Jesus's sufferings were unique in their quality, intensity, extent, and effect. In many ways, his sufferings are inaccessible and unfathomable to us. We have no idea what impact the incarnation and self-emptying had on Jesus's personal experience. What was it like for a perfect divine being to assume humanity, enter a fallen world marked by pain, sickness, and decay—and to sense it fully in his own human mind, body, and spirit? We are not told, and we have no way of finding out.

Jesus's sufferings were unique as he freely chose to suffer complete identification with our sin while remaining sinless himself. We, on the other hand, identify with our own sins only, and rightly so. Only Jesus's sufferings have a substitutionary effect and are therefore of atoning quality.[69] By the way, it is at this point that we part with Bonhoeffer, who was prepared to speculate: "Whether this suffering of Christians also has power to atone for sin (1 Peter 4:1) remains an open question."[70] The task of atoning for sin, in my view, is reserved to Christ alone.[71] "But he was pierced for our transgressions," writes

---

67. DBWE 8:501 [DBW 8:558].

68. By faithfully clinging to the Father right in his absence, Adolf Schlatter notes, Jesus demonstrates his divinity as he establishes fellowship with God in and through forsakenness. Schlatter writes: "Because he does not deny God while denied by him, does not forsake God while forsaken by him, his godforsakenness becomes the basis of communion with God; having his spirit undone and being disgraced become the condition of his being made spiritual and glorified; and the futility of his mission becomes the root of its fruitfulness. What God took from him, he freely and willingly gave up to him, and because he turns the divine taking into his free giving, it becomes the basis of God's return-gift, which brings him into perfect communion." Schlatter, "Jesu Gottheit," 65. I have dealt with this in more detail in Bräutigam, *Union with Christ*, 152–61.

69. See Horton, *Gospel-Driven Life*, 151.

70. DBWE 4:222.

71. One notes a certain ambivalence in Bonhoeffer regarding classic theories of the

the prophet Isaiah in anticipation of the Messiah, "he was crushed for our iniquities; upon him was the chastisement that brought us peace, and with his wounds we are healed" (Isa 53:5). Our sufferings do not have any propitiating, God-appeasing effect. Only Christ suffered "as vicarious representative for the world," notes Bonhoeffer. "Only his suffering brings salvation," he writes, and here we are in complete agreement with him.[72]

No one else suffered rejection, opposition, and persecution as Jesus did. "Jesus Christ is *the* Rejected of God," writes Karl Barth, "for God makes Himself rejected in Him, and has Himself alone tasted to the depths all that rejection means and necessarily involves."[73] The temptations that Jesus endured are beyond our capacity to comprehend. This is so not necessarily because of their quality or quantity, but because they were endured by the Christ, the One who always lived in perfect communion with the Father yet who assumed human nature.

And only Jesus endured crushing godforsakenness. While we might at some points in our life feel forsaken by God, it is what it is at the end of the day, namely merely a feeling, albeit a very forceful one at times. The only One who suffered true godforsakenness was the person of Jesus Christ—so that we would never have to experience it. For these reasons—and we could mention many more—Jesus's cross is indeed the cross that eclipses our crosses. It is the cross par excellence. "What sets him apart is his cross: not only a cross, but his cross," writes Donald Macleod, "a road no-one had travelled before and no-one has travelled since."[74] Only Jesus cried the cry of dereliction; only Jesus exclaimed, "It is finished!" (John 19:30), and only he spoke these last words, "Father, into your hands I commit my spirit!" (Luke 23:46).

At the same time, however, we recognize that in taking up his cross, pain was mixed with joy in Jesus's experience. By taking up his cross, he embraced the ultimate tension of joy in the presence of suffering. The aspect of joy in Jesus's inner life when he took up his cross, Adolf Schlatter argues, has been more or less ignored in theological history.[75] Yet in his view it is clearly portrayed in the New Testament documents. In Jesus's farewell discourse in the Gospel of John, Schlatter argues, one finds no instances

---

atonement, and this certainly affects our retrieval of his ideas. Bonhoeffer's strong emphasis on the incarnation and our sharing in his new humanity at times overshadows aspects of the atonement. For a nuanced discussion, see Burkholder, "Violence."

72. DBWE 4:90.

73. *CD* II/2:496 (emphasis original).

74. Macleod, *Christ Crucified*, 18.

75. Schlatter explores this aspect in Schlatter, "Jesu Gottheit," 74–75. The following observations are based on his insights.

of lament—rather, joy and Jesus's desire to glorify the Father is the predominant sentiment that gives hope to the distressed disciples (e.g., John 16:20–24). In the Gospel of Matthew, the Passion story is illustrated with the parable of the king preparing a wedding banquet for his son (Matt 22:1–14), a picture of celebration and rejoicing. And at the Last Supper, Jesus's "Take, eat; this is my body" (Matt 26:26) "is not a word of wailing but has in it the triumphant jubilation of the Savior's conquering power."[76] Never does Jesus present himself as one who seeks pity. On the contrary, "do not weep for me" (Luke 23:28), is his appeal to the bystanders.[77] Disciples who seek to follow the great high priest, who endured his cross "for the joy that was set before him" (Heb 12:2), then have much cause to hope that their painful experience, too, will be mixed with joy as they pick up their cross. As they follow their Master, they will join in his triumph and victory in the midst of what seems to be defeat and failure.

CONCLUSION

We conclude the first important step on our journey to figure out the meaning of cross-bearing. In this chapter we set out to find answers to the important question of what Jesus means when he calls us to take up our cross. First, it was suggested that we understand cross-bearing in light of our participation in Christ's sufferings. We then managed the initial segment of our route as we provided a clearer picture of Jesus's sufferings. This exercise of recapitulating Jesus's sufferings was sobering but vital since radical disciples need to be intimately familiar with Jesus's sufferings on their behalf as they seek to participate in his sufferings. "Christians cannot suffer with Christ before they have embraced the full benefits of Christ's sufferings for them," writes Ronald Rittgers, "they cannot act like Christ until Christ has acted upon (and in) them."[78] The idea of Christ acting for us in his sufferings is prominently illustrated in the Eucharist. When discussing self-denial earlier, we noted that its sacramental equivalent was baptism, the celebration of our constant dying and rising with Christ. When it comes to the demand of cross-bearing, we have the Eucharist as a tangible reminder of Jesus's ultimate cross-bearing on our behalf and our share in it. Partaking in the Lord's Supper, we receive his body, given for us, and we receive in the cup his blood, the promise of sins forgiven and covenant renewed (Luke 22:19–20; Matt 26:26–28). The tension here is obvious: festive celebration in light of

76. Schlatter, "Jesu Gottheit," 74.
77. Schlatter, "Jesu Gottheit," 74.
78. Rittgers, *Reformation of Suffering*, 115.

our redemption is mixed with the realization that our Beloved had to die in order to procure it for us. The live-giving meal with the elements of bread and wine take on a macabre flavor as it is the body and the blood of the Savior of which we are called to partake. Yet it is in exactly this tension that we receive the new life offered to us through Jesus Christ. New life comes to us, literally, by partaking of his suffering, his blood and body given to us on the cross. And that brings us back to our original question. Having established key aspects of Jesus's experience of cross-bearing we are now in the position to compare his cross to our own. And in so doing we will see how taking up our cross will result in positive transformation.

PERSONAL REFLECTION

How does it make you feel to read about Jesus's sufferings? Is there anything that stands out, that is new to you? What is it?

What effect does it have on you to read about Jesus's sufferings *in your place*? How does it make you grow in your appreciation and love for Christ?

Which aspects of the Lord's Supper appear in new light as you ponder the sufferings of Christ for you?

What does it mean for your own walk of discipleship as you consider the way in which Jesus walked? How could Jesus's cross empower you to take up your own cross and follow him?

How do you want to pray for yourself right now?

6

Sharing in Christ's Sufferings

HAVING EXPLORED JESUS'S SUFFERINGS, we go a step further in this chapter and examine how radical disciples actually do share in his sufferings. How and to what extent does our own cross compare to Christ's? Answering (even posing!) this question comes with particular challenges. While one can indeed draw parallels between Christ's suffering and ours, we must reiterate, based on our explorations so far, that in many ways Christ's suffering is unparalleled and thus not transferable to our own situation. Only his suffering has substitutionary and God-appeasing quality. There are important moments when the parallels break down. In what follows we connect the aspects of Christ's sufferings identified in the previous chapter with our own condition and context, and we seek to do so with appropriate diligence and care, bearing in mind the "infinite qualitative difference" (Kierkegaard) between Jesus's suffering and ours. As we draw near to investigate our own cross, it is vital that we always see it in the shadow of Christ's grand cross.

SELF-EMPTYING AND REPRESENTATION

Great care is needed when comparing Jesus's self-emptying to our own condition and context.[1] For the Logos, the act of emptying himself meant taking on human nature. He clothed himself with human nature. When we are

---

1. I am deeply indebted to Bruce Pass who helped me clarify important nuances in this section and the following one.

called to be like-minded with Christ in our self-emptying (Phil 2:5), we are not required to assume a new nature. That is an impossibility, of course. We have already seen in the previous chapter that we are clothed with our new self through union with Christ by the Holy Spirit. However, we are called to imitate Christ in his obedience as a faithful servant of God the Father. The Logos put on human nature and we put on Christ.

For us, then, self-emptying means that we dump the aspirations of our old self and imitate Jesus's example of putting God and others first. We ignore impulses from the bloated, old, self-centered self, that is infatuated with self-importance and shows a constant need for self-aggrandizement. Instead, we embrace the inclinations of the new self that is Christ-shaped, the self that is happy to adopt the position of a servant, and desires to serve God and others in love and humility as we count others more significant than ourselves (Phil 2:3). The common denominator of Christ's self-emptying and ours is that servanthood is the true form of humanity, and some would say divinity too. In self-emptying, we thus imitate Christ according to his divine nature as well as his human nature.

In the previous chapter, we referred to Jesus's substitutionary and representative roles as he fully identified with us. A few words by way of reminder are appropriate at this point. It is important to note a distinct asymmetry of agency here. We have already established that only Jesus's suffering is of a substitutionary quality. Only Christ died for our sins and reconciled us to the Father, and we are completely and categorically inactive here. And only Jesus represents us in his perfectly lived life before God. In representation, Christ acts on our behalf as the perfect human being, always in close communion with the Father and through the Spirit. However, there is a sense in which we, too, have a representative role, albeit in a different manner. According to Bonhoeffer, the community of the disciples presents the world before God the Father. He writes,

> But the church-community itself knows now that the world's suffering seeks a bearer. So in following Christ, this suffering falls upon it, and it bears the suffering while being borne by Christ. The community of Jesus Christ vicariously represents the world before God by following Christ under the cross.[2]

Bearing the suffering of the world vicariously as a community of disciples is central to Bonhoeffer's mind.[3] Suffering is "God's judgment over sin," he notes.[4] Sharing in Christ's suffering now means that disciples par-

2. DBWE 4:90.
3. DBWE 4:90–91.
4. DBWE 15:409.

ticipate in Christ's bearing the "guilt of the world"—not in a substitutionary, expiating sense, but in a vicarious, representative sense.⁵ In this sense, the community of the disciples' presentation of the world to God supplement Christ's representation of the church to God. This is a highly significant aspect of Bonhoeffer's thinking. The church, as the fellowship of the disciples, not only mirrors Christ's action through the Spirit, Bonhoeffer claims, but somehow actually *is* Christ embodied in time and place, existing for others.⁶ "Christ existing as church-community" is how he prefers to put it.⁷ The church, he writes, is the *"new human being"* that is identical with Christ.⁸ Bonhoeffer here certainly stretches Paul's teaching on the church as the body of Christ to its limits (e.g., Rom 12:5; 1 Cor 12:27), but we note his intention to put into relief that the community of Jesus's disciples indeed acts out his new humanity through the Spirit.

In more practical terms, disciples thus bear each other's burdens, and they lament together, presenting the needs of this world before the Father and through the Spirit who "himself intercedes for us with groanings too deep for words" (Rom 8:26). They love the world with the sacrificial love of Jesus Christ, and they alleviate suffering wherever possible even when it comes at a personal cost (we return to this idea at a later stage when we discuss the disciples' calling to befriend the world in chapter 9). One wonders whether it is exactly this kind of "representative vicarious action" that the apostle Paul alluded to when he writes that he is in his flesh "filling up what is lacking in Christ's afflictions for the sake of his body, that is, the church" (Col 1:24). As radical disciples share in Jesus's active love for a fallen world, suffering with and serving others, they share in Christ's afflictions for the sake of the church, filling up what is lacking, and in that way become truly human.⁹

---

5. "It is the guilt of all flesh that the Christian bears until the end of life, but beyond this it is at the same time the guilt of the world in Jesus that Christians must bear and endure in suffering. In this way the Christian's suffering of judgment in communion with Jesus Christ becomes a vicarious suffering for the world." DBWE 15:409. "Participation in Christ thus draws the follower into the Christ-reality of 'vicarious representative responsibility.'" Zimmermann, "Dietrich Bonhoeffer," 645.

6. Joel Lawrence explains: "For Bonhoeffer, the church is a unique community because it has a unique nature: it *is* the Body of Christ, the presence of Christ on earth in history." Lawrence, *Bonhoeffer*, 40 (emphasis original).

7. DBWE 1:121 [*Christus als Gemeinde existierend*, DBW 1:76].

8. "The 'new human being' is thus at the same time Christ and the church. Christ is the new humanity in the new human being. Christ is the church." DBWE 4:219 (emphasis original).

9. See Bonhoeffer to Eberhard Bethge, July 18, 1944. DBWE 8:480 [DBW 8:535].

PHYSICAL AND SPIRITUAL SUFFERING

Jesus suffered physically, emotionally, and spiritually, and so do we. Again, we note that one cannot quite draw a straight line between Jesus's sufferings and ours. As mentioned earlier, Jesus was "clothed with our flesh"—yet not sinful flesh.[10] Other than Christ, we suffer as those who carry a fallen, corrupt, and sinful human nature. Our own suffering is intimately woven together with the properties of our sinful old self and the manner in which we participate in the sins of human society. We are not excluded from suffering from addictions, from cancer, a ruptured appendix, a major depressive episode, or the consequences of a coronavirus infection. We all have our own, intimate experiences with suffering, and we all have our own stories to tell. And we all have discovered the close interrelation between physical and emotional spiritual suffering.[11] One can influence, intensify, and even cause the other. A depressed disciple will often not only feel despondent and lethargic but is also most likely to suffer physical symptoms such as an interrupted sleep-wake rhythm and gastrointestinal problems, for instance.[12] We are composite, psychosomatic beings, and therefore our physiology and psychology impact one another. This insight has been often overlooked in church and theology, Kelly Kapic argues, especially when it comes to suffering.[13] In Kapic's view, one of the few who noticed the connection here was Dietrich Bonhoeffer, who writes, "The body is not the prison, the shell, the exterior, of a human being; instead a human being is a human body. A human being does not 'have' a body or 'have' a soul; instead a human being 'is' body and soul."[14] Suffering impacts the whole human being as a composite unit, not simply some parts.

Martin Luther, too, was keenly aware of the close relationship between physical and emotional suffering and he had his own share in both. Luther suffered from physical illnesses such as gout, vertigo, poor circulation (or probably Ménière's disease), various digestive problems, and gall and kidney stones.[15] These afflictions surely influenced Luther's psychological experience. More with a view to spiritual-emotional suffering, Luther reports that he was regularly affected by serious afflictions, where physical and spiritual suffering somewhat overlapped. In the summer of 1527, Luther

---

10. *Inst.* 2.13.1:474.

11. On the relationship between physical and mental health, see Ohrnberger et al., "Relationship."

12. Trivedi, "Link"; Fava, "Depression."

13. For a helpful discussion, see Kapic, *Embodied Hope*, 43–55.

14. DBWE 3:76–77. Kapic refers to this in Kapic, *Embodied Hope*, 50.

15. Hendrix, *Martin Luther*, 183; Oberman, *Luther*, 328–30.

went through a particularly dark period that lasted for about half a year. The Black Death had reached Wittenberg at that time, and Luther was asked to evacuate, together with the university, to Jena.[16] Luther, however, decided to stay and to care for patients he received and nursed in his home.[17] Even his son Hans fell ill, but recovered.[18] As if that were not bad enough, Luther struggled at that time with his own dark night of the soul—presumably amplified by the onerous circumstances. Right in the middle of this, he writes to his friend and collaborator in the Reformation, Philipp Melanchthon:

> I was for more than a whole week in death and hell, so that I was sick all over, and my limbs still tremble. I almost lost Christ in the waves and blasts of despair and blasphemy against God, but God was moved by the prayers of saints and began to take pity on me and rescued my soul from the lowest hell.[19]

Luther's example illustrates well the fact that we cannot easily isolate different forms of embodied suffering. Suffering often comes as a complex phenomenon, touching our mind, body, and soul—often at the same time and in complex interaction.

Before we turn to the next, and more obvious instances of suffering with Christ, such as opposition, persecution, and temptations, one might wonder: "Where exactly is our suffering cross-bearing—for Jesus's sake, so to speak—and where not?" Does only a certain level of persecution qualify, or can a light migraine also be counted as sharing in Christ's sufferings?[20] It seems plausible, in my view, to adopt a more inclusive perspective here, and I tend to side with Jac J. Müller who offers a more comprehensive definition:

---

16. Hendrix, *Martin Luther*, 184.

17. Hendrix, *Martin Luther*, 184.

18. Hendrix, *Martin Luther*, 184–85.

19. Luther to Philipp Melanchthon, August 2, 1527, in Luther, *Luther's Correspondence*, 409 (Letter 768). The original is in Latin, "Ego sane ultra ea, quae nuper scripsi, plus tota hebdomada in morte et inferno iactatus, ita ut toto corpore laesus adhuc tremam mebris. Amisse fere toto Christo agebar fluctibus et procellis desperationis et blasphemiae in Deum. Sed Sanctorum precibus motus Deus miseri me coepit et eruit animam meam de inferno inferiori." WA Br 4:226.9–11 (no. 1126).

20. Luther argued that, strictly speaking, we do not suffer with Christ in every circumstance. A normal sickness does not count, in Luther's view, only when we carry "shame and persecution for righteousness' sake" do we carry the cross of Christ. ["Wann ich ym betthe unnd binn kranck, odder so eyner umb seyner missetat willen wirdt getoedt durchs fewer, wasser odder schwert, ist nit das creutze Christi, sonder die schande und vorfolgung umb der gerechtikeit willen ist das creutze Christi."] WA 10/3:368.17–20.

> Sharing the sufferings of Christ is, therefore, more than just suffering for the sake of Christ (in tribulation and persecution), or in imitation of Christ. It means all suffering, bodily or spiritual, which overtakes the believer by virtue of his new manner of life, his "Christ life" in a world unbelieving and hostile to Christ.[21]

Thus, in a sense *all* suffering that the disciple faces on her pilgrimage falls under the category of cross-bearing because her faith in a good and trustworthy God is challenged.[22] Bonhoeffer writes that the disciple "recognizes in suffering a temptation by Satan to separate him from God. Here lies the origin of murmuring against God . . . The Christian's trust in God's love is jeopardized."[23] Christ experienced the very same challenge, and it is right here that we follow in his footsteps. Here, radical disciples engage in the fight of faith as they put their faith into action and, against all odds, confess their trust in a faithful God who draws near to them in Christ in their sufferings.

OPPOSITION AND PERSECUTION

"Be imitators of me, as I am of Christ," writes the apostle Paul to the disciples in Corinth (1 Cor 11:1; 4:16). For Paul, this meant, first and foremost, living life "in conformity with the Crucified One," and it included opposition and persecution.[24] "If they persecuted me," the Master tells his disciples, "they will also persecute you" (John 15:20). While I live a sheltered and comfortable life in modern Western society, many of my fellow pilgrims do not. According to Open Doors, currently over "340 million Christians are living in places where they experience high levels of persecution."[25] A recent review commissioned by the United Kingdom's Foreign Secretary revealed that persecution of Christians is currently at a level that can be compared to genocide.[26] Innumerable intimate stories of misery and torture are being written every day in every corner of the earth. This is not a novel phenomenon, of course. Many of Jesus's disciples died the martyr's death, and the early church suffered waves of persecution under several cruel

---

21. Commenting on Phil 3:10–11, Müller, *Epistles of Paul*, 117.
22. If I remember correctly, John Piper makes this very point in some of his sermons.
23. DBWE 15:406.
24. "Paulus ruft also konkret dazu auf, ein Leben in der Konformität zum Gekreuzigten zu führen." Schrage, *Der erste Brief*, 358.
25. Open Doors, "Christian Persecution."
26. See Mounstephen, "Bishop of Truro," and BBC, "Christian Persecution."

Roman emperors.[27] Discipleship has always been, from the very beginning, *radical* discipleship.[28] Even Martin Luther, and that is a detail one not ought to forget, risked his life at the Diet of Worms in 1521 when, facing the powerful secular and ecclesial rulers, he would not recant. Only about a hundred years earlier, John Hus had been burned at the stake for beliefs very similar to those of Luther.[29] Our thoughts turn also to Bonhoeffer, of course, who suffered and died under the National Socialist regime. For Bonhoeffer, suffering for the sake of Christ in this way was a privilege, and it is here that sharing with Christ's sufferings is made manifest in the ultimate sense. "Christ honors only a few of his followers with being in the most intimate community with his suffering, that is, with martyrdom," Bonhoeffer writes. "It is here that the life of the disciple is most profoundly identical with the likeness of Jesus Christ's form of death."[30] Clearly, disciples are prompted to "count the cost" as they hit the narrow road of radical discipleship (Luke 14:28). Taking up the cross might translate for some to the ultimate readiness to die for Jesus's sake. "The taking up of the way of the cross," writes Ulrich Luz, "means that the prerequisite for discipleship is the readiness to be martyred."[31] Or, as another commentator rephrases Jesus's call even more bluntly, "If you wish to be my disciple, you must put your head on the chopping block."[32]

As we have seen so far, though, we seek to understand sharing in Christ's sufferings more broadly, that is, that it involves more than this ultimate form of persecution. There are various degrees of opposition, rejection, and persecution. I am thinking of one of my relatives who served as a Protestant pastor in the German Democratic Republic under the anti-Christian communist regime. While neither she nor her family members suffered physical harm, they were all exposed to subtle, yet distinct reprisals due to her calling, until the day the iron curtain was lifted. Perhaps we might want to arrive at a more inclusive understanding of the nature of opposition and how radical disciples are to deal with it.[33] In this context, we are thinking primarily of an opposition that comes from a world that is hostile

27. See De Ste. Croix et al., *Christian Persecution*.
28. See Frank, "Nachfolge Jesu."
29. Schäufele, "Luther," 113.
30. DBWE 4:285–86.
31. "Es geht beim Antreten zum Kreuzesweg um die Bereitschaft zum Martyrium als Bedingung zum Jüngersein." Luz, *Das Evangelium nach Matthäus*, 144.
32. Nolland, *Luke 9:21—18:34*, 482.
33. All sorts of suffering, not only with a view to actual persecution, as Klaus Wengst argues, but "feindlich erfahrenes Handeln jedweder Art" ["treatment of any kind that is experienced as hostile"] is meant here. Wengst, *Das Johannesevangelium*, 442.

to Christ and his followers (Matt 10:24–25; John 15:20)—in the following section we elaborate on opposition that might come from within, from the adversary, or even God himself.

It might start early in our discipleship career with bullying in the school playground due to our allegiance with Christ, and it continues with mobbing experiences at the workplace later in life. Since this world presents cause for tribulation for the disciples (John 16:33), they do not expect to be received with open arms wherever they go (see Matt 10:12–14). And in every situation, we are challenged: Do I want to stick with my faith and continue on the bumpy road of discipleship? Do I want to persevere, even if it means loss of reputation, influence, power, and perhaps fame? Am I content to suffer with Christ, the rejected One, and to share the shame of the cross? Sverre Bøe notes,

> Crucifixion, and by all probability also cross-bearing, was heavily associated with shame in antiquity . . . A call to voluntary cross-bearing can therefore be seen as a call to self-stigmatization, to putting oneself in a position of social shame as an outcast. In this respect the call to cross-bearing may therefore indirectly have suggested to Luke's readers that disciples ought to share the shame of Jesus.[34]

This form of suffering, when we are "insulted for the name of Christ" (1 Pet 4:14), is a particular challenge, as Bonhoeffer writes, for it can be easily avoided through denial of Christ.[35] Peter's denial, of course, is the classic example here. "This is a genuine temptation toward apostasy," Bonhoeffer notes.[36] Yet it is also right here where the Christian is "led into the communion of the sufferings of Jesus Christ (1 Pet 4:13)."[37] This brings us to our next instances of cross-bearing.

TRIALS AND TEMPTATIONS

Jesus experienced trials and temptations, and so will we. Times of testing should not come as a surprise to us, the apostle Peter reminds his readers (1 Pet 4:12). Trials and temptations take various forms and come from different sources. When we meet challenges described so far, an internal appraisal process is set in motion: "Shall I really continue to trust in God?"

---

34. Bøe, *Cross-Bearing*, 223.
35. DBWE 15:408.
36. DBWE 15:408.
37. DBWE 15:408.

"Who is this God who allows suffering anyway?" Seeds of doubt are sown and threaten to overgrow the delicate plantlet of our faith.

Martin Luther is undoubtedly the grand master of dealing with all sorts of trials and temptations, what he called *Anfechtungen* in German. The term derives from the German verb "*fechten*" (fencing) and evokes associations of a fight or a struggle.[38] On their pilgrimage, radical disciples battle their way through the tangled undergrowth of doubt and despair as their faith is challenged. Comparing them to soldiers, the apostle Paul summons believers to wear the whole armor of God (Eph 6:10–18), with the expressed hope that they may stand.[39] Testing and affliction are a significant part of our journey as disciples. "A theologian needs to be made by trial and testing and by practice," writes Luther, "not only by reading sacred texts."[40] Against what or whom are we fighting? What are the sources of *Anfechtung* for us? Looking again at the ultimate cross-bearer, we gain important insights. We note that while there are certain parallels between Christ's temptations and ours, the analogies break down at some points. As seen earlier, Christ has been severely tempted by the evil one (e.g., "If you are the Son of God, tell this stone to become a loaf of bread," Luke 4:3), by cruel human beings ("If you are the Son of God, come down from the cross," Matt 27:40b), and even by God himself in the forsakenness on the cross ("My God, my God, why have you forsaken me?" Matt 27:46). We, too, are being tempted by evil forces, by fellow humans, and even in a sense by God himself.

In the remainder of this chapter, we investigate various sources of temptations for us, focusing on the following candidates: first, we deal with ourselves as sources of temptation. Other than in Jesus's case, who lived as the flawless One, we trip ourselves up by giving in to the distorted desires of our old self.[41] Second, we deal with the temptations presented to us by the devil, or a mix of the two sources. Third, having already explored some causes of temptation by the world—in the brief section on opposition and

---

38. An *Anfechtung*, writes Martin O. Dietrich, is "an assault on either the body, mind, or soul, involving fear, conscience, sin or guilt, and is always a test of one's faith." Dietrich, "Introduction to Luther," 181. See also Bayer, *Martin Luther's Theology*, 19–20. Loewenich, *Luther's Theology*, 117–39.

39. Peppiatt, *Disciple*, 96.

40. Luther in Bayer, *Lutheran Way*, 242n310. The original is in Latin, "Theologum oportet fieri experimentis et usu, non lectione tantum sacrarum rerum." WA Tr 5:384.5–6 (no. 5864).

41. In the summer of 1938 Bonhoeffer held a Bible study on temptation, where he expanded on the section of the Lord's prayer, "And lead us not into temptation, but deliver us from evil" (Matt 6:13). In it he suggests as key sources of temptation "*the devil, the desires of human beings, God himself.*" DBWE 15:397 (emphasis original).

persecution—we take some more time to analyze how and in what sense one might speak of being forsaken or tested by God.

First, then, we acknowledge that often we are our own worst enemy as we succumb to our distorted desires. Emerging from the shadow of the past, remnants of our old mode of existence afflict us and distract us from the urgent tasks of loving and serving God and neighbor. Old self impulses continue to tempt us with the desire for self-reliance, which was also the enemy's preferred tactic against Jesus Christ, as we have seen earlier (see chapter 5). It has already been pointed out at the very outset that our default attitude as fallen human beings is self-centeredness and self-reliance. When tempted to live in the mode of our old self, we easily grow anxious, quickly become frustrated, and we are mostly sorrowful yet rarely rejoicing. It is in this mode of existence that our faith in God's providence and superintendence over all evil and suffering is questioned, and we are tempted to give in and give up. Old illicit desires rise from the ashes and afflict and tempt us to sin. It is, in particular, temptation to sexual sin that has destructive effects in our lives. The disciple's "body is a temple of the Holy Spirit" (1 Cor 6:19), Paul writes, and must not be profaned. Sexual sin, in fact, is not simply an issue of the individual disciple but it defiles Christ's body as a whole. "Even the body of the disciple belongs to Christ and discipleship;" writes Bonhoeffer, "our bodies are members of his body. Because Jesus, the Son of God, assumed a human body, and because we are in communion with his body, that is why infidelity is a sin against Jesus' own body."[42] In this sense, he argues, sexual immorality defiles the whole community.[43]

Secondly, radical disciples follow in the footsteps of their Master who has, in his own life, experienced the attacks of the evil one. They take seriously the apostle Paul's statement that we do "not wrestle against flesh and blood, but against the rulers, against the authorities, against the cosmic powers over this present darkness, against the spiritual forces of evil in the heavenly places" (Eph 6:12). As the disciples pick up the fight, they "continue to bear the death of their Lord—in their spiritual disappointments and frustrations, in their struggles with the prince of darkness."[44] Of course, balance is key here. While the enemy's attacks are real, we do not suspect the devil behind every corner. C. S. Lewis has some wise counsel:

> There are two equal and opposite errors into which our race can fall about the devils. One is to disbelieve in their existence. The other is to believe, and to feel an excessive and unhealthy interest

---

42. DBWE 4:127.
43. Bonhoeffer offers some insightful thoughts on this. See DBWE 4:264–65.
44. Silva, *Philippians*, 165.

in them. They themselves are equally pleased by both errors and hail a materialist or a magician with the same delight.[45]

So on the one hand, we acknowledge that there is an evil power that tries to attack our faith in a good God, our sense of peace and serenity, that wants to rob us of our joy in Christ, and make us feel insecure about our new identity in him.[46] On the other hand, though, we know that we share in Christ's triumph over the evil forces (Col 2:15), and we rest assured that the One who is in us "is greater than he who is in the world" (1 John 4:4b).

While some attacks and temptations are easily identifiable, some others are not, and at times our wrong desires forge an unholy alliance with the evil one and the resulting feeling can be complex. Bonhoeffer describes in a letter to his parents the ominous sensation of feeling strangely unhinged without obvious cause or reason:

> However, I have never understood as clearly as I have here what the Bible and Luther mean by "temptation" [*Anfechtung*]. The peace and serenity by which one had been carried are suddenly shaken without any apparent physical or psychological reason, and the heart becomes, as Jeremiah very aptly put it, an obstinate and anxious thing that one is unable to fathom. One experiences this as an attack from the outside, as evil powers that seek to rob one of what is most essential. But even these experiences may be good and necessary in order to learn to understand human life better.[47]

According to Bonhoeffer, then, there seems to be an upside to temptations, in other words, temptations provide us with an occasion to flourish in tensions. Experiencing temptations not only helps us to "understand human life better," as Bonhoeffer writes, it is also a form of suffering that connects us with Jesus Christ. In his notes for a Bible study on temptations,

---

45. Lewis, *Screwtape Letters*, 9.

46. "The temptations of the disciples are various. Satan attacks them from all sides and tries to bring them down," Bonhoeffer notes. "False security and godless doubt tempt them severely." DBWE 4:157.

47. Bonhoeffer to his parents (Tegel, May 15, 1943), DBWE 8:79. "Allerdings ist mir nie so deutlich geworden wie hier, was die Bibel und Luther unter 'Anfechtung' verstehen. Ganz ohne jeden erkennbaren physischen und psychischen Grund rüttelt es plötzlich an dem Frieden und der Gelassenheit, die einen trug, und das Herz wird, wie es bei Jeremia sehr bezeichnend heißt, das trotzige und verzagte Ding, das man nicht ergründen kann; man empfindet das wirklich als einen Einbruch von außen, als böse Mächte, die einem das Entscheidende rauben wollen. Aber auch diese Erfahrungen sind wohl gut und nötig, man lernt das menschliche Leben besser verstehen." DBW 8:70.

Bonhoeffer provides some vital clues as to how we enjoy fellowship with Christ as we deal with temptations.

Bonhoeffer contrasts the temptation of Adam and the temptation of Christ and concludes that the former has been terminated by the latter. He writes,

> Adam's temptation has been brought to an end through the temptation of Jesus Christ. Just as all flesh fell in Adam's temptation, so likewise all flesh has been extricated from Satan's power through the temptation of Jesus Christ. For Jesus Christ bore our flesh, he suffered our temptation, and he has gained victory. Therefore, all of us today bear the flesh that overcame Satan in Jesus Christ. In the temptation of Jesus, even our flesh, we ourselves, have overcome.[48]

Since we share in Christ's (victorious!) humanity, Bonhoeffer argues, we now overcome temptation in and through him. In this sense then, radical disciples can say about themselves, "It is not we who are tempted, *but Jesus Christ who is tempted in us.*"[49] Since Jesus Christ has already won the decisive victory on the cross, and as we are now intimately united with him, we share in his victory (Col 2:15; 1 John 4:4). "To participate in the temptation of *Christ*, however, means at the same time to participate in the overcoming and the victories of Christ."[50] Similarly to Bonhoeffer, Karl Barth stresses that disciples attest to Jesus's victory over temptation in their own lives.[51] Every obstacle or adversary they meet on their pilgrimage, whether it comes from inside or outside, works out for their good as their faith is tested, refined, and purified (1 Pet 1:7). Radical disciples experience Christ's help in temptation and are rescued from their trials (Heb 2:18; 2 Pet 2:9). On this basis, it is understandable why Paul, Peter, and James make the case that disciples have reason to rejoice when they suffer times of testing (Rom 5:3–4; 1 Pet 1:6; Jas 1:2). Tried in the furnace of affliction, they come out at the other end wiser, more mature, having their eyes opened even wider for the glory of Christ, having an even more profound grasp of their new life in and through him. They thrive in the tension of temptation—and we pick up this important idea in the subsequent chapter on taking up the cross. Finally, though, we turn to the third source of temptation, namely the one that arises through God himself.

---

48. DBWE 15: 395–96.
49. DBWE 15:396 (emphasis original).
50. DBWE 15:396 (emphasis original).
51. *CD* IV/2:545.

FEELING FORSAKEN

The most severe form of suffering for Jesus was undoubtedly the forsakenness he endured on the cross. While both Luther and Bonhoeffer seem to indicate that we, too, endure godforsakenness in some measure, it is important to reiterate that we do not suffer *actual* forsakenness the way Jesus did. We would not be able to tolerate godforsakenness for one second since we are at every moment sustained by God—"[i]n him we live and move and have our being" (Acts 17:28). Separated from the One who gives us "life and breath and everything" (Acts 17:25) for just a blink of an eye would lead to our complete disintegration. Plus, radical disciples have been promised that God will never leave or forsake them (Heb 13:5).

However, we might *feel* as though we were forsaken by God. And feelings are real. Believers throughout the ages have witnessed to times of serious spiritual distress. We could call it an extreme form of *Anfechtung*, or a particular spiritual crisis, a "Dark Night of the Soul" (St. John of the Cross). As we have seen earlier, Luther was intimately familiar with these moments of profound spiritual darkness. Severe thoughts of despair and forsakenness were even accompanied by physical symptoms. What makes the experience particularly threatening is the feeling that the all-powerful and gracious God seems to have forgotten or forsaken us.[52] Even worse, we might even feel that God himself is up against us. Luther sees a prime example in King David's experience as expressed in Psalm 6:[53]

> O Lord, rebuke me not in your anger, nor discipline me in your wrath. Be gracious to me, O Lord, for I am languishing; heal me, O Lord, for my bones are troubled. My soul also is greatly troubled. But you, O Lord—how long? (Ps 6:1–3)

For Luther, this is the most serious form of temptation, namely "the terror the individual feels in the moment he is confronted with some dark aspect of God," writes C. Warren Hovland.[54] The disciple for some reason thinks that "God himself is the assailant," as Luther scholar Karl Holl put it.[55]

---

52. Bonhoeffer describes this experience in the following words: "This is the decisive fact in the temptation of a Christian, namely, that one is being *forsaken*, forsaken by all his strengths, indeed attacked by them, forsaken by all human beings, forsaken by God himself. The heart trembles and is engulfed by total darkness. The self is nothing. The enemy is everything. God has taken his hand away . . . has forsaken the Christian for a brief moment (Isa. 54:7)." DBWE 15:387 (emphasis original).

53. See Beintker, *Die Überwindung*, 89–93.

54. Hovland, "Anfechtung," 48.

55. Holl, "Was verstand Luther?," 69. Beintker writes, "Holl hat den Blick darauf gelenkt, daß bei Luther mehr noch und ernsthafter als der Teufel der in Christus

Here, the disciple is challenged to "overcome the God who seemed to be forsaking him with the God who had given his child a definite promise."[56] In Luther's view, several figures in the Old Testament, Abraham, Jacob, Moses, Job, and David, experienced this severe form of temptation.[57] One thinks of the "dreadful and great darkness" that fell upon the sleeping Abraham (Gen 15:12), and the impossible demand to take his long-desired son and sacrifice him on the mountain (Gen 22:2).[58] Joseph, when sold into slavery by his brothers and later imprisoned for two years, surely felt forgotten and even forsaken by God (Gen 40:23; 41:1). "Why do you forget us forever," the author of Lamentations prayed, "why do you forsake us for so many days?" (Lam 5:20). Then there is the uncanny episode told in Genesis, where Jacob struggles with the angel (Gen 32:22–32). In the most confronting way imaginable, Jacob is here literally opposed by God himself. At least, this is how Martin Luther reads the passage—God disguises himself as an angel and fights with Jacob.[59] The direction is important here. "From this image one might infer that it is not that God desires to struggle with us," Simon Podmore writes, "but that God desires us to struggle with God."[60]

These examples are certainly unique, and unrepeatable events that form part of salvation history. Yet what present-day disciples learn is that they, too, are called to engage to some degree in this enigmatic struggle.

Like Jacob, God might lead us, too, into this struggle where he takes away all self-reliance, all self-confidence, and any trace of comfort and strength—this is where we truly feel forsaken.[61] In the end, God "takes the

---

offenbare Gott in Anfechtung setzt, so widerspruchsvoll dieser Gedanke zu sein scheint." Beintker, *Die Überwindung*, 41–42.

56. Holl, *What Did Luther Understand?*, 89.

57. "Ich find wol ynn der schrifft. das Christus. Abraham. Jacob. Moses. Job Dauid. Ezechias vnnd ettlich mehr. ym leben. die helle vorsucht habenn." Luther, WA 7:450.13–15.

58. "Take your son, your only son Isaac, whom you love, and go to the land of Moriah, and offer him there as a burnt offering on one of the mountains of which I shall tell you" (Gen 22:2).

59. Luther discusses this passage in his sermons on the First Book of Moses (*Über das 1. Buch Mose. Predigten. 1527*), WA 24:573–81. I was made aware of Luther's treatment of this topic through my reading of Simon Podmore's work.

60. Podmore, *Struggling with God*, 18.

61. Luther observes, "So wrestling with God is none other than wrestling with the angry God who sets himself against the human as an enemy, who wants to be not only the judge, but (which is even more horrible) also the disciplinarian and take our life . . ." ["So ist nu mit Gott ringen nichts anders denn mit dem zornigen Gott ringen, der sich widder den menschen setzt als ein feind, wil nicht allein richter sein, sondern (das noch greulicher ist) auch der stockmeister sein und umbs leben bringen . . ."] WA 24:577.28–31.

human's heart away from him, so that he cannot see anything anywhere that would be on his side," Luther writes.[62] However, God does not intend to destroy us, but to help us rely on what we do not see, and it is in this way, our little plant of faith grows stronger.[63] Our faith becomes more resilient as we overcome in this struggle by trusting God's goodness in spite of supporting experimental evidence. "Jacob's struggle becomes [in Luther, M. B.] a cypher for the struggle to recognize the love of God in the face of God's apparent wrath," writes Podmore.[64] Luther speaks here of overcoming God with God himself:

> So when I overcome God in myself, then I have overcome God by seizing and holding onto the word of his grace and by casting away what will arouse his wrath. Hence, one does not overcome his majesty, but the work that he does in us. Because of this we learn that it is meant to be written for our instruction, in case we too encounter such a thing, that we knew God to act like that, that we too would become Israel.[65]

The result of the struggle is a completely new vision of God and of self. Luther explains, "Pniel or Pnuel means 'God's face' or 'knowledge,' for through faith in the struggle of the cross one learns to know and experience God properly. So there is no more distress, and so the sun rises."[66] We also think of Job, who, after struggling with God for most of the book that bears his name, also arrives at a new self-understanding and a new vision of God:

---

62. "Also nympt er dem menschen das hertz, das er nyrgend nichts sihet, das auff seiner seitten stuende." *WA* 24:578.6–8.

63. This is what God does "when he wants to strengthen his own [people] completely." ["So thut nu Gott, wenn er wil die seinen vollig starck machen, legt sich widder das guetige troestliche wort und wil sehen, wie feste sie daran hangen, stellet sich, als woelte er yhn nymer gut thun, So fuelet der mensch, das es Gott thut, das thut auch am aller wehesten . . ."] *WA* 24:578.22–25. Luther adds that if the devil or another human being were the source of our discomfort and unease, the pain would be bearable. But if our conscience tells us that God is at work here, "anxiety and misery arise." ["Aber wenn das gewissen sagt, das Gott thut, so ist angst und not da."] *WA* 24:578.26–27.

64. Podmore, *Struggling with God*, 15.

65. "Wenn ich yhn also ynn mir uberwinde, so habe ich Gott uberwunden, dadurch das ich das wort von seiner guete ergreiffe und halte und schlage das hynweg, das yhn zornig wil machen, Also uberwindet man nicht seine Majestet, sondern sein werck, das er an uns thut. Derhalben last uns lernen, das solchs uns zu unterweisen geschrieben ist, ob uns auch solchs begegnet, das wir wuesten Gott also zu halten, das wir auch Israel wuerden." *WA* 24:579.7–13.

66. "Pniel odder Pnuel heyst 'Gottes angesicht' odder 'erkentnis,' denn durch den glauben ym streyt des creutzes lernet man Gott recht erkennen und erfaren, so hats denn kein not mehr, so gehet die Sonne auff." *WA* 24, 579:22–25.

"I had heard of you by the hearing of the ear, but now my eye sees you; therefore I despise myself, and repent in dust and ashes" (Job 42:5–6).

Radical disciples embrace the tension they face as their faith is being tested and tried. They seek to thrive in seeming contradictions and ultimately long to experience fellowship with this marvelous God "whose face is presence-in-absence."[67] Only with a more refined understanding of God that avoids lopsided and simplified accounts of God as discussed earlier, is it possible to thrive in tension here. Dietrich Bonhoeffer summarizes well the disciple's perplexing task with the following words in a letter to his friend Eberhard Bethge,

> God would have us know that we must live as those who manage their lives without God. The same God who is with us is the God who forsakes us (Mark 15:34!). The same God who makes us to live in the world without the working hypothesis of God is the God before whom we stand continually. Before God, and with God, we live without God. God consents to be pushed out of the world and onto the cross; God is weak and powerless in the world and in precisely this way, and only so, is at our side and helps us. Matt. 8:17 makes it quite clear that Christ helps us not by virtue of his omnipotence but by virtue of his weakness and suffering![68]

As Bonhoeffer points out, disciples are strengthened and sustained in this struggle through Christ: "Only the suffering God can help."[69] Since Jesus endured real godforsakenness on the cross, and transcended it, he sustains us in our own afflictions when we feel that God has turned his face away.

CONCLUSION

Living as radical disciples in this world we "will have tribulation" (John 16:33), especially as we follow in the footsteps of the Crucified One. In this chapter we have examined how our suffering is deeply associated with Jesus's own suffering, and yet also very different from it. In many ways, we recognized that the road that Christ traveled is unique; it is not only the path "less traveled" (Robert Frost), but not traveled at all by us. Self-emptying applies only to Christ in the sense that he took on something that did originally

---

67. "Through the struggle, Jacob is reconciled to the other, to a deeper sense of self," Podmore notes, "and to a God whose face is presence-in-absence." Podmore, *Struggling with God*, 16.

68. Bonhoeffer to Bethge, July 16, 1944. DBWE 8:478–79 [DBW 8:533–34].

69. Bonhoeffer to Bethge, July 16, 1944. DBWE 8:479 [DBW 8:534].

not belong to him. Only Christ suffered in a substitutionary sense, carrying our guilt as the sinless One and nailing it to the cross. However, as we are so intimately united with him by faith, we continue in his active obedience even today through his Spirit, filling up what is lacking in his sufferings—and we write and read this sentence with a sense of awe and wonder. Ours is the privileged role of continuing in Jesus's active obedience in his love for God and the world that did not love him back. Suffering rejection, opposition, and even persecution at the hands of a world that is often against Christ, we fill up what is lacking in Christ's sufferings. As we love this world, in spite of opposition, serving the poor, seeking justice, offering hospitality to the stranger, we present this fallen world to God the Father. This is how the fellowship of the disciples becomes alive as "Christ existing as community," as Bonhoeffer put it. The most difficult challenge, of course, arises when we do so even though we feel that God himself is against us. Continuing and persevering in our vocation as radical disciples despite feelings of forsakenness is the most exquisite temptation of all. And it is right here where disciples experience a breakthrough to a new vision of God and self. In the next chapter, we deal in more detail with the positive, transformative effects that we enjoy as we pick up our cross and persevere in various trials and temptations.

PERSONAL REFLECTION

In which areas of your life are you challenged by any of the various forms of suffering that we discussed in this chapter? Do you sense that there is a way in which you share in Christ's sufferings—and his victory? How could this insight transform your present experience?

Looking back at your life, are you, in hindsight, grateful for any episodes of trials and testing? Lucy Peppiatt writes, "The victory is when we are able to say, 'without this, that would never have happened' . . . When the most difficult events become the means for something good, we then reinterpret the past, and sufferings and hardships are transformed in our minds."[70] Where do you detect this in your own spiritual biography?

Have you ever felt forsaken by God? What made you persevere with God and remain on the path of discipleship anyway? What have you learned and how has your faith grown through this experience? How have you changed as a person, a disciple?

How do you want to pray for yourself right now?

---

70. Peppiatt, *Disciple*, 99–100.

7

Taking Up the Cross

ON 20 JUNE 1939, Dietrich Bonhoeffer took a momentous decision. Six years earlier, the National Socialists had seized control over Germany, steadily extending their influence over all areas of social life, including the church. Bonhoeffer rejected their attempt from the very beginning, and he played a vital role in the Confessing Church movement, which opposed the German Christians, a group within the Protestant church that was hijacked by and sympathetic to the National Socialists. Bonhoeffer's activities put him in the line of fire and his friends arranged for him a position in New York, far away from the risks and dangers in his homeland. He arrived in New York in early June 1939—it was his second visit to the Big Apple—having spent a year as visiting fellow at Union Theological Seminary almost ten years before. Bonhoeffer considered the prospect of working among German Christian refugees who left for the United States due to the dire conditions back home.[1] By then, the situation in Germany had taken a turn for the worse. About a year earlier, on November 9, 1938, the day that became known as *Kristallnacht* (Night of Broken Glass), the National Socialists had burned synagogues and smashed Jewish buildings all over the German-speaking lands. Henry Leiper, Executive Secretary of the Federal Council of Churches, had imagined that Bonhoeffer would serve in his new position for at least the next three years, and he had already secured some initial funding for the work.[2] It would have

---

1. Bethge, *Dietrich Bonhoeffer*, 651–52.
2. Bethge, *Dietrich Bonhoeffer*, 651–53.

meant a relative safety away from the church struggle (*Kirchenkampf*) in Germany and the risk of being drafted into military service in an imminent war that Hitler started only two months later with the invasion of Poland.[3] Yet while spending his first days in New York, Bonhoeffer could not stop thinking about Germany and his "German brothers."[4] And on that June 20, 1939, Bonhoeffer decided to go back to his homeland, admitting a certain unease about his decision in his diary:

> Visited Leiper. The decision has been made. I have refused. They were clearly disappointed . . . It is remarkable how I am never quite clear about the motives for any of my decisions. Is that a sign of confusion, of inner dishonesty, or is it a sign that we are guided without our knowing, or is it both?[5]

In a letter to Reinhold Niebuhr, Bonhoeffer explains that by a refusal to return to Germany at this point, he would have, in his view, forfeited his right to rebuild Germany after the war.[6]

Bonhoeffer was clearly aware of the risks that a return to Germany involved. Yet he was prepared to take up his cross and suffer the consequences of his actions. It is one thing to consider one's cross theoretically. We can reflect with some detachment about its form and shape. But it is a completely different story when we do actually take it up, when the cross becomes tangible in real life. In this chapter we explore first some basic aspects of the cross that we are called to bear, examining its various sizes and the countercultural call to cross-bearing. We then discuss, secondly, how radical disciples experience fellowship and transformation through suffering, and how they gain, thirdly, new life in the ultimate act of surrendering to God.

SHAPES OF THE CROSS

Jesus does not call his disciples merely to consider or examine their cross. He expects them to take it up. Not just any cross, but their own, individual cross. For each disciple has his or her cross tailor-made. There is no one-size-fits-all, but crosses vary in size, shape, and weight. Bonhoeffer's cross is

---

3. Schlingensiepen, *Dietrich Bonhoeffer*, 227–34.
4. Bethge, *Dietrich Bonhoeffer*, 652.
5. Bethge, *Dietrich Bonhoeffer*, 653.
6. "I have made a mistake in coming to America. I must live through this difficult period of our national history with the Christian people of Germany. I will have no right to participate in the reconstruction of Christian life in Germany after the war if I do not share the trials of this time with my people." Bethge, *Dietrich Bonhoeffer*, 655.

different from mine, which is again different from yours, but all crosses are made to fit, as Bonhoeffer notes:

> From the beginning, it lies there ready. They need only take it up. But so that no one presumes to seek out some cross or arbitrarily search for some suffering, Jesus says, they each have *their* own cross ready, assigned by God and measured to fit.[7]

There is a particular cross available according to each disciple's situation, strength and stamina, and God will make sure that we will be able to carry it. "God is faithful," writes St. Paul, "and he will not let you be tempted beyond your ability, but with the temptation he will also provide the way of escape, that you may be able to endure it" (1 Cor 10:13).

Radical disciples do not covet their brother's or sister's cross; they do not go looking for a different cross, one seemingly lighter or heavier; but they are determined to take up *their own* cross. They do not look away and ignore their cross on the wayside, but they courageously pick it up.

Of course, we are faced here with the serious conundrum that Jesus calls us to take up a torture instrument. There is clearly a tension involved here that disciples do not wish to avoid but embrace by faith. Again, any attempts at reducing the tension by either ignoring the cross with apathetic stoicism or embracing it with enthusiastic masochism are uncalled for. Radical disciples approach the cross carefully, with sobriety and a touch of curiosity and courage. They "first sit down and count the cost" (Luke 14:28), and draw nearer with prayerful consideration—at times, possibly mixed with apprehension, as Bonhoeffer confessed, and yet also determined and hopeful as they expect that their faith will grow as they take it up.[8]

Taking up one's cross is therefore never a passive-Stoic acceptance of one's fate. Rather, it is a decisive action of faith that expects God to glorify himself in the radical disciple as she bears her cross. In the moment of friction, when disciples are audacious enough to take up their crosses, they will

---

7. DBWE 4:87 (emphasis original). Martin Luther notes, similarly, "It deliberately says: take up *his* cross. For he [Jesus] teaches us not to carry the cross that he himself carried, but that everyone ought to carry his own. A cross of his own stands ready for everyone, for each according to the measure of his strength; for we cannot all suffer the same, since we are not all equal in the measure of faith and spirit." ["Mit Absicht heißt es: der nehme *sein* Kreuz auf sich. Denn er lehrt uns, nicht das Kreuz zu tragen, das er selber getragen hat, sondern ein jeder soll sein eigenes tragen. Für einen jeglichen steht ein eigenes Kreuz bereit, für jeden nach dem Maß seiner Kraft; denn wir können nicht alle das Gleiche leiden, weil wir nicht alle an Kraft des Glaubens und des Geistes gleich sind."] Luther, *Zweiter Teil*, 567–68 (emphasis original).

8. DBWE 4:91.

experience it becoming an agency of blessing to them—like Moses when he picked up the staff turned snake at the tail (Exod 4:4).

Also, carrying one's cross is not a one-off experience. Radical disciples carry their crosses patiently throughout their pilgrimage on earth.[9] Cross-bearing then becomes part of the radical disciple's lifestyle. Taking up the cross is "not [about] passive acquiescence," writes Ulrich Luz, "but an active form of life."[10] As mentioned earlier, Luke inserts the word "daily" in Jesus's command to pick up the cross (Luke 9:23). This is clearly a reference to cross-bearing as a continual experience in the disciple's life—a call to perseverance and patience.

We bear in mind, too, that cross-bearing is always counterintuitive and countercultural. Recognizing the seemingly foolish nature of cross-bearing, radical disciples still decide to take up their cross again and again.[11] It goes without saying that it is a "challenge to have one's whole existence determined by and patterned after a crucified messiah," John Nolland notes.[12] If not regarded through the lens of faith, bearing one's cross must look foolish to any observer whose eyes are not opened to the gospel (1 Cor 1:18, 23). The disciple who carries her cross is being slowed down and it is certainly not a glamorous activity that, should it be posted on social media, would attract a high number of likes. On the contrary, the one who carries the cross exposes her weakness and vulnerability to the world. Yet it is exactly through this weakness that God intends to work, to exercise his power, and to glorify himself in the life of the disciple (2 Cor 12:9). The blind man whose story John the apostle tells in his gospel carried the cross of blindness since birth. And Jesus makes clear that this was not on account of his own or his parents' sin, but so "that the works of God might be displayed in him" (John 9:3).

While every disciple has his own cross to bear, no one bears his cross in isolation. Radical disciples carry their crosses *together* as they follow the

---

9. See DBWE 4:88.

10. Luz argues "daß Leiden nicht passives Hinnehmen, sondern aktive Lebensform ist." Luz, *Das Evangelium nach Matthäus*, 491.

11. "The disciples' conflict with the world pervades their whole life and requires an ever-new decisiveness," writes Adolf Schlatter. "This cannot be replaced by a one-off decision, no matter how earnest." ["Der Konflikt der Jünger mit der Welt zieht sich durch ihr ganzes Leben hindurch und verlangt von ihnen die immer neue Entschlossenheit. Diese läßt sich nicht nur durch einen einmaligen Entschluß ersetzen, und sei er noch so ernst. Die Begehrungen, die aus der menschlichen Gemeinschaft und aus der natürlichen Bedürftigkeit entstehen, haben nicht auszurottende Wurzeln. Sie müssen unaufhörlich abgewiesen werden. Das macht aus dem Verhalten der Jünger immer wieder 'den Griff nach dem Kreuz.'"] Schlatter, *Das Evangelium des Lukas*, 99.

12. Nolland, *Luke 9:21—18:34*, 482.

cross-bearer par excellence.[13] In times where nonstop entertainment and the constant pursuit of health, wealth, and prosperity prominently feature not only in the public square but also in many churches, the call to cross-bearing is easily drowned and ignored. Perhaps the most important task of the church today is to recover her self-understanding as the community of cross-bearing disciples. A significant part on the road to recovery is to retrieve the lost notion of lament, as Matt Jacoby argues. "The discarding of the genre of lament from our corporate worship repertoire is, I believe, the greatest omission in the worship practices of the church today," he writes.[14] It seems, there is not sufficient space in the church for every disciple to place her cross next to herself when worshipping God. We will return to this—literally—crucial aspect of bearing our own and one another's burdens in the next chapter where we explore the notion of following Jesus *together* in more depth. For now, we direct our attention to the vital question of how our action of taking up the cross by faith turns into a blessing, even new life. At the very moment that radical disciples pick up their cross, they experience, right in this painful friction, intimate fellowship with Jesus Christ, they are transformed into the image of Christ, and they receive true life as they surrender to God. We will look at each aspect in turn.

FELLOWSHIP THROUGH SUFFERING

The disciple who decides to take up the cross enjoys an intimate relationship with the One who went before her on the way of the cross.[15] Radical disciples rejoice in the privilege of suffering "for the sake of Christ" (Phil 1:29). "The suffering in the way of the cross is . . . an expression of the believers' existential connection with their Lord," writes Friedrich Lang. "It is in particular in suffering that the Christian experiences fellowship with the crucified and risen Christ in a special way."[16] By taking up our cross, we

13. "Perseverance and praise through hardship and suffering is not something we are able to do as individuals," notes Lucy Peppiatt, "but is something we can only do as a community." Peppiatt, *Disciple*, 97.

14. Jacoby, *Deeper Places*, 58. Kelly Kapic notes, similarly, "When contemporary churches cease to sing laments as part of their regular catalog of songs, instead only choosing happy or upbeat music, the people of God lose their ability to lament well. When the homes of believers are hit by chronic pain or mental illness, they often find the contemporary church strangely unhelpful, even hurtful." Kapic, *Embodied Hope*, 38.

15. "The cross is neither misfortune nor harsh fate," writes Bonhoeffer. "Instead, it is that suffering which comes from our allegiance to Jesus Christ alone." DBWE 4:86.

16. "Das Leiden in der Kreuzesnachfolge ist keine äußerliche Nachahmung des Kreuzestodes Jesu und hat auch nicht dessen soteriologische Bedeutung, aber es ist Ausdruck der existentiellen Verbundenheit der Glaubenden mit ihrem Herrn. Gerade

identify most intimately with Christ and we demonstrate to God and the world that we are indeed prepared to lose our life for Jesus's sake.[17] The very act of taking up the cross establishes an intimate bond between the disciple and the Master, who is intimately familiar with their trials and afflictions.[18] In the action of taking up the cross and patiently bearing it, we do meet with Christ and the cross therefore becomes a blessing to us, as Bonhoeffer argues. He notes,

> Bearing the cross does not bring misery and despair. Rather, it provides refreshment and peace for our souls; it is our greatest joy. Here we are no longer laden with self-made laws and burdens, but with the yoke of him who knows us and who himself goes with us under the same yoke. Under his yoke we are assured of his nearness and communion. It is he himself whom disciples find when they take up their cross.[19]

How exactly do we experience fellowship with Christ as we take up our cross? It seems to me that the decisive factor here is that the disciple intentionally invites Christ into her own experience of cross-bearing. When all attempts at carrying the cross with a stiff upper lip have been relinquished, the disciple finally allows Christ to draw near, to become the supreme co-sufferer. When every impulse of self-fabricated bravery has waned, the disciple discovers honest lament as a key skill in her arsenal of suffering. This is where joint suffering occurs, and this is where the disciple enjoys the unique experience of having Christ alongside herself.

The following story might help to illustrate what I have in mind. I was born with a rare genetic disorder that entails urinary and kidney abnormalities due to a lack of abdominal wall muscles. If it were not for the specialist surgeon who happened to serve in my local hospital at the time of my birth, I would most likely not be writing these lines today. He performed several critical surgeries in the first three years of my life and by the grace of God achieved an outcome that allows me to live a relatively normal life. For the first twenty-odd years of my life though, I regularly suffered from

---

im Leiden darf der Christ die Gemeinschaft mit dem gekreuzigten und auferweckten Christus in besonderer Weise erfahren." Lang, *Die Briefe*, 253.

17. "Now the Christian understands his own suffering as the temptation of Christ in the self," writes Bonhoeffer. "This leads him to patience, to endure temptation in stillness and silence, and fills him with thanks, for the more the old human being dies, the more certainly the new one lives; the deeper one is cast into suffering, the closer one comes to Christ." DBWE 15:407.

18. The call to take up the cross indicates "their [disciples'] identification with and faithfulness to the way of Jesus himself." Edwards, *Gospel*, 256.

19. DBWE 4:91.

very painful colic; doctors were unable to locate the source of the pain, and medication proved ineffective. I endured severe stinging pain in my right lower abdomen between anything from a few hours to a whole day or night. Growing up as a young believer, I struggled to process the presence of the pain together with my belief in God who, as the Scriptures and my fellow disciples told me, loved me, and cared for me. In my view, the only way to reduce my cognitive dissonance was to separate the pain from my God-experience. My solution was that I compartmentalized the two, so that whenever the pain attacked, I excluded the notion of God from my discipleship experience. Once it subsided, I invited God back into my life. In my early twenties, though, I slowly began to realize the futility of my approach, and I decided to try something new. On several occasions, I avoided reducing the tension, embraced it by faith, and intentionally invited Jesus into my suffering and allowed him to co-suffer with me. And, indeed, the Master who carried his cross before me drew near and I enjoyed the liberty both to lament and to worship God throughout the painful episodes. Right in these painful moments intimate fellowship with Christ was being established and I was sustained by the One who was present with me, even in the darkest hour. In Bonhoeffer's words, "The disciples bear the suffering laid on them only by the power of him who bears all suffering on the cross. As bearers of suffering, they stand in communion with the Crucified."[20] Radical disciples then always suffer *with* Christ, and never in isolation from him. They are happy to invite Jesus right into the midst of their misery and by faith experience not estrangement from God but precious communion with him.[21]

A most suitable role model for what it means to suffer in fellowship with God, is of course, the Old Testament figure of Job. Job did not exclude God from his suffering, but invited him right into his own pain, again and again, chapter by chapter. Tim Keller, in his *Walking With God Through Suffering and Pain*, captures Job's attitude well:

> Yes, he complained, but he complained to *God*. He doubted, but he doubted to *God*. He screamed and yelled, but he did it in God's presence. No matter how much in agony he was, he continued to address God. He kept seeking him. And in the end, God said Job triumphed.[22]

---

20. DBWE 4:104.

21. "So all suffering must lead the Christian not to apostasy but to the strengthening of faith," Bonhoeffer notes. "While the flesh shies away from and rejects suffering, the Christian recognizes his own suffering to be just the suffering of Christ in himself." DBWE 15:407.

22. Keller, *Walking with God*, 287 (emphasis original).

Similarly, Kathryn Greene-McCreight notes that when the prophet Isaiah is at the end of his wits, he still cries to God; he does not pray: "Truly he is a God who hides himself," but "*Truly, you are a God who hides himself, O God of Israel, the Savior*" (Isa 45:15).[23] When lament is honestly and unashamedly addressed to God, the result is lived fellowship with God in and through suffering. If we invite Jesus as co-sufferer into our own suffering, we will experience that his presence, even if veiled at times, brings us comfort. We are promised that God "comforts us in all our affliction," and are told that those who share in Jesus's sufferings "share abundantly in comfort too" (2 Cor 1:4–5).

What is the basis of this comfort? Of course, on the one hand, the sheer knowledge and experience of having Christ suffer with us is a source of encouragement. However, the disciples' real ground for hope is the fact that Christ has overcome suffering and death and has risen to new life in which the disciples share already now. Radical disciples identify with the crucified Savior, but they also identify with the risen Christ who has triumphed victoriously on their behalf (Col 2:15). Our fellowship with Christ's suffering and death goes hand in hand with our fellowship in his resurrection and our enjoyment of new life here and now. As we endure the tension of participating in suffering and resurrection life, we experience positive transformation, and to this we turn next.

TRANSFORMATION THROUGH SUFFERING

At the very instant that we take up the cross, we are given the opportunity for profound transformation. Maturation and growth in character usually happen *not* when life is sweet and easy, but when we meet challenges and obstacles on our way. Since the early beginnings of the discipline of psychology, scholars have pointed out that human beings develop through friction, as they are required to master crises. Sigmund Freud, for instance, assumed that as we grow up, we undergo five stages of psychosexual development.[24] At each stage, we need to resolve and master certain conflicts, and if we fail to do so, we are at risk of developing mental health problems such as neuroses. Building on Freud, Erik H. Erikson suggested eight stages of psychosocial development.[25] Each stage presents us with various conflicts and

---

23. Greene-McCreight, *Darkness*, 13–14 (emphasis original).

24. For an overview, see Ellis et al., *Personality Theories*, 103–10.

25. For a brief summary, see Wirtz and Strohmer, *Dorsch*, 492–93. A more extensive discussion of Erikson's stages is found in Conzen, *Erik H. Erikson*, 63–95. See also Ellis et al., *Personality Theories*, 205–7.

crises that require to be mastered. To avoid what Erikson called an "identity crisis," we need to have formed an identity in adolescence.[26] Again, successful maturation is linked to effective dealings with tensions. We could go on and refer to Jean Piaget's theory of cognitive development, or, expanding on Piaget, Lawrence Kohlberg's stages of moral development, but the key point is sufficiently clear: we mature by dealing successfully with crises.

Without doubt, there is a difference between going through various stages in our development and the voluntary act of taking up our cross. Plus, of course, all humans suffer various degrees of afflictions and meet challenges in their walk of life, and many report that they grow through them, irrespective of whether they are following Christ or not. Yet for disciples, their tailor-made cross has a particular function as it serves as an instrument of transformation, so that they will be conformed to the image of Christ.[27] Radical disciples walk in the footsteps of their Master who himself was perfected through suffering. This, at least, is the astonishing claim that the author of the Letter to the Hebrews makes. The writer mentions that Jesus was made "perfect through suffering" (Heb 2:10), and that Jesus, "[a]lthough he was a son, he learned obedience through what he suffered" (Heb 5:8). These statements raise some serious questions: How can one imagine that Jesus Christ, the already perfect One, could be made perfect through suffering? Or, what could be an appropriate criterion of progress in Jesus's development? This whole idea seems "nonsense," as one commentator put it.[28] Obviously, Jesus's goal is not about developing a striking "personality, full of character."[29] The parallel between our growth through suffering and Jesus's being made perfect through suffering breaks down at this point. "To make perfect" here in this passage in Hebrews is therefore not to be understood in terms of moral perfection but is linked with Jesus being crowned "with glory and honor" (Heb 2:7). It thus refers to his exaltation and entry into the presence of God on account of his perfect sacrifice on our behalf.[30]

Only Jesus has been perfected through suffering in this sense; what we experience, on a different level, is transformation through suffering.

---

26. See Ellis et al., *Personality Theories*, 206–7.

27. John Calvin writes, "The reason why He preached about bearing the cross was that, although man's life is subject to all the common troubles, yet God exercises His own in a special way to conform them to the image of His Son, and so it is not surprising that He gave this law to them." Calvin, *Harmony*, 194.

28. Gräßer, *An die Hebräer*, 306.

29. "Lernziel ist natürlich nicht seine Festigung als charaktervolle Persönlichkeit." Gräßer, *An die Hebräer*, 306.

30. I am grateful to Greg Forbes for his helpful comments regarding this passage in Hebrews.

"Not only so, but we also glory in our sufferings," writes St. Paul, "because we know that suffering produces perseverance; perseverance, character; and character, hope" (Rom 5:3). Growth in character of course is a significant objective of discipleship. "Discipleship," Medi Ann Volpe argues, "is all about formation: to be a disciple, by definition, is to be in a process of becoming like the Master."[31] Disciples who courageously take up their cross, therefore, expect to make progress in sanctification, as they are being transformed into the image of Christ. John Stott notes that "[t]here is always an indefinable something about people who have suffered. They have a fragrance which others lack. They exhibit the meekness and gentleness of Christ."[32] Much like self-denial, the call to cross-bearing is *not* a threat to our existence, as challenging as it may sound, but it is in in fact leading to fresh life with a new sense of purpose and meaning as we discover and grow in our identity in Christ.

Believers throughout all the ages actually embraced afflictions for what they are: opportunities for growth in Christlikeness. In fact, what many saints throughout church history feared most was not the affliction per se, but its absence, for this meant spiritual standstill, or worse, entropy, and decay. A member of the early Christian community of desert fathers reportedly prayed, "Lord, send me an affliction, for, being healthy, I am not obedient to you."[33] Martin Luther, likewise, highlighted the beneficial effects of trials and temptations: they keep us in the fear of God, and teach us to pray and to grow in our knowledge of Christ and his word.[34] In his view, then, much worse than experiencing testing of the faith, was to experience none at all.[35] As radical disciples take up their crosses, they not only consent to

---

31. Volpe, *Rethinking Christian Identity*, 228.

32. Stott, *Cross of Christ*, 319–20.

33. "There was a brother at The Cells who had attained such a degree of humility that he was always offering this prayer: 'Lord, send me an affliction, for, being healthy, I am not obedient to you.'" Wortley, *"Anonymous" Sayings*, 339.

34. "Es sind uns aber solche Anfechtungen nicht allein nöthig, sondern auch gut und nützlich, sonst gingen wir sicher dahin, ohn alle Gottesfurcht, ruften ihn nicht an um Hülfe. Denn wer gesund und fröhlich ist, der darf keines Arzts noch Trösters nicht; so könnte der Teufel uns auch leichtlich betrügen. Darnach dienet die Anfechtung auch dazu, daß wir in Gottes Furcht leben, fursichtiglich wandeln, ohn Unterlaß beten, in der Gnad und Erkenntniß Christi wachsen und die Kraft des Worts lernen verstehen. Und ob wir gleich noch schwach sind, so ist doch unsers Herrn Christi Kraft in den Schwachen mächtig, 2. Cor. 12." WA Tr 1:407.9–16. Ronald Rittgers offers a helpful discussion of Luther's view on this in Rittgers, *Reformation of Suffering*, 93–94.

35. "Qia omnium devotorum iudicio et experientia teste maxima tentatio est nullam habere tentationem. Et omnium summa adversitas nulla adversitas." WA 3:420.16–18. "Nulla tentatio omnis tentatio, Nulla persecutio tota persecutio." WA 3:424.11. On Luther's view on overcoming *Anfechtung* through Christ and God himself, see Beintker,

being exposed to the storms of life that will help them grow stronger, but they also intentionally submit to being trimmed in their character. This is often a painful experience, but in the end turns out to be a fruitful endeavor. The principle of pruning that Jesus mentions in John 15 is illuminating in this respect.

In this picture, Jesus compares himself to the true vine, the Father to the vinedresser and the disciples to the branches. We abide in Jesus, and that is how we bear fruit—without our life-giving connection to him, we could do nothing (John 15:5). Jesus explains that the Father prunes every branch that bears fruit so "that it may bear more fruit" (John 15:2). Apparently, more fruit is what is desired. The Father is simply not satisfied with stagnation or decay. His kingdom is ever expanding, compared to a tiny mustard seed that grows into a majestic plant covering the whole earth. Similarly, the disciple is expected to grow. As a contrasting picture, we call to mind the occasion where Jesus cursed the fig tree when he saw only leaves but no fruit (Matt 21:18–22). And the slave who buried his talent in the ground, failing to produce a return on the investment, is punished (Matt 25:24–30). Bearing fruit is key—it is *the* distinctive mark of disciples: "By this my Father is glorified, that you bear much fruit and so prove to be my disciples," Jesus says in John 15:8. Yet growing fruit is no picnic. The kind of fruit that we desire to see sprouting in us does not grow in the greenhouse. Rather, we are fragile little branches in the vineyard, exposed to the seasons, neither shielded from wind nor rain nor storm. And the vinedresser is clearly not the helicopter parent who wraps the branches in cotton wool. Quite the contrary. At the appointed time, he comes along, takes his pruning knife, and cuts back some of our shoots—not with the intention to hurt us, but with a view to seeing even more fruit growing in us.

Radical disciples are therefore invited to embrace, by faith, the strange notion that the God who loves them at times hurts them in order to bring about growth. God disciplines those whom he loves (Heb 12:6). Foreign to them is the view of their "snowflake generation" contemporaries, where God is portrayed as protective daddy, always there for us and shielding us from every harm. In this sanitized and simplified caricature of God, he might perhaps handle a cake slicer, but certainly not a sharp pruning knife. Today, the concept of a God who might wound us does not seem to register anymore. And we leave behind the God of whom Job could say: "For he wounds, but he binds up; he shatters, but his hands heal" (Job 5:18). Or

---

Die Überwindung, 145–73. Again, the writings of the desert fathers echo this sentiment: "There was an elder who was continually sick and unwell, but then for one year he was not sick. He was terribly upset and wept, saying: 'God has abandoned me and not visited me.'" Wortley, *"Anonymous" Sayings*, 149.

about whom Hosea speaks, "Come, let us return to the Lord; for he has torn us, that he may heal us; he has struck us down, and he will bind us up" (Hos 6:1). Foreign is the God who struggled all night with Jacob and left him with a dislocated hip,[36] or who should send the beloved apostle Paul a "thorn in the flesh" in order to keep him "from becoming conceited" (2 Cor 12:7)—or who calls us to take up our cross.

Radical disciples walk against the stream though, and embrace the biblical, more complex, and perhaps even more confronting, vision of God. They draw closer and trust that whatever the Father does is for their best and for his glory. They accept that painful experiences lead to growth and humility and that these forms of suffering, such as Paul's "thorn," as he writes, are actually "[f]or the sake of Christ" (2 Cor 12:10). In some mysterious way, their suffering might even turn out to become a blessing not only for themselves but also for their fellow disciples. Kathryn Greene-McCreight, who writes with refreshing (and often shocking) honesty about her painful struggles with mental illness, notes in the preface to her book: "It is my way of offering up my own pain to Christ, that it may be redeemed as it touches the lives of others."[37] We conclude our reflections on cross-bearing with a closer look at the idea of not only offering up our suffering to Christ, but even our whole person, which is the ultimate act of cross-bearing.

NEW DESIRE THROUGH SURRENDER

Radical disciples, as they come to grips with their cross bend down to take it up. Their very posture reflects an attitude of humility and surrender. Here is humble submission under the will of God. "Here I am, O Lord, do to me as you please, I trust you in everything," is the prayer of the disciple who is ready to take up the cross. In German, the word *Hingabe* captures well this idea of giving oneself completely over to either a cause, an idea, a partner, or—as in our context—God. *Hingabe* reflects the combination of passionate commitment and dedication, as well as self-sacrifice. The English terms, surrender, commitment, and devotion all go in the right direction, and we shall use them interchangeably in the remainder of this chapter, bearing in mind their interconnectivity. We practice surrender when we have entirely

---

36. Having prevailed in the fight with the angel, Jacob's hip is dislocated, resulting in a limp that he will carry for the remainder of his life. Yet as he perseveres in the struggle, Jacob is rewarded: he receives a new name, a new identity from God. "The stranger bestows this gift of a new name—one sanctified by its unison with the name of God (*El*)," writes Simon Podmore. Podmore, *Struggling with God*, 13–14.

37. Greene-McCreight, *Darkness*, xxiii.

emptied ourselves, when we have completely given up on ourselves, on our ambition, a particular career, a certain reputation, or a particular achievement. Once the disciple was "neighbor to himself," writes Barth, but "When he is called to discipleship, he abandons himself resolutely and totally."[38] The act of surrender happens when we place ourselves, head, heart, and hand, fully and irrevocably, again and again, into the care of God.[39] It is the natural step that disciples take when they realize that they, anyway, do not own themselves but belong to God, "You are not your own, for you were bought with a price" (1 Cor 6:19b–20a). Surrender is courageous commitment as it reflects utter readiness to expose the self to the vinedresser's pruning knife. Surrender in the *Hingabe* sense echoes Jesus's ultimate, "not my will, but yours be done" (Luke 22:42).

Of course, one could not hand oneself over to *any* god. A fool surrenders to a domesticated god, a god of process theology or open theism who is limited in his knowledge of the future and in his power to control what is happening in his creation and in our little lives. This god might pity us and offer some words of encouragement, but he has no ultimate means to intervene on our behalf. Surrender to such a god would be futile. Yet radical disciples know that they hand themselves over to a God who is both perfectly trustworthy and all-powerful. Anything else would be not only foolish but suicidal. Radical disciples gladly give themselves over to God since he practiced surrender first as he gave his only Son for them (John 3:16). Having received the gift of his Son, they return the gift by presenting themselves to God, the creator and possessor of everything. They are happy to surrender to the God who calls the stars by their name (Ps 147:4), and who is supremely in charge over every atom in the universe. In these hands, they know, they are secure. Only under his protection and care will they experience peace that surpasses understanding (Phil 4:7). To abandon oneself to *this* God, then, is not a fatalistic act performed with a degree of resistance. Rather, it is done freely and cheerfully, because the disciple is confident that God is merciful and sovereign.[40]

---

38. *CD* IV/2:539. "Er war sich selbst der Nächste. Eben als solchen läßt er sich, in die Nachfolge gerufen, resolut und gänzlich fallen." *KD* IV/2:610.

39. "Thus cross-bearing expresses a readiness to *surrender* one's entire life to Jesus," notes Sverre Bøe, "both in the Lukan and Pauline expressions." Bøe, *Cross-Bearing*, 226 (emphasis original).

40. Adolf Schlatter explains, "Surrender accomplished its goal only when it occurred resolutely and cheerfully. Only faith, however, could cheerfully surrender its own right and the expression of its own conviction, and this required the certainty for the disciples that divine grace would help them when they went the path of renunciation. Jesus did not give them merely the weighty commandment that was full of sacrifices but also what made 'his load light' for them: a confidence in the rich God."

Ultimately, radical disciples come to realize that as they die to self and completely surrender to God, they gain new life. As the disciple gives herself away to God, she emulates Jesus's ultimate act of devotion. Telling his disciples about his imminent death through which he would glorify the Father, Jesus says, "Truly, truly, I say to you, unless a grain of wheat falls into the earth and dies, it remains alone; but if it dies, it bears much fruit. Whoever loves his life loses it, and whoever hates his life in this world will keep it for eternal life" (John 12:24–25). Only at first sight does surrender appear to be loss of life, then. Yes, the disciple loses herself as she hands herself over to God—but this act of devotion is instantly rewarded by the gift of new life. Loss of life by surrender to God ushers into new life that spills over into eternity.[41] In the high-priestly prayer that Jesus prays for his disciples, he explains the nature of this new kind of life: "And this is eternal life, that they know you, the only true God, and Jesus Christ whom you have sent" (John 17:3). This, then, is the definition of real life, eternal life: knowing God and knowing his Son Jesus Christ. John puts it very clearly in his first letter: "Whoever has the Son has life; whoever does not have the Son of God does not have life" (1 John 5:12). True life, life that deserves to be called life, germinates in intimate relationship with Jesus Christ, even in and through suffering.

We have already touched on the important idea that disciples who take up the cross participate not only in Jesus's suffering but also in his resurrection. Christ's new resurrection life shapes and defines the disciple's newness of life.[42] Rudolf Bultmann speaks in this context of a "new form of existence" (*neues Existieren*) that disciples experience as they rise with Christ.[43] This new existence involves—next to the gifts already mentioned, such as a new identity, a refined character, and a new prospect—a new desire. This, perhaps, is the most profound change that happens in the disciple who surrenders herself to God. Having given ourselves over to the Master, we experience a reorientation of our desires and there is one particular desire that repositions everything else: now, we long after Jesus Christ. Now, we pray with the psalmist: "Whom have I in heaven but you? And there is nothing

---

Schlatter, *History*, 304.

41. "God commands us to lose our lives so that he may exalt us," writes John Webster. Webster, "Discipleship and Obedience," 17.

42. Through the resurrection of Christ, discipleship has changed in its essence, so much so, "daß es nach Ostern nicht mehr einfach um Nachfolge Jesu geht, sondern daß Jesus als Erhöhter die Nachfolge verwandelt und verändert." Luz, "Nachfolge Jesu," 685.

43. Rudolf Bultmann notes with a view to the disciples: "... werden sie nur vermöge der Verbundenheit des Leidenden mit Christus, d.h. durch das neue Verständnis der eigenen Existenz (nicht ein theoretisches, sondern ein existentielles ist ein neues Existieren, da das Sich-Verstehen ein Strukturmoment des Existierens ist)." Bultmann, *Der zweite Brief*, 29.

on earth that I desire besides you. My flesh and my heart may fail, but God is the strength of my heart and my portion forever" (Ps 73:25–26; cf. 16:2; 119:57). Having handed themselves over to God they have received, in turn, Christ himself. Their new, true life is "now hidden with Christ in God" (Col 3:3). Having Jesus Christ is everything to the disciple. Whatever may come, whatever they might gain or lose on their pilgrimage, they are at peace, for they will never lose their ultimate object of desire.

Julian of Norwich lived most of her life as an anchoress. She decided to retreat to a small cell that was built against the wall of the church; the cell was sealed and she was dependent on others for vital support.[44] While confined to her cell, Julian experienced several visions and words, which she wrote down, and they were later published as *Revelations of Divine Love*—in fact the first book in English written by a woman. A key theme are the encouraging words, "all shall be well, and all shall be well, and all manner of things shall be well" (ch. 27).[45] Reading her writing, one gets the impression of her strong sense of being loved and kept by Jesus Christ. Here is someone who has surrendered her freedom, living voluntarily in solitary confinement, and yet experiencing true life. When reflecting on her own pilgrimage as Christ's disciple, the difficult life in this world and the eternal bliss of heaven, she said the following: "For I often considered the misery that is here, and the joy and the blessed existence that is there. And even if there had been no pain on earth except the absence of our Lord, it seemed to me sometimes more than I could bear."[46] Surrendering herself to God has definitely resulted in a reorientation of her desires. Even if everything on earth were pleasant and pain-free, but Christ was not at the center of her life, it would have been unbearable for her. Julian clearly reflects here the attitude of the apostle Paul, who writes: "Indeed, I count everything as loss because of the surpassing worth of knowing Christ Jesus my Lord" (Phil 3:8). We expand on this vital insight in the next section where we discuss important aspects of the command, "Follow me," which involves a new desire to contemplate the face of the friend.

CONCLUSION

The demand to take up the cross sounds foolish at first. Everything in us wants to avoid the tensions that come with it: the cross stands for pain and shame, it slows us down, and we wonder why we ought to take it up. Yet

---

44. Windeatt, "Introduction," in Norwich, *Revelations*, ix–xvi.
45. Norwich, *Revelations*, 75.
46. Norwich, *Revelations*, 28.

as we conclude our reflections on Jesus's call to cross-bearing, we remind ourselves of the foundation on which we stand as radical disciples and of the promise that is associated with cross-bearing. We take up the cross as the ones who have already moved from death to new life in Christ. Already now we do share in Christ's resurrection life.[47] And we are promised that in and through our suffering we are being sustained in the intimate fellowship with our great co-sufferer, Jesus Christ. Even more than that, the promise is that our suffering serves a grander purpose. By surrendering ourselves to God completely, neck and crop, we are being transformed and experience a breakthrough to a new vision of self and God. We get a new taste for the newness of life that is ours in Christ and the greatness of God who leads us on our way. In the friction that the act of cross-bearing brings, we are being refined in our desires. Now our focus is on Christ—and we long to see his face.

PERSONAL REFLECTION

How does your cross feel today? What is its shape, size, and weight? Is it different from yesterday? Last month? Have you discovered new aspects of it?

Is there anything you appreciate about your cross? Do you detect any tangible evidence that the cross shapes you into the image of Christ?

What does it mean for you to invite Christ into your suffering? Can you think of concrete examples where you have experienced intimate fellowship with Jesus Christ in your suffering?

What are the ways in which God is pruning you right now? If you could ask for some areas in your life that need further pruning, which are they? Do you see new fruit of the Spirit growing in you?

What does surrendering to God look like in your own life? Do you sense the presence of new resurrection life in you through the Holy Spirit? Knowing and having this life, how does this change your perspective on your present troubles and challenges?

How do you want to pray for yourself right now?

---

47. "Since the Christ is at work in the glory of God," Adolf Schlatter writes, "he creates the church of the eternally living and risen [people]." ["Denn wenn der Christus in der Herrlichkeit Gottes wirksam ist, schafft er die Gemeinde der ewig Lebenden und Auferstandenen."] Schlatter, *Markus*, 163.

III
Follow Me

8

Following Personally

IN OUR JOURNEY so far, we have explored how radical disciples flourish in the tension of constant rejection of the old self and embrace of the new self as Jesus in his role as Prophet calls us to self-denial. We highlighted how Jesus in his office as Priest invites us to take up our cross, and we noted the differences and similarities between Christ's cross and ours and faced the conundrum that by taking up our cross we gain true life. Having arrived at the third stage of the call to discipleship, we probe Jesus's call "Follow me," issued in his role as King. Disciples hear in the voice of the sovereign also the voice of their greatest friend (John 10:5), and we consider how by following Christ they meet the great friend and grow up in their relationship with him and their fellow disciples. It is important to remember that with the call, "Follow me," Jesus invites a group of followers into discipleship. Disciples always follow their Master *together* as the community of believers. At the outset, though, we zoom in on the intimate encounter that each disciple faces with Jesus as she personally listens to his call and counts the cost of discipleship. In a first step, then, we scrutinize what the call to discipleship involves as the life of the one who gives heed to it is turned upside down. Much of what is dear to the disciple, be it things or even relationships, is to be relinquished, and, in return, the disciple gains a new perspective for the things of God. As the disciple follows Christ, she begins to imitate Christ and to witness the spectacular work of the Spirit in the most ordinary of circumstances. We focus, secondly, on the fellowship of the disciples who follow their Master *together*; here, the aspect of spiritual friendship is central as disciples imitate their great friend, establish spiritual friendships with one other, and ultimately, also befriend the world. The third and final section looks at the link between seeking the friend's—Jesus's—face and being changed into his image. Contemplating the friend's face, the disciple learns, leads to transformation into the image of the Beloved.

THE CALL TO DISCIPLESHIP

"Speech is silver, silence is golden," goes the old proverb. The wisdom of the sages in the book of Proverbs lends support to this attitude. The one who "restrains his words" is lauded and even "a fool who keeps silent is considered wise; when he closes his lips, he is deemed intelligent" (Prov 17:27–28). James admonishes the readers of his Epistle to be "quick to hear, slow to speak" (Jas 1:19). From the very beginnings of Christianity, practicing the art of listening, of silence and solitude, of waiting upon God in quiet reflection was deemed vital to the disciple's spiritual health. Today, as we are more and more surrounded by a cacophony of voices and sounds that compete for our attention, it seems that listening has become something of a lost art.

When my wife and I moved from Germany to Scotland's capital Edinburgh almost twenty years ago, we joined the church closest to our home, and it happened to be a Free Church of Scotland. As we soon found out, this church and the denomination with which it was affiliated, were known for its austere services, consisting simply of prayer, Scripture reading, children's address, sermon, and, back in the day, only *a capella* Psalm singing. This took us by surprise, since we were used to a fairly cluttered German evangelical church service with various distractions throughout, such as multiple announcements or (more or less) entertaining interactions. Yet this very basic Scottish worship service, stripped of everything that we had considered essential but later came to recognize as rather superfluous, made listening to God's voice in Scripture reading, sermon, and sacraments, so much easier. Less is more, we noted to our surprise. In his book on *Silence: A Christian History*, Diarmaid MacCulloch speaks of the "Word-centered noisiness of Evangelical Protestantism," that he identified in contemporary practices, and I think he has a point.[1] Sometimes we simply produce too many words. We make too much noise and are at risk of committing the sin of loquacity. Even

---

1. MacCulloch, *Silence*, 223. Michael Casey makes the very same point. "Sometimes we feel that the Church is awash with words," Casey laments. "Like the society in which we live, there is so much talk, so much paper, that even the liturgy is often threatened by verbosity." Casey, *Sacred Reading*, 17.

the background noise of beautiful church choirs, well-crafted sermons, and pious prayers can sometimes drown out the voice of Jesus.

Our tendency to be rather selective when it comes to listening presents another obstacle. So often, we hear what we want to hear, we love to have our "ears tickled" (2 Tim 4:3). As a consequence, "all of us in some way stop listening to the divine Word," writes John Webster, and the result is that ". . . we become selectively deaf."[2] Yet God is the God who speaks and we, his people, are supposed to listen. This is the core of the Shema, "Hear, O Israel" (Deut 6:4). This call is taken up by Jesus Christ who exclaims, "He who has ears to hear, let him hear" (Mark 4:9).

The radical disciple's first step into discipleship begins by listening to Jesus's call, and, as she continues to follow Christ, her whole journey is marked by constant listening to his word. "Listen diligently to me," God calls his people. "Incline your ear, and come to me; hear, that your soul may live" (Isa 55:2–3). Throughout her walk of discipleship, she refines her listening skills. She emulates Mary who enjoyed sitting at the "Lord's feet and listened to his teaching" (Luke 10:39). Jesus calls each of his disciples individually. The disciple is being singled out from the masses, acknowledged, named, and called as an individual.[3] One by one we seek "to enter through the narrow door" (Luke 13:24). Several elements of this call deserve closer scrutiny. The divine call, "Follow me," is an authoritative, effective, and irresistible call, and we look at each of these important aspects in turn.

First, the call is authoritative in the sense that Jesus Christ, in his role as King, calls his subjects to himself. Having redeemed them by his work on the cross, they are forever his. Jesus's call, therefore, writes Webster, "has *absolute* force; it is beyond comparison; it occurs with true, legitimate, divine authority."[4] From our perspective, then, discipleship is always a matter of listening first, not of speaking or rushing into action. We acknowledge that the call to discipleship is based on God's initiative. There is a distinct passivity involved here, as we pay attention to the authoritative call and our response, which is, of course, required, follows, but only in a secondary sense. We cannot open our ears ourselves and we depend on the call coming to us from the outside. "None can call themselves," Dietrich Bonhoeffer insists,[5] and Karl Barth asserts that discipleship is not "self-selection."[6] The one

---

2. Webster, "Discipleship and Calling," 146.

3. Bonhoeffer deals with this in great detail under the section entitled, "Discipleship and the Individual," in his *Discipleship*. See DBWE 4:92–99.

4. Webster, "Discipleship and Calling," 139–40 (emphasis original).

5. DBWE 4:60.

6. *CD* IV/2:535.

who came to Jesus and tried to initiate discipleship on their own, boldly claiming, "I will follow you wherever you go," received the rather uninviting response, "Foxes have holes, and birds of the air have nests, but the Son of Man has nowhere to lay his head" (Luke 9:57–58).

Secondly, this call is also an effective call. God himself says about the word that goes out from his mouth that it "shall not return to me empty, but it shall accomplish that which I purpose, and shall succeed in the thing for which I sent it" (Isa 55:11). Everything depends on the One who calls us to follow him. God is to open our deaf ears so that we can truly hear (Isa 35:5). The stirring command of "*Ephphatha*" ("Be opened!") is included in every call to discipleship (Mark 7:34). The stubborn plug of indifference that clogged our ears needs to be removed first. Once we are able to hear, and actually do listen, our ears are called blessed "for they hear" (Matt 13:16). As the divine call, "Let there be light," brings light into being (Gen 1:3), the divine call, "Follow me," brings the disciple to life. John Webster argues that the "command of Jesus is sheerly *creative*. It *makes* disciples and makes them out of nothing."[7]

Thirdly, Jesus's call to discipleship is always an irresistible call.[8] When Jesus calls, the disciple *will* follow. The call is irresistible because it is rooted in the grace of God which the disciple cannot resist. No one is entitled to receive the call, and no one has earned the privilege of following Jesus Christ. It does not depend on what we might consider our special qualifications or accomplishments.[9] Discipleship is never "the meritorious achievement of individuals," but it is always based on the unmerited divine act of grace, Bonhoeffer insists.[10] "You did not choose me, but I chose you," Jesus tells his disciples (John 15:16). The call to discipleship, then, as Bonhoeffer put it, is "not a human possibility."[11] And Karl Barth notes that disobedience to the command to follow Jesus Christ "is a phenomenon which is absolutely terrifying in its impossibility."[12]

At this point we touch on the important connection between discipleship and election. In fact, discipleship, John Webster notes, "is a matter of election."[13] "Those who are encountered by Jesus and his call to follow him

---

7. Webster, "Discipleship and Calling," 143 (emphasis original).

8. "This call, this grace," writes Bonhoeffer, "is irresistible." DBWE 4:60.

9. "[N]othing can be said about the competence, suitability, or readiness of those who are called," John Webster observes. Webster, "Discipleship and Calling," 143.

10. DBWE 4:47.

11. DBWE 4:83.

12. *CD* IV/2:535.

13. Webster, "Discipleship and Calling," 143.

are faced by an unconditional determination and appointment."[14] If this is true, if indeed then the call to discipleship depends on God's purposeful determination—and not on our own initiative—we might need to reconsider the ways we think and talk about discipleship. Some material used in Christian worship, for instance, needs closer inspection. Phrases found in songs, such as, "I have decided to follow Jesus," surely only portray half the truth, and are in dire need of being balanced with a statement where the disciple praises God for his action to which we humbly and gladly respond.

In her new mode of existence, the radical disciple in fact welcomes God laying his claim on her. The authoritative, effective, and irresistible nature of the call to discipleship rings offensive only in the ears of our old self that craves independence, self-control, and self-efficacy. "Should *I* not be the one initiating *my* discipleship?" the old self murmurs. "*I* am the one who is following, after all!" However, from the perspective of the new self the call to discipleship is gladly received. The disciple enjoys the freedom in giving heed to the irresistible call that slips into her opened ear like a hand into the tailor-made glove. Faced with *this* call, the radical disciple cannot even begin to imagine listening to someone or something else instead. "Lord, to whom shall we go? You have the words of eternal life," we echo Peter's reply (John 6:68).

Before we even consider articulating a careful response to this call, we might want to ponder first the wonder of being called by Jesus Christ in his role as King. Jesus calls *us*—and we consider the magnitude of it. He knows us most intimately, our worst fears, greatest hopes, and most serious flaws. But he calls us anyway. "The sheep hear his voice, and he calls his own sheep by name and leads them out" (John 10:3). All our futile old self attempts to achieve recognition, acknowledgment, and appreciation are put to rest by this gracious calling. Jesus's call calms our desperate attempts to declare our perceived self-worth to others and we discover the soothing and liberating gift of being named and loved by the great shepherd. As we have already seen earlier, the naming of God establishes and sustains our identity as those chosen by God (see chapter 3). The radical disciple then has a distinct way of talking about herself: "I am known and called by God. I am Christ's." The possessive here is significant, for it signifies that disciples are

---

14. Webster, "Discipleship and Calling," 143. In Webster's words, "The call of Jesus does not look to a future decision on part of the disciple, by virtue of which it might become effective. Rather, the call sets before its hearer a decision which has *already* been made. It places the one called under a conclusion. Here in Jesus's call we do not have the first stages of the gathering of a voluntary assembly of those who choose discipleship; we have the outworking of the eternal divine purpose: he destined us in love." Webster, "Discipleship and Calling," 143 (emphasis original).

their Master's possession; they are his, they belong to him. As noted earlier, Christian talk about the self is always Christ-infused; we have coined the term, Christothentic self. When the radical disciple talks about herself, she cannot but refer to herself but in vital connection with Christ. This, and this alone, brings about composure and peace that surpasses all understanding (Phil 4:7).

The call to discipleship may be authoritative, effective, and irresistible, but each disciple is still required to answer. In issuing the call, "Follow me," Jesus presents a challenge to each disciple. We are tasked with a response and no one else can speak for us here. Dietrich Bonhoeffer writes,

> Jesus' call to discipleship makes the disciple into a single individual. Whether disciples want to or not, they have to make a decision; each has to decide alone. It is not their own choice to desire to be single individuals. Instead, Christ makes everyone he calls into an individual. Each is called alone. Each must follow alone.[15]

Discipleship, then, is an intimate matter between the disciple and Jesus. Jesus calls, we listen, and we respond knowing full well that our resolution to follow Christ might involve serious consequences for our life. We might have to leave behind our nets and take a courageous step into unknown territory. "Immediately they left their nets and followed him" (Matt 4:20). Following Jesus requires this "definite first step," as Karl Barth put it.[16] We might need to leave behind possessions, certain habits, dreams, status, privilege, health, even relationships—and yes, even our own self, in order to follow Jesus. The costs are high. Confronted with the costs of discipleship, we read in John's Gospel that "many of his disciples turned back and no longer walked with him" (John 6:66). This is clearly one of the most sobering verses in the New Testament.

Having established the important elements of the theological basis of Jesus's call, "Follow me," we turn our attention next to our response. This response involves mastering the art of letting go that radical disciples learn on their first steps into discipleship. We move, in a second step, to the important question of imitation, exploring the ways in which we emulate the Master whom we follow.

---

15. DBWE 4:92. Bonhoeffer apparently alludes here to Søren Kierkegaard who insisted that we need to become "*the single individual.*" "As *the single individual* he is alone," Kierkegaard notes, "alone in the whole world, alone—face-to-face before God." Kierkegaard, *Point of View*, 123 (emphasis original). Cf. DBWE 4:92n2.

16. *CD* IV/2:538.

LETTING GO AND FLOURISHING

Following Jesus involves a clear "break," Karl Barth notes.[17] This break consists in leaving behind a whole range of old self preferences, desires, and ideals. Disciples are being led into a tension here as they are asked to let go without knowing the consequences. As we shall see, though, the promise attached to the action of letting go is that disciples receive recompense in astonishing ways as their vision and love for the Master grows, and as they begin to flourish in the company of the other disciples. In what follows we explore how radical disciples relinquish their desire for self-determination, are prepared to let go of their possessions and even relationships, and thrive in the midst of these tensions as they are being rewarded in multiple ways.

From Self-Determination to Freedom

The first item that disciples release as they make their first step into discipleship is the map. We relinquish our desire to set the course for discipleship ourselves. Radical disciples are courageous enough to renounce their need for autonomy and self-determination. We are content to give up our position in the driver's seat of our life. In our old mode of existence, we sought to determine the direction ourselves. Yet here, and this is a major step of courage, we relinquish control and step into the unknown.[18] "Self-loyalty, self-disposition, self-affirmation, obedience to that intense impulse to survive: in the movement of discipleship, all this is to be laid aside," John Webster writes.[19] Dietrich Bonhoeffer speaks in this context even of a death of self, and we are here reminded of our earlier discussion of the urgency to put to death the impulses of the old self.[20] Disciples who have entered this new path of discipleship follow not their own plans and ideas, but Jesus Christ. Wherever Christ goes, they follow.

---

17. *KD* IV/2:614.

18. "Loss of self," John Webster argues, "is the most fundamental abandonment" as we make the initial step into discipleship. Webster, "Discipleship and Obedience," 15.

19. Webster, "Discipleship and Obedience," 15.

20. Bonhoeffer writes: "It is laid on every Christian. The first Christ-suffering that everyone has to experience is the call which summons us away from our attachments to this world. It is the death of the old self in the encounter with Jesus Christ. Those who enter into discipleship enter into Jesus's death. They turn their living into dying; such has been the case from the very beginning. The cross is not the terrible end of a pious, happy life. Instead, it stands at the beginning of community with Jesus Christ. Whenever Christ calls us, his call leads us into death." DBWE 4:87.

It is important to highlight this obvious fact: Disciples always follow, they never go ahead. The Greek word for "to follow" (*akoloutheō*) refers to the act of walking behind someone, to follow someone as a companion.[21] We walk behind Christ, not in front of him or even next to him. As John Webster puts it, "the command is to follow at a distance."[22] There is "always an unbridgeable distance—like the cloud and the pillar of fire in the wilderness, Jesus goes ahead of his followers."[23] The disciple "never moves beyond the condition of following."[24] To follow behind Jesus is then very different from imitation, argues Karl Barth (we focus on the question of imitation further below).

> In the first place it is descriptive of someone who accompanies another, who takes the same road as he does. But more pregnantly, it indicates the follower who respectfully walks behind a master or prince, the scholar who strides along at a distance behind his teacher. And in cases like this imitation is not only unnecessary, but impossible.[25]

Throughout their journey, radical disciples continue to be vigilant, since ambitious old impulses might entice them to take the lead, to set the agenda and determine the direction. In our old mode of existence, we might even speed ahead with inappropriate spiritual vigor and overtake the Master. Once the enthusiasm has waned, though, and we are out of breath, stopping and looking around us, we notice that Jesus is out of sight. We have left him behind. Stubborn lost sheep, we are stuck in the thicket of thorns and thistles and need to wait for our patient guide, who will come to our rescue, in his own time. He will catch up with us, find us, and carry his lost and disoriented sheep back to the fold (Luke 16:3–6).

Radical disciples might have left behind a comfortable life, a convenient rhythm, and familiar rituals. Yet once they have entered the condition of following Christ, they avoid looking back with nostalgia like Lot's wife. "No one who puts his hand to the plow and looks back," Jesus says, "is fit for the kingdom of God" (Luke 9:62). Instead, they look ahead with a mix of apprehension and eager expectation. On the one hand, they know that they

---

21. "Hinterhergehen, nachkommen," "als Begleiter nachfolgen." Bauer et al., *Griechisch-deutsches Wörterbuch*, 60. Karl Barth observes that the New Testament documents always refer to the act of following after Jesus; *akoloutheō* always appears as a verb in the New Testament, and never in its substantival form. CD IV/2:534.

22. Webster, "Discipleship and Calling," 141.

23. Webster, "Discipleship and Calling," 141.

24. Webster, "Discipleship and Calling," 141.

25. CD I/2:277.

have just made a serious step into the unknown. They do not see clearly the way before them. The difficulty, as Heinz Schürmann recognized, is that "the call to the discipleship of the cross only ever shows a path and not the destination."[26] On the other hand, though, they move ahead with courage, since following Jesus always comes with a great sense of freedom. As we follow Jesus and leave behind our net of self-determination, entangled with all its various perceived self-related desires and needs, we become truly free. Indeed, disciples are "called to freedom" (Gal 5:13). Serenity, composure, and poise follow those who embrace the tension of letting go. These disciples follow Jesus with a light readiness, for Jesus assures them of his grace in each step they take.[27]

From Possessions to Prosperity

On the road of discipleship one travels lightly, leaving behind any excess baggage. Disciples step into this new path having emptied their pockets. The conditions are set out very clearly: "So therefore, any one of you who does not renounce all that he has cannot be my disciple" (Luke 14:33). This is obviously a radical call that we may want to put into perspective (and some have argued that it was issued only to the itinerant disciples in this particular context).[28] We remember, for instance, the other Lukan passage where Zacchaeus, the chief tax collector (and chief fraudster), started out as a fresh follower of Jesus "only" giving away half of his possessions. Still, Jesus responded positively, "Today salvation has come to this house" (Luke 19:9). Essential, it seems, is not the quantity of what we renounce, but the qualitative change of attitude toward our possessions that takes place in us. Bearing this in mind, we still note the recurrent theme: Jesus's call to a radical denial of the things we own clearly touches a sore spot in our materialist default mentality.[29] "I have bought a field, and I must go out and see it. Please have me excused," is our classic pretext (Luke 14:18). Every fiber of our being reacts against the condition of letting go of our possessions, perhaps even more so today in our culture of consumerism than back then.[30] If we are

26. As Schürmann notes, "der Ruf in die Kreuzesnachfolge weist ja immer nur einen Weg, nicht das Ziel." Schürmann, *Das Lukasevangelium*, 539.

27. Jesus asks for complete renunciation of our own volition, yet "he wanted it to be exercised and borne cheerfully, not as a misery and misfortune but as gain." Schlatter, *History*, 313.

28. I am indebted to Greg Forbes for a stimulating conversation on this question.

29. Karl Barth writes that "Jesus' call to discipleship challenges and indeed cuts right across the self-evident attachment to that which we possess." *CD* IV/2:548.

30. On this see Reimer, "Biblical Perspectives."

honest, we will be ready to admit that we are too much in love with things. We have accumulated things, and even more things. Superabundance and excess in the West abound, opulence and material goods overkill wherever one looks. The average US-American household today apparently counts around a staggering amount of 300,000 items.[31] We own so much that our homes are spilling over with things and we are now building storage facilities in prime locations of our inner cities to hoard our superfluous belongings. In Australia, for instance, one observes a "relentlessly increasing demand for off-site storage."[32] These storage facilities represent modern shrines to things, worship centers to the material.

Of course, there is nothing to be said against the material in and of itself. Christianity is a very material, physical faith. Christian believers highlight the goodness of creation and look forward to God's refashioning of his redeemed creation in the eschaton. We are physical beings and we embrace the blessings of materiality. Yet once the material moves from the periphery of our existence right into the center, it is at risk of becoming an idol. We then worship the dead thing instead of the living God. In materialism and consumerism, the thing itself becomes an idol as it "wrongly centres the meaning of life," David Reimer writes.[33] This was the case with the rich young man whom Jesus once encountered (Matt 19:16–23). He was definitely curious about following Jesus. Yet at the heart of his life were his possessions. So Jesus puts his finger in the wound and gives him the following condition for discipleship: "[G]o, sell what you possess and give to the poor, and you will have treasure in heaven; and come, follow me" (Matt 19:21). The young man walked away, "sorrowful, for he had great possessions" (Matt 19:22).

Why are we so much in love with our possessions? Why do we so often fail to let go? Dietrich Bonhoeffer has a plausible answer here. In his view, possessions, we tend to think, give us as sense of security. If I just own enough, I shall be safe and content, our old self thinks. "And I will say to my soul, 'Soul, you have ample goods laid up for many years; relax, eat, drink, be merry'" (Luke 12:19). There is, however, a serious misconception and the gentleman in Jesus's parable is called a "fool" for that very reason. "Earthly goods," Bonhoeffer explains, "deceive the human heart into believing that they give it security and freedom from worry. But in truth, they are what cause anxiety."[34] More possessions do not reduce, but fuel, anxious thoughts and worries.

31. Macvean, "Many People."
32. Baum, "Lock-and-Leave."
33. Reimer, "Biblical Perspectives," 17.
34. DBWE 4:165.

In a study conducted with over 400,000 participants, Daniel Kahneman and Angus Deaton offered empirical evidence that money really does not buy peace and happiness.[35] Of course, they found that very low income was, as one would predict, closely associated with low scores in well-being. Nevertheless, a moderate income that covered most of life's expenses (in this case, 75,000 US dollars at the time) was actually more than sufficient to contribute to personal contentment. Beyond this amount, that is, an income that puts one in the "rich" category, fails to produce an equivalent boost in well-being, Kahneman and Deaton concluded. In fact, more possessions even seem to be associated with more problems: more loneliness,[36] lower life-satisfaction, and reduced well-being, as various researchers found.[37] The more possessions, the more the worry is the old truism. This kind of worry is part of our old mode of existence. "Worry is the concern of nonbelievers," writes Bonhoeffer, "who rely on their strength and work, but not on God."[38]

Today's storage facilities are modern versions of the barn built by the rich fool in Jesus's parable. They grow out of the old, insecure, and self-reliant self. Jesus reprimands this attitude of laying up treasures for oneself and instead encourages us to be "rich toward God" (Luke 12:21). Richness toward God is expressed in the ability to let go and to put our trust in God. We surrender our assumed need for self-control through acquiring possessions and instead trust in God. "Only those who put tomorrow completely into God's hand and receive fully today what they need for their lives are really secure," writes Bonhoeffer.[39] True prosperity, in the sense of security, well-being, and comfort follow the one who has made God her provider.

A candidate seeking to become a Benedictine monk or nun leaves behind everything at the door of the monastery—even his or her own clothes—as one is being provided with new ones.[40] The candidate is not allowed to have any personal possessions, not even a book or a pen.[41] While there is much to learn from those who join a monastery and renounce literally *all* their possessions (as they go over into the possession of the cloister),

---

35. Kahneman and Deaton, "High Income."

36. "Rik Pieters of Tilburg University," writes Robert Muller, "has established a link between materialism and increasing loneliness over time." Muller, "Minimalism."

37. Jebb et al., "Happiness."

38. DBWE 4:167. "Nonbelievers are worriers," he continues, "because they do not know that the Father knows what their needs are. So they intend to get for themselves what they do not expect from God." DBWE 4:167.

39. DBWE 4:165.

40. See Pax CSPB, "Regula Benedicti 58.26/27."

41. Pax CSPB, "Kapitel 33.3."

we cannot and should not all become monks and nuns.[42] "We need not become ascetic or sell every possession," notes Chuck DeGroat. "But we must learn the posture of the ascetic and be ready to be without. In fact, what we relinquish is the need to possess."[43] Thus, as radical disciples we might want to lead our lives as if we were monks and nuns, that is, we aim at possessing our things, as Bonhoeffer put it, "as if I did not possess them."[44] Or, in the words of the apostle Paul, radical disciples live as "those who buy as though they had no goods, and those who deal with the world as though they had no dealings with it" (1 Cor 7:30–31). In this way, we are only loosely attached to our belongings; they do not weigh us down, we are happy to let go if need be, and we experience freedom and contentment in the process. As our hearts are untied from the false promise of security and happiness that material possessions pretend to bring, we joyfully follow the one who "had no place to lay his head" (Luke 5:58). The heart that clings to Jesus and not to things does not break if the thing falls away, for Jesus is its portion and security. In this way, the disciple, by renouncing her attachment to possessions, experiences true prosperity.

From Relations to Intimacy

Following Christ also involves a reappraisal of our priorities when it comes to relationships. "If anyone comes to me and does not hate his own father and mother and wife and children and brothers and sisters, yes, and even his own life, he cannot be my disciple" (Luke 14:26; cf. Matt 10:37). "Hate" is certainly a strong word here (and we have already pointed to the particular radicality that we find in Luke), but one realizes that there is a risk that some relationships can get in the way of discipleship. "I have married a wife, and therefore I cannot come," is one of the excuses put forward in that passage (Luke 14:20). "The coming of the kingdom of God means an end of the absolute of family no less than that of possession and fame," Karl Barth observes.[45] He explains that relationships may become a stumbling block for the disciple on account of "the impulsive intensity with which he allows himself to be enfolded by, and think that he himself should enfold, those who stand to him in these relationships."[46] There is a risk that the disciple

---

42. For Bonhoeffer's discussion of asceticism, see DBWE 4:160.
43. DeGroat, *Wholeheartedness*, 137.
44. DBWE 4:78.
45. *CD* IV/2:551.
46. *CD* IV/2:550.

might become imprisoned and taken captive in these relational ties.[47] In some places of this world, radical disciples leave their families because their faith in Jesus collides with their family's allegiance to another religion, or to a religious or political leader. However, today this might not be the most pressing problem for the readers of this book. Our temptation in the West might be more subtle, but equally challenging: even those closest to us, our partner, children, and friends can become stars around which we orbit.

Dietrich Bonhoeffer experienced in his own life the pain of letting go of intimate relationships. When in prison, he was not only cut off from family and friends, but even from his fiancée. He was engaged to Maria von Wedemeyer in January 1943, only three months before his arrest.[48] While in prison, Bonhoeffer was only allowed to communicate with his fiancée via censored mail and they spoke in person only with supervisors present.[49] Today we have some insight into their challenging circumstances through the publication of their correspondence, *Love Letters from Cell 92*. In one of her moving letters, Maria writes to Dietrich,

> Sometimes, when I wake up in the night and can't help thinking of you so much, I wonder if I've been woken by a thought of yours. And that would be lovely. When I get up at half-past five in the morning, I always try to think of you very gently and cautiously, so as to let you sleep on a bit. I've chalked a line around my bed roughly the size of your cell. There are a table and a chair standing there, the way I picture it, and when I sit there I almost believe I'm with you. If only I really were.[50]

Whomever they leave behind, radical disciples are assured of Jesus's promise that "[E]veryone who has left houses or brothers or sisters or father or mother or children or lands, for my name's sake, will receive a hundredfold and will inherit eternal life" (Matt 19:29). While still in this life, radical disciples, equipped with a new desire, want to make sure that their intimate relationship with Jesus enjoys priority over all other relationships.[51] They constantly come up with new answers to the question, "How is your beloved

---

47. *CD* IV/2:550.
48. Schlingensiepen, *Dietrich Bonhoeffe*, 310.
49. Schlingensiepen, *Dietrich Bonhoeffer*, 336.
50. Letter to Dietrich, April 26, 1944, in Bonhoeffer and von Wedemeyer, *Love Letters*, 191.
51. This is, as Hahn notes, "eine Frage der Priorität, wobei die Lebensgemeinschaft mit Jesus eindeutigen Vorrang vor allen familiären Bindungen besitzt." Hahn, *Theologie*, 77.

better than others?" (Song 5:9, NIV).[52] Faced with the decision of what and whom to let go when, considerable deliberation and care is required, and to this we turn next.

IMMEDIACY AND DELIBERATION

Radical disciples respond without delay to the call to discipleship. "Brothers, what shall we do?" was the urgent question on the minds of those who listened to Peter's sermon (Acts 2:37). Disciples do not incubate for a period of time, deferring the decision, but respond immediately (e.g., Mark 2:14; Matt 4:20; 9:9).[53] Those who seek to postpone their decision—"I will follow you, Lord, but let me first say farewell to those at my home"—are declared unfit for the kingdom of God (Luke 9:61–62). Immediacy is key. "Obedience is immediate obedience," John Webster writes.[54]

I wonder whether we are overcomplicating things a little in our churches today. One can get the impression that only those who have signed up for the three-week discipleship course or the six-week discipleship training seminar can legitimately call themselves disciples. One might think that only when one has worked through the "Ten Steps to Discipleship" one is qualified to follow Jesus. The New Testament, however, does not know anything of the sort; it portrays simple obedience as the first step into discipleship and many churches today would do well in rediscovering a healthy dose of simplicity and immediacy.

While the response is immediate, the path on which we follow may differ from disciple to disciple. There is no one-size-fits-all solution to discipleship; how our particular follow-ship pans out in detail looks different from disciple to disciple. When the apostle Peter inquired about the path ahead for his fellow disciple John—"Lord, what about this man?" (John 21:21)—Jesus did not offer any clues. He made sure that Peter was focused on his own walk of discipleship, not squinting at his friend and wondering

---

52. Kris Lundgaard repeatedly uses this question from the Song of Solomon with a view to christological application in his highly recommended book, Lundgaard, *Looking Glass*, 13, 28, 43, 55, 68, 82, 105, 21, 36, 51, 67.

53. Karl Barth insists that there is "no interval, i.e., that they first believed in Him, and then decided to obey Him." *CD* IV/2:538. Dietrich Bonhoeffer, too, emphasizes this prompt act of obedience when he notes: "The call goes out, and without any further ado the obedient deed of the one called follows. The disciple's answer is not a spoken confession of faith in Jesus. Instead, it is the obedient deed." DBWE 4:57.

54. Webster, "Discipleship and Obedience," 9.

what his way might look like.⁵⁵ Obeying the command "Follow me!" may look different for disciple A and disciple B, as Karl Barth writes:

> In obedience to the command we may just as well do something else and even the very opposite. For example, instead of giving all that we have to the poor, we may maintain and increase our possessions; or instead of turning the other cheek, we may return the blow which we have received. . . . All in a grateful appropriation of the salvation which comes with Jesus' call to discipleship!⁵⁶

My fellow disciple might need to renounce habit X while I ought to work on bidding farewell to person Y. In Barth's words: "To *this* man He *now* gives—and this man now receives—*this* command as the concrete form of the call to discipleship now issued to him."⁵⁷ The nets we are to leave behind might look different for each and every one of us. Ferdinand Hahn offers some balanced insights here:

> As much as Jesus's call to discipleship is a demand that claims the human in his or her totality, it is not about legalistic rules and does not expect human perfectionism. The way in which discipleship is specifically realized differs case by case. It is pivotal, though, that there does not remain a reservation based on worldly attachments or goods that would make following Jesus impossible . . . Everyone who answers Jesus's call is completely under orders; for everyone it is about a total surrender of life to Jesus, howsoever this might play out in practice.⁵⁸

Karl Barth makes the case that disciples of Christ need to ask the question, "What should we do?" again and again, in all seriousness and

---

55. "Jesus said to him, "If it is my will that he remain until I come, what is that to you? You follow me!" (John 21:22).

56. *CD* IV/2:541.

57. *CD* IV/2:547.

58. "So sehr Jesu Ruf in die Nachfolge eine den Menschen total beanspruchende Forderung ist, geht es dabei nicht um gesetzliche Bestimmungen oder um einen vom Menschen erwarteten Perfektionismus. Wie sich Nachfolge konkret realisiert, ist von Fall zu Fall verschieden. Entscheidend ist, daß nicht um irdischer Bindungen und Güter willen ein Vorbehalt bleibt, der letztlich die Nachfolge Jesu unmöglich macht . . . Hinzu kommt, daß Nachfolge nicht nur in außergewöhnlichen Lebensformen realisiert wird, und entsprechend lassen die jeweiligen Lebensformen auch keine Unterscheidung zwischen guten und weniger guten Jüngern zu. Jeder, der Jesu Ruf annimmt, ist ganz gefordert; für jeden geht es um eine totale Lebenshingabe an Jesus, wie immer sich das konkret auswirkt. Aus diesem Grunde gelten auch alle Forderungen allen Menschen, aber es ist nicht von jedem alles gleichzeitig gefordert." Hahn, *Theologie*, 79.

"complete openness."[59] Yet we do so not as those who are foreign to God and his commandments, but as those, Barth asserts, who are God's covenantal partners.[60] The question about the concrete expression of our follow-ship, so to speak, is always embedded in the comforting context of our intimate relationship with the God who loves us in Christ and who leads us through his Holy Spirit. "By seriously asking: What should we do?" Barth writes, "we confess that we, as the ignorant, have known of God that his eternal eye is fixed on our being, willing, doing and not doing; we then place it trustingly in his hands as it is; we will then entrust it to him."[61] Our discernment and deliberation, in that sense, always stands under the sovereign decision of God to be gracious to us in Jesus Christ.[62] In Bonhoeffer's words, our decision how and where to follow lies in the person of *Jesus Christ himself*. It is he who calls. That is why the tax collector follows. This encounter gives witness to Jesus' unconditional, immediate, and inexplicable authority."[63] We turn our attention next to the gravitational pull that the person of Christ exerts on those who are called into discipleship.

FOLLOWING AND IMITATION

Radical disciples follow the person of Jesus Christ.[64] It was always a distinguishing mark of the people of God that they walked with God, "Enoch walked with God, and he was not, for God took him" (Gen 5:24); "Noah walked with God" (Gen 6:9); and Moses tells God, "Is it not in your going with us, so that we are distinct, I and your people, from every other people on the face of the earth?" (Exod 33:16). Likewise, the mark of radical disciples is that they walk with Christ and Christ with them. It is important to stress this point, since there has been some misunderstanding about the nature of discipleship in this regard. Christian disciples do not unite around an influential idea, a worthy cause, or a virtuous purpose.[65] This, in fact,

---

59. *KD* II/2:720.

60. *KD* II/2:713.

61. "Indem wir ernstlich fragen: Was sollen wir tun? bekennen wir, daß wir als die Nichtwissenden von Gott gewußt, daß sein ewiges Auge auf unser Sein, Wollen, Tun und Lassen gerichtet ist; wir legen es dann, wie es ist, vertrauend in seine Hand; wir lassen es dann ihm anbefohlen sein." *KD* II/2:722.

62. *KD* II/2:727.

63. DBWE 4:57 (emphasis original).

64. DBWE 4:94.

65. We follow not "some cause, principle or truth beyond or behind Jesus," John Webster reminds us. Webster, "Discipleship and Calling," 141.

would run counter to the very idea of discipleship, as Bonhoeffer remarks. "An idea about Christ, a doctrinal system, a general religious recognition of grace or forgiveness of sins does not require discipleship," he writes. "In truth, it even excludes discipleship; it is inimical to it."[66]

There are, of course, many good causes we could (and ought to) pursue. Yet whenever the good cause overshadows the person we follow, we might need some recalibration and reconsideration of our priorities. John Webster lists some of the good causes that could tempt us and therefore distract us from focusing on the person before us, such as "justice; spirituality; inclusiveness; orthodoxy; moral truth."[67] Caring for creation, too, is a worthy objective, and we could add many others. Yet, again, once any of these goals begins to overshadow our zeal to follow Jesus, we might need some readjustment.[68] Radical disciples do not follow great ideals, but they follow the one who *personifies* all these ideals. And only through our intimate relationship with Jesus can we begin to pursue these worthy ideals. We follow not an idea of love but love incarnate—and through our intimate union with him, we will be inspired and empowered to imitate Jesus's love for God and humanity.

Following Jesus, then, obviously carries the notion of imitation. Radical disciples imitate their Master. In fact, this idea was central to interpretations of discipleship throughout theological history.[69] Thomas à Kempis, *The Imitation of Christ*, written in the early fifteenth century, is a prime example here.[70] As we constantly look to Jesus who goes ahead of us, we see him act in a certain way and we seek to imitate his example. However, it is vital in this context to examine the nature, and in particular, the limits of imitation, and thus to parry lopsided understandings of the concept.

---

66. DBWE 4:59.

67. Webster, "Discipleship and Calling," 142.

68. Karl Barth writes: "Again, discipleship is not the recognition and acceptance of a programme, ideal or law, or the attempt to fulfil it. It is not the execution of a plan of individual or social construction imparted and commended by Jesus." CD IV/2:536. ["Und so ist Nachfolge auch nicht die Anerkennung und Übernahme eines Programms, eines Ideals, eines Gesetzes, nicht der Versuch, ein solches zu verwirklichen. Nachfolge ist nicht die Ausführung eines dem Menschen von Jesus mitgeteiltem und zur Nachahmung empfohlenen Planes individueller oder sozialer Lebensgestaltung." KD IV/2:607].

69. See Riches, "Nachfolge Jesu."

70. Kempis has a great deal to offer in this devotional work and I have learned much from him. Michael Horton refers to a significant drawback of the work, though, in that he laments that "most glaringly, *Christ in his saving office*" is somewhat missing. Horton, *Gospel-Driven Life*, 146 (emphasis original).

First, the disciple recognizes certain limits of imitation. There are aspects of Jesus's person and work that we *cannot* imitate. It reminds us of the fact that we walk behind Jesus, and that even though we are intimately united with him, he remains over and above us.[71] We always follow "the transcendent Lord," John Webster notes, and we will remain "*unlike* him and so *behind* him."[72] We have already pointed to various limitations in this regard, such as that we cannot imitate Jesus's incarnation, his perfect life in obedience to the Father as the divine human being, or his salvific, substitutionary work on our behalf. Here, we are categorically inactive and all we do is benefit from the gifts that flow to us through our intimate union with him.

Second, many a time in theological history Jesus was reduced to a moral example that his followers were supposed to emulate. Of course, Jesus is in many ways our moral role model and we are called to do as he did—"For I have given you an example," Jesus tells his disciples, "that you also should do just as I have done to you" (John 13:15); and the apostle Paul writes, "Be imitators of me, as I am of Christ" (1 Cor 11:1). The core issue here, though, is that we adopt an adequate understanding of imitation. We have already touched on the "What would Jesus do?" (WWJD) movement earlier. This surely well-intended desire to imitate Jesus can easily turn into legalism, as Andrew Purves observes:

> [M]y main problem with the theology of WWJD is that it turns Jesus into the teacher of fixed moral ideas which must be imitated. Everything is now cast back upon us to achieve. Even with a little help from the Holy Spirit, it sounds like a religion of obedience to moral laws.[73]

The New Testament picture of imitation, however, points to our intimate union with Christ, which secures our declaration of righteousness and renewal in sanctification. This is the solid basis on which the disciple stands. Only from the vantage point of being in Christ, enjoying the benefits of Christ's active and passive obedience as our representative and substitute, can we begin to consider what imitation is. The indicative of our union with Christ is the basis for the imperative of imitation. Viewed from this perspective, we are not standing from afar, observing Jesus and desperately trying to copy his actions; rather, we are with him, even in him (1 Pet 5:14; Phil 1:1; Rom 8:1; Col 3:3) and he in us (John 14:20, 17:23; Col 1:27; Gal 2:20). In this

---

71. CD I/2:277.
72. Webster, "Discipleship and Calling," 141 (emphasis original).
73. Purves, *Crucifixion of Ministry*, 51.

vital union through the Holy Spirit, we are empowered to live according to the character who reigns in us. Michael Horton writes,

> The Spirit's work of uniting us to Christ makes us not mere imitators but living members of his body. We are incorporated—baptized—into Christ's death, burial, and resurrection. Paul does not say, "Be like Jesus." He says, "You *are* like Jesus. He is the head, and you are part of his body."[74]

Taking seriously the liberating truth of "Christ in you, the hope of glory" (Col 1:27), we move from the rather blunt question, "What would Jesus do?" to the more refined, "What does the Spirit prompt me to do in this particular situation?" or "How does the Spirit nudge me to Christ-like action in this very moment?" Imitation correctly understood, then, takes as its foundation our union with Christ that supports, through Christ's work on our behalf, the basis of our agency as spiritually renewed disciples who grow up into the image of Christ through the Spirit who works in us.

In short, imitation is by grace. "Jesus's actions," writes Adolf Schlatter, "were not dependent on the question of how he could be useful as our example but how he could become the giver of grace."[75] And the nature of grace is that it restores human nature. God's grace does not lift us into a super-human state but as we benefit from Jesus's active obedience, our human nature is healed and restored. "If you love me, you will keep my commandments," Jesus says (John 14:15). And Jesus's commandments, the apostle John explains "are not burdensome" (1 John 5:3). Obeying and imitating is light, because it is empowered by grace. "It is a grace which commands" as Barth put it.[76] As a consequence, we might not even be aware that we are slowly growing more into the likeness of our Master. "Sometimes imitation is unconscious. Without knowing it, a disciple may begin to mimic a mentor's style or mannerism," Michael Casey writes. "What this sometimes amusing behavior indicates is that a bonding is taking place between disciple and master."[77] By living in close relationship with Jesus Christ, the disciple experiences transformation, change in character, outlook, and attitude—we will return to this important organic principle in chapter 10.

---

74. Horton, *Gospel-Driven Life*, 150 (emphasis original).

75. "Darum war das Verhalten Jesu nicht von der Erwägung abhängig, wie er uns als Beispiel nützlich sei, sondern wie er für uns zum Spender der Gnade werde." Schlatter, *Das christliche Dogma*, 314. And Dietrich Bonhoeffer notes, "Blessed are they for whom following Jesus Christ means nothing other than living from grace and for whom grace means following Christ." DBWE 4:56.

76. *CD* IV/2:535.

77. Casey, *Sacred Reading*, 37.

As we draw to a close of this present chapter, we are left with some open questions, such as "What is the actual content of imitation?" or "What is it in Jesus Christ that his followers imitate?" and "How does this play out in real life?"

LOVING GOD AND NEIGHBOR

Radical disciples imitate Jesus in their love for God and neighbor. Jesus's love was always directed toward his Father and human beings. Adolf Schlatter highlights that Jesus continuously lived in the double orientation of his "service to God" and his "service to humanity."[78] Radical disciples follow him in this double orientation and apply it to their own lives and contexts. Empowered by the spirit of Christ in them, they fulfill the greatest commandment, namely, to love God with heart, soul, mind, and strength, and to love their neighbor as their own self (Mark 12:30–31). Since Christ reigns, too, in their fellow disciples, they realize that when they serve and love them, they have also served and loved Christ. "Truly, I say to you, as you did it to one of the least of these my brothers, you did it to me" (Matt 25:40). It is here that they discover their true vocation. Loving God, their fellow disciples, and neighbors, they find their purpose of being, in fact, they become "real human beings," as Bonhoeffer put it.[79]

Grace-empowered love of God and neighbor plays out in concrete acts in daily life. In fact, it is *all* about love made concrete.[80] Whereas in our old mode of existence we might have put forward many a lame excuse for why we could not or must not do this or that, in our new self-existence our love will be made concrete in tangible action. As usual, Bonhoeffer takes us out of our comfort zone:

> You should not ask; you should act. The question Who is my neighbour? is the final question of despair or hubris, in which

---

78. Schlatter, "Christi Versöhnen," 161; *Aus meiner Sprechstunde*, 29–30.

79. Bonhoeffer argues that as we live out the commandment to love others, we will become "real human beings" and also help others to become "human beings before God." He writes: "Christ does not teach an abstract ethic that must be carried out, cost what it may. Christ was not essentially a teacher, a lawgiver, but a human being, a real human being like us. Accordingly, Christ does not want us to be first of all pupils, representatives and advocates of a particular doctrine, but human beings, real human beings before God . . . Christ was not concerned about whether 'the maxim of an action' could become 'a principle of universal law,' but whether my action now helps my neighbour to be a human being before God." DBWE 6:98–99.

80. See DBWE 4:123.

disobedience justifies itself. The answer is: You yourself are the neighbour. Go and be obedient in acts of love.[81]

This is a wake-up call for disciples who might have started out on their way of discipleship full of enthusiasm, but are now, half-way down the road, grown lukewarm and tired. There is always the temptation that radical disciples morph into tepid consumers who sit comfortably in church and enjoy listening to accessible preaching, while neglecting to put into practice what was proclaimed. "God will not ask us someday whether our confession was evangelical," Bonhoeffer addresses this dull disciple, "but whether we did God's will."[82] Or, in Adolf Schlatter's words, "The church is being assessed, by those who do not attend it, not on the basis of what the church *says*, but according to what it *does*."[83] (Both Bonhoeffer and Schlatter clearly valued the importance of the church's confessions, so one ought to take these statements with a pinch of salt as they have been drafted provocatively, in an attempt to wake up slumbering disciples.) Of course, life can be comfortable when one is encased in the cocoon of pious coziness. But here, discipleship has atrophied and does not deserve the name discipleship anymore. Radical disciples are called to simple, yet concrete obedience through the spirit of God. "Little children, let us not love in word or talk but in deed and in truth" (1 John 3:18).[84] Disciples become *radical* disciples when their grace-enabled love for God and neighbor spills over in concrete action on behalf of others. Bonhoeffer writes, "[D]o what is good! You do it. That is the only thing that counts. It is not important for you what others might do, but what you will do. Do what is good, fearlessly, unreservedly, and unconditionally."[85]

When disciples are moved into action to love God and neighbor, extraordinary things happen. Astonishing deeds of love, however, go often unnoticed by the general observer. Yet the spectacular happens right in the presence of what seems to be ordinariness, and radical disciples are called to recalibrate their vision as they look at the world through Jesus's eyes.

Extraordinary deeds of love happen right in what we perceive to be quite ordinary circumstances.[86] Bonhoeffer asserts,

---

81. DBWE 4:76.

82. DBWE 4:179.

83. Schlatter, *Die Dienstpflicht*, 11 (emphasis mine).

84. "Jesus knows only one possibility: simply go and obey," Bonhoeffer writes. "Do not interpret or apply, but do it and obey." DBWE 4:181.

85. DBWE 4:241.

86. Michael Horton pursues this very same idea in his highly engaging and accessible work, Horton, *Ordinary*.

> What are you *doing* that is special? The extraordinary—and that is what is most offensive—is a *deed* the disciples do. It has to be done—like the better righteousness—and done visibly! Not in ethical rigor, not in the eccentricity of Christian ways of life, but in the simplicity of Christian obedience to the will of Jesus.[87]

Few are the newspaper articles, blog posts, or TV newsrounds reports about seemingly insignificant deeds of love; but the most extraordinary things take place on a daily basis in the most ordinary of circumstances. David Brooks writes:

> All around the world there are people out there humbling for God. They are making themselves servants. They are on their knees, washing the feet of the needy, so to speak, putting themselves in situations where they are not the center; the invisible and the marginalized are at the center. They are offering forgiveness when it makes no sense, practicing a radical kindness that takes your breath away.[88]

The extraordinary deed is visibly performed, but remains inconspicuous to the public, and often to the disciple herself. Mark the evangelist reports the episode where Jesus and his disciples watch others as they put money in the offering box at the temple (Mark 12:41–44). This happens in public for everyone to see, and "[m]any rich people put in large sums" (v. 41). And indeed, many are distracted and stand in awe as they observe old selves perform their boasting parade. Jesus's focus lies elsewhere though. A widow comes by, and she is clearly an emblem of insignificance, so ordinary and almost invisible. Here she stands: poor, of low status, no rights, no hope, no future. The disciples would have completely ignored her, blinded by the impressive sums that the rich put in the offering box. However, Jesus draws their attention to this particular person: "Truly, I say to you, this poor widow has put in more than all those who are contributing to the offering box. For they all contributed out of their abundance, but she out of her poverty has put in everything she had, all she had to live on" (Mark 12:43–44).

While the observer needs open eyes to see the extraordinary deed of love performed in front of him, the deed itself is often inconspicuous to the actor. One wonders whether the poor widow in the episode realized that suddenly she was at the center of attention for Jesus and his group of disciples. She, of course, did not seek to impress anybody. The disciple does not act in order that either she or the deed might be perceived to be

---

87. DBWE 4:145 (emphasis original).
88. Brooks, *Second Mountain*, 260.

spectacular.[89] "The extraordinary is not supposed to happen in order to be seen," Bonhoeffer writes.[90] Quite the contrary. In our love for God and others we completely forget about ourselves (and we are reminded of the disciple's attitude of quiet self-awareness we touched on earlier). "The goodness of Christ, the goodness of discipleship takes place without awareness," notes Bonhoeffer. "The genuine deed of love is always a deed hidden to myself."[91] The widow would not have imagined in her wildest dreams that she would become an example for her fellow disciples who would talk about her extraordinary deed still many centuries later and praise God for her. The astonishing nature of her deed was completely inconspicuous to her.

CONCLUSION

Radical disciples follow Jesus Christ personally and they do so joyfully. Responding to the authoritative, effective, and irresistible call, they follow their Master with what David Brooks describes as the "kind of permanent joy that animates people who are not obsessed with themselves but have given themselves away."[92] They rejoice because they have been freed from their need for self-determination and the burden of their possessions, and they are now experiencing true prosperity and intimacy in fellowship with the great friend. Radical disciples gladly imitate their Master in his love for God and others. As pointed out, though, it is vital that disciples correctly understand the modus, and, especially, the basis of imitation. They are not called to imitate Jesus based on their own strength, but, standing on the solid foundation of Christ's work for them in his representation and substitution—living the perfect life on their behalf and eradicating their guilt on the cross—they are now free to explore what it means to be truly human as Christ lives in them through his Spirit, restoring their nature and enabling them to love God and neighbor. Throughout this chapter we focused on the individual disciple who listens to Jesus's call, obeys, follows, and imitates him. While we make the first step into discipleship as individuals, we join at the same time a group of followers. Bonhoeffer writes:

> Everyone enters discipleship alone, but no one remains alone in discipleship. Those who dare to become single individuals trusting in the word are given the gift of church-community. They

---

89. Bonhoeffer's "call to be extraordinary" is not to be mistaken for a desire to be perceived as extraordinary. DBWE 4:148.
90. DBWE 4:148.
91. DBWE 4:151.
92. Brooks, *Second Mountain*, xi.

find themselves again in a visible community of faith, which replaces a hundredfold what they lost.[93]

In the next section, we turn to the important aspect of following Jesus Christ together as a community of disciples. We explore first, in particular, how radical disciples express their love for God and neighbor in the sphere of spiritual friendship. They follow their great friend, continually making new friends and befriending the world.

PERSONAL REFLECTION

Where and when have you first listened and responded to the call to discipleship? How has your life changed since then?

What do you find particularly surprising or thought provoking regarding the nature of the call to discipleship?

Where have you experienced in your own life how letting go has led to a deeper sense of fulfillment and intimacy with Jesus Christ?

"For where your treasure is, there your heart will be also" (Matt 6:21)—how does this verse speak to you?

How is your new desire to imitate the Master expressed in your own life? In which concrete situations have you realized that imitating Jesus is "not burdensome" (1 John 5:3), but grace-fueled?

---

93. DBWE 4:99.

9

Following Together

In 2018 Swinburne University, Melbourne, asked 1678 Australian adults whether they felt lonely.[1] According to their findings, one out of four Australians express feelings of loneliness and one out of three "never or rarely feel part of a group of friends."[2] This phenomenon was further exacerbated during the COVID-19 pandemic with its various measures of social distancing. Studies suggest that lockdown-induced social isolation and loneliness were closely associated with psychological distress, depression, and anxiety.[3] This confirms pre-pandemic research outcomes which suggest that isolation and loneliness go hand in hand with mental and physical health problems,[4] and are also associated with a higher risk of mortality.[5] Social neuroscientist John Cacioppo and his team showed in various studies that the damaging effects of loneliness are comparable to those of smoking or obesity and it highlights the importance of social connection for human survival and flourishing.[6] The government of the United Kingdom has already, in 2018, recognized these harmful effects and thus appointed a

---

1. Abbott et al., "Impact of Loneliness."
2. Abbott et al., "Impact of Loneliness."
3. Hwang et al., "Loneliness"; Loades et al., "Rapid Systematic Review."
4. Cacioppo et al., "Loneliness."
5. Holt-Lunstad et al., "Loneliness."
6. Cacioppo and Patrick, *Loneliness*.

Minister for Loneliness.[7] We have touched on some of the obvious causes of loneliness at the outset of our journey, namely our tendency to focus too much on our self. In the words of David Brooks,

> Our society suffers from a crisis of connection, a crisis of solidarity. We live in a culture of hyper-individualism. There is always a tension between self and society, between the individual and the group. Over the past sixty years we have swung too far toward the self.[8]

The more focused we are on our self, the lonelier we get. Our bias toward our self has obscured our view of the community and has turned us into lonely individuals. Although we might be connected with—in some cases, literally—a myriad of friends via social media, we tend to be much lonelier than in previous times. "[J]ust three decades ago," writes Michael Hendrix, "the typical American had a little over three close friends. Today, he or she barely has one confidant."[9] The inflation of individualism in Western societies has serious effects on everyday life and, of course, our expressions of faith. When what *I* feel, think, and want is more important than the needs of the community, I ought not to be surprised when, at the end of the day, I feel lonely and isolated. The disciple's calling then is to swim against the stream of individualism and to instill a sense of community where relationships thrive. David Brooks is again spot on: "The only way out is to rebalance, to build a culture that steers people toward relation, community, and commitment—the things we most deeply yearn for, yet undermine with our hyper-individualistic way of life."[10]

Radical disciples are at the forefront of this undertaking as they are intentionally oriented toward creating and sustaining meaningful relationships, and, even more than that: friendships. For some reason, the important theme of friendship is under-researched in psychology, anthropology, and related disciplines.[11] In theology, too, one observes a strange neglect of the topic, although it is so very central to the Christian life. For it is through lived-out friendships that radical disciples disseminate God's love in this world and contribute toward healing the plights of self-centeredness, loneliness, and isolation.[12] "Friendship," writes Brian Edgar, "is the essential coun-

---

7. Yeginsu, "U. K. Appoints."
8. Brooks, *Second Mountain*, xvii.
9. Hendrix, "Lonely America," 10.
10. Brooks, *Second Mountain*, xvii.
11. Denworth, *Friendship*, 39, 190.
12. On this important topic of friendship, see Edgar, *God is Friendship*.

ter to the individualism and egoism of modern society."[13] In this chapter, we first explore the theological foundation of the art of what twelfth-century Cistercian monk Aelred of Rievaulx calls "spiritual friendship."[14] Secondly, and more practically, we investigate how we grow up as disciples as we "[l]ove one another with brotherly affection" in everyday life (Rom 12:10). In a third step, we broaden our perspective by considering how disciples befriend the world.

SPIRITUAL FRIENDSHIP

Following their Master, disciples enjoy something greater than simply a mere teacher-student relationship. They savor the gift of Jesus's friendship. The New Testament story of Jesus and his disciples is in fact a story about the great friend laying down his life for his friends (John 15:13), drawing them even closer to himself, and turning them into loving friends through his love for them. "In this is love," writes the apostle John, "not that we have loved God but that he loved us and sent his Son to be the propitiation for our sins. Beloved, if God so loved us, we also ought to love one another" (1 John 4:10–11). It is a tale about radical friendship through sacrificial love and profound personal transformation.

It seems that Christian theology and the church have often overlooked the important role of Jesus as the disciples' great friend. While we have so far connected Jesus's role as Prophet with the call to self-denial, his role as Priest with the invitation to cross-bearing, and his role as King with the call to follow-ship, we expand this third office by including here also his role as Friend. The One who calls us into followship is not only King, but also Friend. Jesus's role as Friend, Jürgen Moltmann argues, even supersedes the other offices.[15] Through the "death of the friend," he notes, "they [his disciples] become forever his friends."[16] (One ought to add, though, that he is Friend only because of his role as the great high priest in the order of Melchizedek; Christ's priesthood is the basis of his friend-hood.) The most profound self-designation of the radical disciple then is this: "I am Jesus's friend." "What a friend we have in Jesus," is the opening line of Joseph M. Scriven's well-known hymn. This is the core of the disciple's self-understanding.

It seems that disciples are often at risk of losing sight of this significant title. As they walk on the path of discipleship, over time, in some disciples'

13. Edgar, *God is Friendship*, 259.
14. Rievaulx, *Spiritual Friendship*.
15. Moltmann, *Kirche*, 138–39.
16. Moltmann, *Kirche*, 137.

minds an alternative role might be more prominent, such as "Jesus's employee," for instance. Tragically, many of us are so busy trying to follow Jesus as "professional" disciples that the privilege of amity becomes obscured. As Eugene Peterson put it, "We become so diligent in learning about and working for Jesus that our relationship with Jesus erodes. The constant danger—and this has been going on a long time in church—is that we take on a role, a religious role, that gradually obliterates the life of the soul."[17] Cultivating this special friendship and growing up as Jesus's friend is therefore the disciple's constant pursuit. This pursuit is inspired and empowered by the great friend himself, who transforms us into his own image, turning us into radical friends ourselves so that we love others with his own love (we will expand on this critical aspect of transformation in the final chapter). In what follows, we explore the nature of spiritual friendship more carefully. Spiritual friendship between radical disciples is defined by love for one another, a love that is inspired by Christ and his Spirit, and that unites the disciples with one another, moving them to make ever new friends.

Love

Spiritual friendship is characterized by the love disciples have for one another. "You are my friends if you do what I command you," Jesus tells his disciples (John 15:14). "This is my commandment," he says, "that you love one another as I have loved you" (John 15:2). In fact, their mutual love makes the community of the disciples stand out in this world: "By this all people will know that you are my disciples, if you have love for one another" (John 13:35). Radical disciples, who have learned the skill of listening well—as discussed earlier—understand the terminology correctly, here. They are not put off by the term "commandment," because they understand themselves as friends, and as such they naturally embrace what their friend asks them to do. The King who commands is also Friend. In this way, duty of loving others turns into our delight.[18] "The language of friendship frees the idea of command from its suggestion of subservience," notes Oliver O'Donovan. "The friend cooperates precisely because he or she has been allowed to understand, has been made party to the great purpose."[19]

---

17. Peterson, *Practice Resurrection*, 190.

18. John Piper establishes the important connection between duty and delight in Piper, *Dangerous Duty*.

19. O'Donovan, *Entering into Rest*, 154.

Inspired

This love in spiritual friendship is informed and inspired by Jesus Christ.[20] Jesus invites us into intimate friendship with himself and as we enjoy his love for us, we are enabled to love him in return and extend his love to others. Our ability to thrive and flourish as Jesus's friend and the friend of others depends entirely on Jesus Christ. It is precisely at this point where Christian views on friendship move beyond traditional Greco-Roman and Western philosophical concepts, as, for instance, developed by Aristotle, Cicero, and Plutarch.[21] To Christian believers who thought carefully about friendship, it was always clear that true (spiritual) friendship was enabled only by Christ.[22] In discipleship-friendship there is someone else present who lifts friendship to a whole new level. Aelred of Rievaulx articulates this important aspect in his work, *Spiritual Friendship* (*De spirituali amicitia*).[23] Right at the outset, Aelred points to Jesus Christ as the sustaining source of friendship: he is the bond that unites the friends. "Here we are, you and I," he writes, "and I hope a third, Christ, is in our midst."[24] Oliver O'Donovan refers in this context to the organic picture of the vine and the branches in John 15.[25] The branches are friends with one another since they are all connected to the one life-giving vine. "The life to which the parable points is a life at once divine and human," O'Donovan notes, "articulated on an ascending scale as joy, mutual love, and sacrificial friendship (vv. 11–13)."[26]

Dietrich Bonhoeffer offers some further terminological clarification regarding the nature of our divinely inspired love for others. He writes:

> Christ has become the mediator who has made peace with God and peace among human beings. Without Christ we would not know God; we could neither call on God nor come to God. Moreover, without Christ we would not know other Christians around us; nor could we approach them. The way to them is

---

20. In the New Testament, Brian Edgar argues, we find "a new form of friendship based on the experience of Jesus Christ so that friendship is no longer based on the self, but upon the presence of God." Edgar, *God Is Friendship*, 142.

21. On Greek and Roman philosophers' accounts of friendship, see Nehamas, *On Friendship*. Oliver O'Donovan traces the development of the concept of friendship from early philosophical to mediaeval theological approaches in O'Donovan, *Entering into Rest*, 140–43.

22. See Edgar, *God Is Friendship*, 81–82.

23. Rievaulx, *Spiritual Friendship*.

24. Rievaulx, *Spiritual Friendship*, 1.1, 51.

25. O'Donovan, *Entering into Rest*, 154.

26. O'Donovan, *Entering into Rest*, 154.

blocked by one's own ego [das eigene Ich]. Christ opened up the way to God and to one another. Now Christians can live with each other in peace; they can love and serve one another; they can become one. But they can continue to do so only through Jesus Christ. Only in Jesus Christ we are one; only through him are we bound together. He remains the one and only mediator throughout eternity.[27]

Like Aelred and O'Donovan, Bonhoeffer insists that Christ is the one who connects us with one another, making spiritual friendship possible. Bonhoeffer also distinguishes between emotional love and spiritual love. The former is defined as love of the other for one's own sake, whereas the latter is the love through which we love "the other for the sake of Christ."[28] This spiritual love is what radical disciples desire to see growing in themselves by the grace of God. Spiritual love, Bonhoeffer explains,

> Comes from Jesus Christ; it serves him alone. It knows that it has no direct access to other persons. Christ stands between me and others.... Jesus Christ will tell me what love for my brothers and sisters really looks like. Therefore, spiritual love is bound to the word of Jesus Christ alone.... It is something completely strange, new, and incomprehensible to all earthly love.[29]

Spiritual love is indeed a "strange, new, and incomprehensible" form of love—it is an other-worldly love, a kingdom of God love that does not shy away to sacrifice the self for the other (we return to some of the practical outworking of spiritual love further below).

Unifying

In spiritual friendship, relational networks between radical disciples are established as they follow their Master together. Given the predominance of our present-day individualism it is critical to highlight this important aspect of unity and togetherness. While Jesus calls us individually as friends, he does not call us so that we would remain isolated individuals.[30] The many who are called individually become one group of friends in and through

27. DBWE 5:32–33 (emphasis original).
28. DBWE 5:42.
29. DBWE 5:43.
30. As Adolf Schlatter put it, the Gospels do not focus on "individual disciples," but portray how Jesus "gathered them into a united group to which he issued the same word of repentance and to which he gave the same task of proclamation." Schlatter, *History*, 106.

Jesus Christ. Although we are many, writes St. Paul, we are "one body in Christ, and individually members one of another" (Rom 12:5). United with our great friend Jesus by faith, we are also united with one another, seeking to serve and love one another. Pope Emeritus Benedict XVI expands on this idea in his encyclical, *Deus Caritas Est*,

> Union with Christ is also union with all those to whom he gives himself. I cannot possess Christ just for myself; I can belong to him only in union with all those who have become, or who will become, his own. Communion draws me out of myself towards him, and thus also towards unity with all Christians.[31]

Radical disciples thus realize that the call, "Follow me," is directed not only to themselves, but to the whole community of Jesus's disciples who follow their Master together. They remember that Jesus's assertion, "I have called you friends," is issued in the plural (John 15:15). "To be friends with the risen Jesus," writes Oliver O'Donovan, "is to have the same friends as he."[32] As radical disciples reflect on this idea, they get a new sense and appreciation for the community, a community that is defined by a common mindset, common goals, and aspirations. "[W]e picture lovers face to face," as C. S. Lewis put it, "but Friends side by side; their eyes look ahead."[33] We collaborate and coordinate our efforts as we serve as co-laboring friends in the kingdom of God.

Expanding

Enjoying the gift and benefits of spiritual friendship, radical disciples continually seek to make new friends. Lived-out spiritual friendship, they realize, comes with the promise of flourishing, since God's blessing rests on it. "How good and pleasant it is when God's people live together in unity" (Ps 133:1, NIV). Radical disciples discern beauty in the other, because Christ is living and active in their fellow disciple friend. Friendship, as C. S. Lewis observed, "is the instrument by which God reveals to each other the beauties of all the others."[34] Discovering the other's beauty, and, in turn, being singled out by the friend and affirmed as beautiful in Christ, radical disciples flourish together. Spiritual friendship, Aelred of Rievaulx argues, therefore surpasses any other form of human friendship. Only here, in the context of

---

31. Benedict XVI, "Deus Caritas Est."
32. O'Donovan, *Entering into Rest*, 159.
33. Lewis, *Four Loves*, 63.
34. Lewis, *Four Loves*, 83.

spiritual friendship do we have the opportunity to converse about spiritual things and to mature together in our shared friendship with Christ. Aelred praises the beauty of spiritual friendship in the following words:

> But what happiness, what security, what joy to have someone to whom you dare to speak on terms of equality as to another self; one to whom you need have no fear to confess your failings; one to whom you can unblushingly make known what progress you have made in the spiritual life; one to whom you can entrust all the secrets of your heart and before whom you can place all your plans! What, therefore, is more pleasant than so to unite to oneself the spirit of another and of two to form one, that no boasting is thereafter to be feared, no suspicion to be dreaded, no correction of one by the other to cause pain, no praise on the part of one to bring a charge of adulation from the other.[35]

Enjoying the promise of spiritual friendship, radical disciples, of course, are ever attentive, ever vigilant as they seek to forge new friendships. They recognize that spiritual friendship offers them a healthy distraction—and, in fact, remedy—from their old self tendency to self-centeredness, and it recalibrates them in their desire to love God and neighbor. Radical disciples, then, are constantly on the look-out to forge new friendships. Establishing and sustaining friendships, psychologists tell us, helps us thrive and flourish in various areas of life.[36] If this is true for regular friendship, it applies all the more to spiritual friendship. "Friendship has to be lived as befits a pilgrimage, a constantly expansive readiness for presence and promise," as Oliver O'Donovan put it. "It must be open to the making of new friends, for its tally is never full."[37] Having considered some central aspects of spiritual friendship, we turn next to the more practical "art" of spiritual friendship, that is, we explore how spiritual love is expressed in real life within the community of friends.

LOVING THE FRIEND

Radical disciples indiscriminately love one another with "brotherly affection" (Rom 12:10), and they exercise "sincere brotherly love" (1 Pet 1:22). Yet among the group of disciple friends there are some with whom we are friendlier than with others. There are different levels of intimacy. Even

---

35. Rievaulx, *Spiritual Friendship*, 2.11, 72.
36. See, for instance, Denworth, *Friendship*.
37. O'Donovan, *Entering into Rest*, 145.

within the close-knit circle of the Twelve, Jesus had a few special friends: Peter, James, and John, the "disciple whom Jesus loved" (John 21:20). Not with every friend do I feel inclined to confess my sins and to share my deepest secrets. But with some friends, I might. "We may be friendly to all," notes Oliver O'Donovan, "but we cannot be a friend to all."[38] We love every disciple of Jesus who walks with us on the way, but within that group there may be two or three to whom we pay particular attention and with whom we develop an even more special bond.[39] I feel drawn to one particular friend when I notice an overlap of interest. "What? You too? I thought I was the only one," is the typical beginning of a friendship characterized by similar likes, as C. S. Lewis put it.[40] Interests may change, though, and so do friendships. Some friends might walk with us through the ups and downs of life for decades, whereas others accompany us only for a certain part of the journey. Changing arrangements in terms of time and location have a significant impact on friendships, too. When I moved from Germany to Scotland and subsequently from Scotland to Australia, some bonds of friendship were weakened, others strengthened, often unexpectedly, and yet again new friendships were initiated and flourished in the new destination.

We are also mindful of the fact that we are all fallen friends who jointly share in their daily tension of rejecting the old self and embracing the new self. This means that we will, sooner or later, disappoint others, experience breaches of trust, and perhaps even betrayal (as Jesus did!). All these reasons make a "reordering of friendships" a part of life's exigency, as O'Donovan observes.[41] Radical disciples thus seek to develop a mature understanding of the preciousness and volatility of friendship. While keeping the whole spectrum in view, they still strive to love their chosen friends with spiritual love. In what follows, we examine some evidence for the presence of spiritual love among disciples.

Fruitful

Fruit of the Spirit flourish in the presence of spiritual friendship.[42] Where spiritual love among disciples prevails, one notices the presence of a whole

---

38. O'Donovan, *Entering into Rest*, 140.

39. This aspect of selective friendship, O'Donovan argues, is a prominent theme in the writings of Greek and Roman philosophers, such as Aristotle, Cicero, and Plutarch. O'Donovan, *Entering into Rest*, 140–41.

40. Lewis, *Four Loves*, 62.

41. See O'Donovan, *Entering into Rest*, 145.

42. The fruit of the Spirit, as Edgar writes, can be regarded as "Christological virtues

cluster of virtues and the marked absence of certain vices.[43] When encountering the friend, the disciple expresses love, joy, peace, patience, kindness, goodness, faithfulness, gentleness, humility, and self-control (Gal 5:22–23; 1 Cor 13:4–6).[44] In so doing they bear witness to their union with the Master whose character traits they imitate. On the other hand, we seek to eradicate in our dealings with one another any weeds of envy, arrogance, rudeness, irritability, impatience, and resentment—and we do so through the Holy Spirit (Rom 8:13). We have already touched on the constant cycle of putting off oldness and putting on newness earlier (see chapter 4).

Growing and delighting in each other's character-fruit is fertilized when we enjoy a trustworthy space where mutual respect, trust, and dependability prevail. Here, we can open up about our own successes, struggles, challenges, and weaknesses. Here, I can honestly share with my disciple friend where their actions or words have hurt me (Matt 18:15), and I am not ashamed to ask for forgiveness of my own errors in turn. With my radical disciple friend, I rejoice in accomplishment without worrying to evoke envy. I express failure without fearing to be crushed or judged. I assume that my disciple counterpart, in whom the Spirit of Christ resides, accepts me as I am and as I accept her—just as Christ himself accepts and loves both of us. Among radical disciple friends I confide in my significant other and my request for her opinion and advice is met with forthrightness and honesty. Jürgen Moltmann summarizes well some of the virtues of friendship that are shared and celebrated among disciples:

> One does not have to bow down in the presence of a friend. A friend one looks into the eyes. One does not look up or down toward him. In friendship, one experiences oneself the way one is, respected and accepted in one's own freedom. Through friendship one respects and recognizes other humans in their humanness and their special personality. Friendship combines affection with loyalty. One can depend on a friend. As a friend, one becomes dependable for others. A friend remains friendly even in disaster, even in guilt.[45]

---

in that they are all demonstrated in the life of Christ." Edgar, *God Is Friendship*, 255.

43. For a thorough discussion of the place of virtues in "holy friendship," see Edgar, *God Is Friendship*, 247–66.

44. Goodness, trust, equality, respect, and justice flourish in the context of what Brian Edgar calls "holy friendships." Edgar, *God Is Friendship*, 251.

45. "Vor einem Freund braucht man sich nicht zu bücken. Einem Freund kann man in die Augen sehen. Man sieht nicht zu ihm auf und auch nicht auf ihn herab. In der Freundschaft erfährt man sich selbst, so wie man ist, geachtet und in seiner eigenen Freiheit angenommen. Durch Freundschaft achtet und anerkennt man andere

A true disciple friend then, is loyal, keeping my secrets and encouraging me in my struggles and challenges, and I seek to reciprocate the gift of integrity and trustworthiness.

Some friendships, as they develop, might even elevate to a more formal commitment. Commitment indeed is the sign of a mature spiritual friendship, as Oliver O'Donovan points out. "Friendship may be sown by the wind of circumstance," he writes, "but it needs the soil of moral commitment to grow."[46] Disciple friends who go through the thick and thin of life together might even make a covenant with one another. Both Ruth and Naomi's and Jonathan and David's covenant forms of friendship are prominent biblical examples here.[47] "[B]ehold," Jonathan swears to David, "the Lord is between you and me forever," putting into a formal commitment the triangular relationship in the sense of Aelred (1 Sam 20:23). This form of commitment is valid even in the case of the death of the friend, and David has honored his covenant with Jonathan by looking after his descendants.

Shaping

Following on from the idea of fruitfulness, we note that it is in friendships that we shape others and are being shaped in turn by our friends. Friends are an integral part of the radical disciples' lives when it comes to personal and spiritual formation. Friends make an impression on us, they know us intimately, share life with us, and form a vital part of our microcosmos.[48] Psychologists Toni Antonucci and Robert Kahn developed what they call a "social convoy" model. It refers to the group of friends who travel with us through life and provide us with emotional connectedness.[49] We pray, eat, simply sit, laugh, and cry with them. As we grow older, the quality of relationships with our friends and confidants takes precedence over quantity, as a recent study showed.[50] We tend to become more selective in choosing

---

Menschen in ihrer Menschlichkeit und ihrer besonderen Persönlichkeit. Freundschaft verbindet Zuneigung mit Treue. Auf einen Freund kann man sich verlassen. Als Freund wird man für andere zuverlässig. Ein Freund bleibt freundlich auch im Unglück, auch in der Schuld." Moltmann, *Kirche*, 134.

46. O'Donovan, *Entering into Rest*, 139.

47. See Edgar, *God Is Friendship*, 134–39.

48. "A stranger is recognized as a human being, another self, or whatever," notes Oliver O'Donovan, "but a friend is recognized as one whom we have known before and hope to know again, not only as 'what' she is, but as 'who,' an identity established in our memory and forming part of our world." O'Donovan, *Entering into Rest*, 139.

49. Kahn and Antonucci, "Convoys."

50. Bruine de Bruin et al., "Age Differences."

our relationships over time; and it seems that we become more confident in choosing whom we allow to shape us, and whom we want to shape in turn.

Friends then enrich our lives as they help us to grow up as disciples. Together we intend to figure out what it means to deny our self, take up our cross, and follow Christ in each of our own circumstances. A friend is perhaps the most important instrument in God's toolbox that he uses in order to prune and shape us, so that we would bring about more fruit. "The fruit of the Spirit simply cannot be learned in isolation; they are essentially relational," writes Brian Edgar, "and growth in the Christian life depends on having close companions who can help develop them."[51] In this sense, then, the community of friends become means of our personal discipleship development plan, or, in traditional theological language, means of our sanctification. After all, it is often only in the intimate space of fellowship with the friend that one learns vital skills. Here, one is most vulnerable, yet here, too, the most significant breakthroughs are achieved. Sanctification is a communal enterprise.[52] Disciple friends recognize in the encounter with their friend an opportunity for personal growth in holiness. As iron sharpens iron, one disciple sharpens another (Prov 27:17). Friends challenge us, they seek to speak "truth in love" (Eph 4:15), they correct, rebuke, and criticize wherever appropriate.[53] Of course, this might at times put a friendship under a particular strain, perhaps stretch it even to breaking point (the disagreement and eventual separation between the apostle Paul and Barnabas is a classic example here, see Acts 15:36–41). Yet often it is right in the midst of these tensions when considerable growth happens, both individually, as well as with a view to the particular friendship.[54] Dietrich Bonhoeffer gives us some insight into the trust he enjoyed in his friendship with Eberhard Bethge to whom he writes:

> And that the two of us could be connected for five years by work and friendship is, I believe, a rather extraordinary joy for a human life. To have a person who understands one both objectively and personally, and whom one experiences in both respects as a faithful helper and adviser—that is truly a great deal. And you have always been both things for me. You have also patiently withstood the severe tests of such a friendship, particularly with

---

51. Edgar, *God Is Friendship*, 75.

52. "Sanctification apart from the visible church-community," writes Bonhoeffer, "is mere self-proclaimed holiness." DBWE 4:262.

53. See Edgar, *God Is Friendship*, 170–76.

54. "Friendship is a sphere where criticism can be free within the confidence of mutual goodwill," notes Oliver O'Donovan, "while flattery is the sign that confidence has been broken." O'Donovan, *Entering into Rest*, 144.

regard to my violent temper (which I too abhor in myself and of which you have fortunately repeatedly and openly reminded me), and have not allowed yourself to be made bitter by it. For this I must be particularly grateful to you. In countless questions you have decisively helped me by your greater clarity and simplicity of thought and judgment, and I know from experience that your prayer for me is a real power.[55]

Disciple friends then stick together and assist each other in the—often strenuous—cultivation of precious character crops, and they also enjoy the fruits of their labors. If indeed fruit of the Spirit grows in my life—praise God for my friend who fertilized my character—it is not mainly me but especially my friend who enjoys its sweetness. It is my friend who helped me cultivate it but now also enjoys my fruit of gentleness, long-suffering, and hospitality. Of course, I expect to relish fruit of kindness in return, too.

Affirming

Confident and secure in the knowledge that they are known and loved by the great friend, radical disciples do not feel the need to seek approval or admiration to boost their self-esteem. Their identity safely rooted in Christ, they "stand up straight" with their "shoulders back," and walk through life with an unpretentious air.[56] Operating from the vantage point of a quiet self-awareness, as seen earlier, they have sufficient headspace to focus on the other disciple. Thinking less often and less intensely about ourselves and our own interests and desires, we instead turn our thoughts and our mind toward the friends and their needs, finding opportunities to elevate and affirm them wherever appropriate. In his little book, *Being Disciples*, Rowan Williams aptly describes the impression one gets upon meeting a true radical disciple friend:

> [H]oly people however much they may enjoy being themselves, are not obsessively interested in themselves. They allow you to see not them, but the world around them. They allow you to see not them, but God. You come away from them feeling not, "Oh, what a wonderful person," but, "What a wonderful world," "What a wonderful God," or even, with surprise, "What a wonderful person I am too."[57]

---

55. Letter to Bethge, February 1, 1941, in DBWE 16:136.
56. Peterson, *12 Rules for Life*, 1.
57. Williams, *Being Disciples*, 52–53.

It is at this point that the apostle Paul's exhortation to "[o]utdo one another in showing honor" finds its full expression (Rom 12:10). Putting this into practice, the disciple knows, demonstrates true greatness, since greatness in the community of the disciples "was achieved by bearing, liberating, and elevating others," Adolf Schlatter notes, "not by binding and humiliating them."[58] In their self-effacing and neighbor-affirming attitude, they reflect the divine Spirit's movement and thus contribute to a flourishing of the friend and a strengthening of the bond of friendship.[59] To radical disciples, then, the call to "count others more significant than yourselves" (Phil 2:3) is not repulsive at all. They receive it with open ears and freely act upon it. Seriously and honestly interested in the wellbeing of their friend, they want to see her thrive and flourish.

Forgiving

Radical disciples express their love for one another in the forgiveness of sins through the grace of Jesus Christ.[60] As already highlighted, walking side by side with our friends as we follow Jesus on a daily basis is not always easy. At times, the other disciple friend can become a burden to me and others, and it is right here where we are called to bear with one another (Col 3:13).[61] I admire, especially, my few old friends who have endured my quirks, eccentricities, and flaws for the past several decades. Indeed, patience is a most formidable fruit of the Spirit. In the past, I have wronged certain disciple friends and there will be times when I offend them again in the future—and vice versa. Yet as a radical disciple I wish to exercise patience and kindness, and extend forgiveness again and again, "seventy-seven times," as the Master insists (Matt 18:22).

Forgiveness, of course, is not optional for the radical disciple. It is compulsory. Since the Lord has forgiven them, Paul reminds the Colossians,

---

58. Schlatter, *History*, 314.

59. Since self-effacement is a key characteristic of the personality of God's Spirit, as Tom Greggs argues, we, who are inhabited by the Spirit, are turned from "self-orientation to self-effacement in relation to God in time and space." Greggs, *Dogmatic Ecclesiology*, 24.

60. Bonhoeffer writes, "Will not another Christian's sin be an occasion for me ever anew to give thanks that both of us may live in the forgiving love of God in Jesus Christ? Therefore, will not the very moment of great disillusionment with my brother or sister be incomparably wholesome for me because it thoroughly teaches me that both of us can never live by our own words and deeds, but only by that one Word and deed that really binds us together, the forgiveness of sins in Jesus Christ?" DBWE 5:11.

61. DBWE 5:100–101.

"so you also must forgive" (Col 3:13). "[F]orgive us our debts, as we also have forgiven our debtors," is a critical line in the disciple's prayer (Matt 6:12). It is right in the moment of disappointment and even disillusionment that I venture into forgiveness. I ask for forgiveness and I forgive, not merely because Christ has forgiven me, but because Christ still stands between me and my friend, as Bonhoeffer put it. Christ is the one who reaches out to both of us, uniting us again and reconciling us through himself.[62] Since Christ is the link between the friend who has hurt me and myself, I will see my friend through the prism of Christ's grace—and I hope that my friend sees me through that same prism, too. Therefore, radical disciples are friends who "no longer see the other as the one who has harmed them," notes Bonhoeffer, "but as the one for whom Christ has interceded on the cross pleading for forgiveness."[63] By embracing and extending forgiveness, we experience transformation in our own person, and reconciliation with the friend through Jesus Christ.[64]

Confessing

In the intimate sphere of spiritual friendship, radical disciples not only forgive one another but they feel audacious enough to confess their sins to one another (Jas 5:16). Confession, though, seems to be a lost art among many Protestant disciples today.[65] This neglect is strange insofar as historically, confession has been an integral part of the Christian Protestant life—in the *Apology to the Augsburg Confession* it is even listed as a third sacrament.[66] Of

---

62. According to Bonhoeffer, there is no immediacy between friends here: "Ever since Jesus called, there are no longer natural, historical, or experiential unmediated relationships for his disciples. Christ the mediator stands between son and father, between husband and wife, between individual and nation, whether they can recognize him or not. There is no way from us to others than the path through Christ, his word, and our following him. Immediacy is a delusion." DBWE 4:95.

63. DBWE 4:269.

64. "People are formed and transformed by friendship," writes Brian Edgar, "particularly in learning about love and forgiveness." Edgar, *God Is Friendship*, 127.

65. I am following in this section closely Bonhoeffer's ideas as laid out in DBWE 5:108–18.

66. "So sind nu rechte Sacrament die Tauff und das nachtmal des Herren, die Absolutio, Denn diese haben Gottes befehl haben auch verheissung der gnaden, wilche denn eigentlich gehöret zum neuen Testament und ist das neue Testament. [Vere igitur sunt sacramenta Baptismus, coena Domini, Absolutio quae est sacramentum poenitentiae. Nam hi ritus habent mandatum Dei et promissionem gratiae, quae est propria novi Testamenti.]" *Apologia Confessionis Augustanae*, Artikel XIII, in Dingel, *Die Bekenntnisschriften*, 512–13.

course, confession is not to be coerced, and Martin Luther always emphasized the freedom that disciples enjoy here.[67] Still, being a Christian, for Luther, involved the confession of one's sin to another disciple.[68] Confession, he writes, is a "splendid, delightful, and consoling" exercise.[69] No doubt, confessing specific sins to another disciple is a daring thing to do—both back then and today—but this is precisely what makes a disciple a *radical* disciple. Dietrich Bonhoeffer admits that confession can be a difficult, even humiliating undertaking, for it "deals a terrible blow to one's pride."[70] Yet we remind ourselves that we confess our sins to someone who is both a fellow fallen sinner and a friend who loves us with spiritual love. In the safe space of spiritual friendship, we feel confident enough to open up and confess our sins of ignorance, rebellion, addiction, despair, and disbelief.[71]

In the moment of confession, the radical disciple has reached the end of the road of pretension, writes Bonhoeffer: "In the presence of another Christian I no longer need to pretend. In another Christian's presence I am permitted to be the sinner that I am, for there alone in all the world the truth and mercy of Jesus Christ rule."[72] As one disciple confesses her sins to the other in the presence of God, hidden skeletons are fetched from one's closet and put on the table. As painful as this might be, an option for serious growth and renewal presents itself. Now, "the light of the gospel breaks into the darkness," writes Bonhoeffer, "and closed isolation of the heart."[73] In this way, he argues, sin loses its power over the disciple and she makes a "*breakthrough to community*."[74] In other words, confession in the presence of the friend is one of the ways we put to death our old self. "By confessing actual sins the old self dies a painful, humiliating death before the eyes of another Christian,"

---

67. "Von der beichte haben wir allzeit also geleret, das sie solle frey sein." WA 30/1:233.20.

68. "Daruemb wenn ich zur beichte vermane, so thue ich nichts anders denn das ich vermane ein Christen zu sein." WA 30/1:238.1–2.

69. "So leren wir nu, wie trefflich, koestlich und trostlich ding es ist umb die beichte." WA 30/1:237.18–19.

70. DBWE 5:111.

71. In my late teens and early twenties, I was part of a German homegroup movement where regular confession of sin was an integral part of the community life. I would meet up once a week with my disciple friend, the "exchange partner" (*Austauschpartner*), to talk, and to pray, and we also confessed our sins to each other. In these critical moments, we clearly felt our own vulnerability and fragility—but it happened in the safe space of mutual friendship.

72. DBWE 5:109.

73. DBWE 5:110.

74. DBWE 5:110 (emphasis original).

Bonhoeffer notes.[75] It is right at this point that we experience what he calls a *"breakthrough to the cross."*[76] We witness how our sins died with Christ on the cross and we share in the victory of his resurrection, rejoicing in a *"breakthrough to new life."*[77] It is important, in Bonhoeffer's view, that what is confessed in the presence of the radical disciple friend are specific, concrete sins. Otherwise we might run the risk of pursuing merely "self-forgiveness," he writes, which "can never lead to the break with sin."[78] True change, true assurance of forgiveness, he argues, comes when we not simply acknowledge our general sinfulness, but admit *"concrete* sins" in the presence of the other disciple.[79] As we confess our specific sins to one another, "the flesh dies together with its pride."[80] Regarding the question, "Who is the disciple that could take my confession?" Bonhoeffer suggests that there is only one quality that helps us discern the right person, and that is whether the other disciple indeed lives "beneath the cross."[81] "Wherever the Word of the Crucified is a living reality, there will be confession to one another."[82]

Suffering

Psychologist Shelley Taylor and her working group showed that human beings tend to connect with one another in stressful situations (the effect is greater in women than in men, interestingly). Taylor and colleagues labeled it the "Tend and Befriend Theory," and they could show that this behavior actively reduces our biological stress response.[83] The effects of psychological stress are cushioned when we stick together, even more so when we have access to our network of close friends. Our social networks, therefore, have a significant effect on our physical health and mental wellbeing. Sheldon Cohen showed in a study that the more social ties the participants in his study had, the less susceptible they were to catching the common cold.[84] Cohen and Wills speak of social buffering in this context: close relationships

---

75. DBWE 5:111 (emphasis original).
76. DBWE 5:111 (emphasis original).
77. DBWE 5:112 (emphasis original).
78. DBWE 5:113.
79. DBWE 5:113 (emphasis original).
80. DBWE 4:270.
81. DBWE 5:116.
82. DBWE 5:116.
83. Taylor, *Tending Instinct*; Taylor et al., "Biobehavioral Responses," 411–29.
84. Cohen et al., "Social Ties."

serve as protective factors.[85] Spiritual friendships, then, serve as buffers; when we go through episodes of suffering, our friendships mitigate the damaging effects.

Spiritual friendship provides holy space for suffering. Here, radical disciples bear each other's burdens. They do not withdraw when their friend is in need, but they suffer with one another. "You are those who have stayed with me in my trials," is the special commendation that Jesus's disciples receive (Luke 22:28). When we see our friend in distress, we come close and offer care and support. Helping my friend through his own dark night of the soul is costly, and at times even penetrating my own mental and emotional world. Still, watching with my friend in his own garden of distress in prayer is exactly how I express my spiritual love. Deeply concerned about my friend, I offer comfort within the modest limits of my own existence, abilities, and gifts.[86] We are generous as we contribute to each other's needs, visit each other, and show hospitality (Rom 12:13; cf. 1 Pet 4:9). "Bear one another's burdens, and so fulfill the law of Christ," the apostle Paul encourages the Galatian disciples (Gal 6:2). The "law of Christ," of course, is that we love one another (John 13:34–35). And by loving the friend, we love Christ who lives and reigns in our fellow disciple through his Spirit. This is why Jesus can say: "*I* was naked and you clothed me, *I* was sick and you visited me, *I* was in prison and you came to me" (Matt 25:36). It was my friend Tim whom I visited when he was ill, yet somehow, I also visited Jesus—and he rejoiced in it. "In that day you will know that I am in my Father, and you in me, and I in you" (John 14:20). The co-suffering of radical disciples, then, happens always in intimate fellowship with Christ (we have already touched on the aspect of fellowship with Christ in suffering at an earlier stage, see chapter 6).[87]

It is important to add, too, that there exists a kind of "friends first policy" when it comes to supporting our suffering friends. My fellow disciple enjoys priority in terms of mutual commitment and care over other members of the human community. Of course, radical disciples love the non, or not-yet, disciple, but their focus is on the other disciple in whom Christ dwells through his Spirit. The community of the disciples enjoys priority when it comes to the expression of spiritual love. In the words of the apostle Paul, "So then, as we have opportunity, let us do good to everyone, and especially to those who are of the household of faith" (Gal 6:10). As we

85. Cohen and Wills, "Stress."

86. See O'Donovan, *Entering into Rest*, 136.

87. "The *being-with-each-other* of the church-community and its members through Christ," writes Bonhoeffer, "already entails their *being-for-each-other*." DBWE 1:182 (emphasis original).

suffer with one another and care for one another we become who we are, namely, as Bonhoeffer put it, "the community of the Crucified,"[88] "the community of his suffering."[89]

Sacrificing

In the final chapter of his letter to the Christians in Rome, the apostle Paul sends greetings to various friends. Among them, he mentions Prisca and Aquila, "who risked their necks for my life" (Rom 16:4). They present to Paul the ultimate gift of spiritual friendship, and that is self-sacrificial love. Jesus, of course, has demonstrated sacrificial love to his disciples as he laid down his life for the friends (John 15:13). There is no greater love than the one that seals the friendship with blood. While a demonstration of this ultimate form of spiritual love remains the exception for most disciples, it reminds us that radical discipleship love is always costly.[90]

I am writing this while forced to stay put in my home in Melbourne's Eastern suburbs. In the air hangs the sinister threat of a dangerous virus and lockdown restrictions only allow me to go out for one hour a day for exercise or shopping essentials. There is much to be learned from the Protestant Reformers who were themselves challenged by a pandemic in their own time. When the plague hit Zurich five hundred years ago, in 1519, Swiss Reformer Ulrich Zwingli heroically cared for the sick and dying, prepared to sacrifice his life for them.[91] At one point Zwingli himself became a victim of the plague. As he fell ill, he composed a prayer-song (*Gebetslied*) where he acknowledges his dependence on God. Zwingli, of course, prays for deliverance from the disease, but ultimately, he surrenders himself to God as he prays: "Do unto me as you wish; nothing is intolerable for me; I am your vessel, restore me or break me."[92] It is the prayer of the one who has courageously taken up his cross and has completely surrendered to God—as we have seen in chapter 5. Zwingli's health was restored, and he was able to continue to reform the church.[93] A few years later, in 1527, Martin Luther was

---

88. DBWE 4:109.

89. DBWE 4:217.

90. Andreas Köstenberger notes that Jesus's "self-sacrificial, self-giving, selfless love . . . will serve as the foundational ethic for the new messianic community." Köstenberger, *John*, 423–24.

91. Campi, "Reformation," 69.

92. "Tu, wie du willst; nichts halte ich für unannehmbar. Dein Gefäss bin ich; stelle es wieder her oder zerbrich es." Opitz and Saxer, *Zwingli lesen*, 19.

93. Campi, "Reformation," 69.

faced with the outbreak of the plague in Wittenberg.[94] Like Zwingli, Luther refused to leave, and he encouraged essential service-workers and clergy to do the same. He even transformed his home into a makeshift hospital, caring for sick friends and family members (Luther himself was affected as well, although apparently not as seriously as Zwingli).[95] During that time, fellow minister Johann Hess from Breslau sent Luther a letter, asking him whether a Christian may flee from death.[96] Luther answered with a long letter that has enjoyed a revival during the height of the COVID-19 pandemic in 2020. In his response to Hess, Luther offers comfort and suggests practical coping strategies as to how one might face the plague. In Luther's view, the plague presented an occasion for the disciple to renounce the devil and to put one's trust in God. Whether one decides to stay or to flee, the disciple remembers that she is always in God's hands and it is to him that one surrenders, echoing Zwingli here. Most remarkably, though, Luther reminds Hess of the Christocentric trajectory on which we have already touched. When we care for our fellow disciple, we also look after Christ who dwells in that person. Luther writes: "If you wish to serve Christ and to wait on him, very well, you have your sick neighbor close at hand. Go to him and serve him, and you will surely find Christ in him, not outwardly but in his word."[97] Having explored the vital elements of spiritual friendship among disciples, we finally broaden our perspective and consider how radical disciples also befriend the world.

BEFRIENDING THE WORLD

The spiritual love with which radical disciples love each other flows to the world. Some might argue at this point though that the very idea of befriending the world runs counter to James's charge that "friendship with the world is enmity with God" (Jas 4:4). And, of course, John tells us that we are *not* to "love the world or the things in the world" (1 John 2:15). It seems there are different ways to talk about the world and about our love for it, as Oliver

---

94. Hendrix, *Martin Luther*, 183.

95. Hendrix, *Martin Luther*, 184.

96. Luther writes: "ob eim Christen menschen gezyme zu fliehen ynn Sterbens leussten." WA 23:338.6. For the English translation of this piece, see *LW* 43:119–38.

97. *LW* 43/2:130. "Wiltu nü Christo selber dienen und sein warten, Wolan so hastu da fur dir deinen deinen krancken nehisten gehe hin zu yhm und diene yhm, so findestu gewislich Christum an yhm, nicht nach der person, sondern ynn seinem wort." WA 23:362.18–21.

O'Donovan explains.[98] In his view, everything hinges upon the question whether we love the world "from the world" or "from the Father."[99] The former is the kind of distorted love that the New Testament writers warn about, namely a love for "what the flesh desires, what the eyes desire, what the vulgar world boasts of."[100] The latter, however, is the sacrificial love of the Father who "so loved the world, that he gave his only Son" (John 3:16). Loving the world "from the Father," disciples look at this fallen world and, instead of being tempted to sin by the "world's phenomena," they love it for the sake of the "ultimate purpose God has for it."[101]

Radical disciples, then, do not ignore the plights of this distorted world; they do not seek to create their own little paradise in a cozy discipleship bubble, but they direct their gaze at a fragile creation that is waiting for its ultimate refashioning and redemption. They love this world with the love of the One who has "overcome the world" (John 16:33). Loving one another and loving neighbor, they carry Christ's love into the world and become what they are, namely salt and light of the world (Matt 5:13–14). As salt, they preserve what is good, true, and beautiful, and as light, they illuminate the darkness around them. Christ himself, in fact, is the mediator for this outgoing, world-embracing love. Radical disciples then look at the world through the Father's eyes and love it through the Son and the Holy Spirit. In everything they do, they are inspired by their great friend who goes before them and shows them what it means to be there for the other.

According to Bonhoeffer, Jesus is the one who "is there for others," "the human being for others," and the community of disciples continues this mission in her orientation toward the other.[102] We have already touched on this important point earlier as we highlighted our mission of presenting the world before God, thereby continuing Jesus's ministry of representation. Understood in this way, one notes that the community of disciples is so much more than a Christian institution. "A prophet and a teacher would not need followers, but only students and listeners," writes Bonhoeffer. "But the incarnate Son of God who took on human flesh does need a community of followers [*Nachfolgergemeinde*] who not only participate in his teaching but also in his body."[103] It is especially in her being for others that the church continues Christ's mission in this world. Radical disciples together actively

---

98. See his helpful treatment in, O'Donovan, *Finding and Seeking*, 72–77.
99. O'Donovan, *Finding and Seeking*, 74.
100. O'Donovan, *Finding and Seeking*, 73.
101. O'Donovan, *Finding and Seeking*, 75.
102. DBWE 8:501 ("Outline for a Book"); see also DBWE 6:6, 85, 95, 430.
103. DBWE 4:215.

follow the One who lived, loved, suffered, and died for others. Only when the community of disciples emulates Christ's move toward the other does it truly become the church.[104] The church as Christ's body in action is moved by the needs of this world and the disciple draws near, just as Christ did. Tom Greggs sums it up well:

> This is what the church's mission is: to love *just as* Christ has loved us; to love in the painful and difficult self-giving, cruciform way; to love in the context of sin and brokenness and enmity; to love in an active sharing by the Spirit in Christ's priestly humanity; to love in active participation in the movements of God's grace in the world.[105]

In which concrete sense does the community of radical disciples exist "for others," as Bonhoeffer insists? What does befriending the world look like in practical terms? In his view, it means that, among many things, the church "must become visible to the world."[106] Or, in Jürgen Moltmann's words, disciples are "called to show Jesus's friendship for others openly and holistically."[107] Looking at the world "from the Father's" perspective,[108] disciples befriend the world by speaking the gospel message of hope and renewal into the lives of others. Their conduct is a living witness to Christ and they "proclaim the excellencies" of the one who has transferred them from darkness "into his marvelous light" (1 Pet 2:9). Wherever they go, they proclaim the good news of salvation in Jesus Christ. They are attentive and outraged at injustice, appalled at inequality, and they yearn, pray and act—through the Holy Spirit—for the establishment of justice. Radical disciples passionately care for this fallen creation that desperately longs for redemption, because Christ cares and acts through them.

With his opposition against the inhumane National Socialist regime, Bonhoeffer has left us an extraordinary example in civic courage. The failure to speak up for the Jews, Bonhoeffer argued, was tantamount to resigning one's faith. "Only he who cries out for the Jews can sing the Gregorian chant," he famously remarked.[109] As disciples become radical disciples in taking their calling seriously and embracing this fallen world with Christ's love,

---

104. "The church is church only when it is there for others," writes Bonhoeffer. DBWE 8:503 ("Outline for a Book").

105. Greggs, *Dogmatic Ecclesiology*, 424 (emphasis original).

106. DBWE 4:236.

107. Moltmann argues "daß Christen die Freundschaft Jesu offen für Andere und ganzheitlich erweisen müssen." Moltmann, *Kirche*, 140.

108. O'Donovan, *Finding and Seeking*, 75.

109. Bethge, *Dietrich Bonhoeffer*, 441.

the church becomes visible, and the world is being transformed. Bonhoeffer writes:

> Where the world despises other members of the Christian family, Christians will love and serve them. If the world does violence to them, Christians will help them and provide them relief. Where the world subjects them to dishonor and insult, Christians will sacrifice their own honor in exchange for their disgrace. Where the world seeks gain, Christians will renounce it; where it exploits, they will let go; where it oppresses, they will stoop down and lift up the oppressed. Where the world denies justice, Christians will practice compassion; where it hides behind lies, they will speak out for those who cannot speak, and testify for the truth. For the sake of brothers or sisters—be they Jew or Greek, slave or free, strong or weak, of noble or common birth—Christians will renounce all community with the world, for they serve the community of the body of Jesus Christ. Being a part of this community, Christians cannot remain hidden from the world. They have been called out of the world and follow Christ.[110]

In light of this, one wonders whether some contemporary disciples may need to recalibrate their plan of action. In the Australian context, for instance, it seems that the vocal protest against COVID-19-vaccination requirements is not always matched by the outcry against the offshore processing of refugees in prisons under dire circumstances. Passionate advocacy for personal freedom is often interpreted along narrow lines and that certainly does not echo the Bonhoefferian spirit.

When I traveled to Leipzig some years ago, one of the sites I visited was St. Nicholas's Church (*Nikolaikirche*), the place of the famous Monday Prayers for Peace (*Friedensgebete*). These prayers originated in the early 1980s, grew in size to up to 1500 attendees in 1989, and spilled over to the churchyard.[111] Ultimately the Monday Prayers led to the peaceful revolution that first brought down the wall that separated the two Germanies and then led to the collapse to the German Democratic Republic. To commemorate the movement of prayer originating from within the church outward to the public square, an artist built a replica of one of the beautifully ornamented church pillars and placed it right on the neighboring market square. The power of this symbol is clear to everyone: the church literally moved beyond the confines of its walls, became visible, transformed society, and made

---

110. DBWE 4:237.
111. Saunders and Pinfold, *Remembering and Rethinking*, 180.

history. Rather than being "conformed to this world" (Rom 12:2), radical disciples contribute toward transforming this world and to spread a forestate of God's shalom. Befriending the world in this way, however, presents them with obstacles and we take up our theme of embracing tensions by faith again at this point.

Jesus sends his friends into this world (John 20:21), "like lambs among wolves" (Luke 10:3). He expects them to flourish in the tension of opposition and conflict. Again, any attempts at reducing the tension will mean that the salt will lose its saltiness. On the one hand, we dismiss any postmillennial attempts "to start building a heavenly kingdom on earth," Bonhoeffer clarifies.[112] And on the other hand, we reject any daydreaming escapism where the disciple is "too heavenly minded for earthly good." Disciples seek to befriend the world as they thrive in tension here: having their minds set clearly on the "things that are above" (Col 3:2), they understand themselves as pilgrims, ultimately, "not of the world" (John 17:14–18), desiring "a better country, that is, a heavenly one" (Heb 11:16). Still, as Bonhoeffer points out, "The 'unworldliness' of the Christian life is meant to take place in the midst of this world."[113] Jesus Christ still goes ahead of them in *this* world, and wherever they are placed, they take their commission seriously to "make disciples of all nations" (Matt 28:19). Radical disciples embrace the tension between deep befriending in the here and now while longing for the "new heaven and a new earth" (Rev 21:1). Their hope for the ultimate reconciliation of all things (Col 1:20) does not render them lethargic. They give in neither to frustration vis-à-vis a fallen world, or nostalgia regarding a paradise lost. Instead, they thrive in the tension of already-not-yet, as it is right here in this friction that their faith grows.

CONCLUSION

Having explored the intimate and personal manner in which we are being called individually into follow-ship by the Master, our attention shifted in this chapter to the community of the disciples who follow Christ together. Through the work of the great friend, Jesus Christ, radical disciples are being turned into friends themselves, loving God, one another, and the world. In the context of spiritual friendship, disciples love one another with spiritual love, seeing the fruit of the Spirit ripening in each other. Shaping and affirming one another, they assist each other in the demolition of the old self and embrace of the new self. Spiritual friendship is the place where forgiveness

---

112. DBWE 4:146.
113. DBWE 4:245.

is extended and received, and where confession takes place; friends love one another with sacrificial love and suffer with one another. Their love is not restricted to the community of the friends, but they also seek to befriend the world, loving the world "from the Father."[114] Spreading the good news of the gospel of Jesus Christ, they make new disciples wherever they go, presenting the needs of this world to the Father. We conclude our section on Jesus's invitation to follow him by taking a closer look, literally, at the face of the great friend whom we are following.

PERSONAL REFLECTION

How has your life changed knowing that the great friend has laid down his life for you?

How do you want to remind yourself on a regular basis of the precious gift of Jesus's friendship to you?

Whom do you wish to thank for the gift of spiritual friendship? And to whom do you want to extent your gift of friendship in very concrete ways?

In which areas of your life have friends shaped, affirmed, or suffered with you?

What does it mean for you, in your own context, to "befriend the world"?

How do you want to pray for yourself as you seek to grow up as a radical disciple friend who loves Jesus and others with spiritual love?

---

114. O'Donovan, *Finding and Seeking*, 75.

10

Seeking the Friend's Face

THE NEW TESTAMENT REPORTS this peculiar episode where Jesus takes his three closest friends, Peter, James, and John, on a mountain to pray (Matt 17:1–8; Mark 9:2–8; Luke 9:28–36). Suddenly he is spectacularly transfigured: his face shines like the sun and his clothes gleam dazzling white. As if this were not astonishing enough, out of nowhere appear two famous Old Testament figures thought to be dead for a long time: Moses and Elijah. Apparently quite alive, they talk with Jesus about the mission he would accomplish in Jerusalem. Of course, the disciples are utterly terrified, and as usual, Peter is the first to recover his voice. He suggests they build three tents—perhaps he was thinking of Moses's encounters with God in the tent of meeting and now similarly intends to shield the divine glory from profane eyes.

At this moment, a cloud that stands for the presence of God (Exod 13:21–22; 40:34–38), overshadows the scene, and a voice from the cloud says: "This is my beloved Son, with whom I am well pleased; listen to him" (Matt 17:5).[1] Upon hearing this, the three friends, now even more terrified, fall on their faces, and Jesus comforts and encourages them. As they open their eyes again, everything is back to normal, and Jesus urges them to remain quiet about what they have seen and heard.

This is the transfiguration account on which the Synoptic evangelists agree. In all three accounts the story follows on Jesus's call to discipleship (Matt 17:1–9; Mark 9:2–8; Luke 9:28–36). Matthew, Mark, and Luke first

---

1. Instead of "my beloved Son" Luke has "my Chosen One" (Luke 9:35).

report how Jesus calls disciples into follow-ship and subsequently portray him as the glorified One in the account of the transfiguration. Surely, this is not a not a coincidence. This connection suggests a vital link between the transfiguration narrative and Jesus's prior call to self-denial, cross-bearing, and following. It is as if the costs of discipleship are balanced with the reward of seeing the glorified Christ. In what follows, we flesh this out in more detail as we turn our attention again on the person and work of the great friend, with a particular emphasis on his humiliation and exaltation that is demonstrated in the transfiguration. We point out, secondly, how disciples share in Jesus's humiliation and exaltation, and thirdly, we note how contemplating the face of Jesus Christ leads to profound transformation in the radical disciple.

THE GLORIFIED FRIEND

On the mountain, the three friends gain a glimpse into the splendor of the glorified Son of God. Here, the Son of God is revealed in true glory. For the very first time, human eyes behold the glory of the One who is the "image of the invisible God, the firstborn of all creation" (Col 1:15). They are given a vision of the beauty of Jesus Christ, who is "the radiance of the glory of God and the exact imprint of his nature" (Heb 1:3). Up to this point Jesus's glory had been hidden from people's eyes. Every intention to proclaim him as the glorious Messiah had been silenced (Mark 8:29–30)—and, in fact, the three chosen friends are instructed not to tell anyone of the special vista they received until Jesus has risen from the dead (Matt 17:9; Mark 9:9).[2] Jesus, the "human being for others," as Bonhoeffer consistently refers to him, clearly intended to teach his disciples something through this extraordinary event.[3] What, then, is the purpose of the dazzling vision that is granted to the disciples?[4]

First, the disciples here encounter the simultaneity of exaltation and humiliation, of glorification in the presence of announced suffering. The content of the conversation on the mountain is illuminating in this respect.

---

2. As Hans Boersma explains, the transfiguration is "a theophany of unprecedented glory, as the divinity of the eternal Son of God is revealed to the disciples in the brightness of the light." Boersma, *Seeing God*, 134. This is the view of those who pursue what Boersma calls a "sacramental reading" of the transfiguration account.

3. DBWE 8:501 ("Outline for a Book").

4. With a view to Jesus Christ himself, the transfiguration clearly served as an occasion to assure the Son of God of the Father's love for him—just prior to the crucifixion. It was also significant to strengthen the faith of the three friends right before the dark events of the passion and the cruel persecution that would follow soon after.

In their brief exchange, the glorified Christ, Moses, and Elijah, Luke tells us, "spoke of his departure, which he was about to accomplish at Jerusalem" (Luke 9:31). In other words, they talked about Jesus's imminent death on the cross—and of course, prior to this conversation, Jesus had already announced his passion to the disciples, multiple times (Matt 16:21; Mark 8:31; Luke 9:22). Jesus's gloriously transfigured state right in front of their eyes coexists with the announcement of impending humiliation on the cross. Exaltation and humiliation go hand in hand throughout Jesus's life, from his birth all the way to the cross. "Glory to God in the highest, and on earth peace among those with whom he is pleased!" are the words with which the multitude of the heavenly host praise God on the occasion of the angel's announcement of Christ's birth to the shepherds (Luke 2:8–14). God's glory is proclaimed in the context of Christ's humble birth in the manger.[5]

The synchronicity of exaltation and humiliation culminates in the cross. In the Gospel of John, Jesus's prayer, "Father, glorify your name," is answered by the voice that comes from heaven, "I have glorified it, and I will glorify it again" (John 12:28). The locus of glorification here, of course, is the crucifixion. The moment of utter humiliation is at the same time the instance of supreme exaltation as the Son glorifies the Father by giving himself as a sacrifice for us, and by being highly exalted in return by the Father. Other than in the transfiguration, though, the aspect of glory is not easily recognizable, it is somewhat hidden.[6] Karl Barth writes,

> This Exalted One is the One who is concealed in the lowliness of His death. He is, in fact, exalted in this concealment. And as He bursts open from within the closed door of His concealment, of His death, He reveals Himself as this exalted One. No one

---

5. "[T]he beauty of Christ while in the form of a slave (i.e., during his earthly career) is an aspect of his glory, which itself involves a dialectic of revealing and concealing," writes Jonathan King. "For in and through the form of Christ crucified is the radiance of his glory, radiating a beauty reflective of and dramatized in the self-giving love of God." King, *Beauty*, 164.

6. According to Martin Luther, God reveals himself in Christ crucified as the hidden God (*deus absconditus*). "Because men misused the knowledge of God through works," Luther explains, "God wished again to be recognized in suffering, and to condemn wisdom concerning invisible things by means of wisdom concerning visible things, so that those who did not honor God as manifested in his works should honor him as he is hidden in his suffering." *LW* 31:52. In Luther's view, Johannes Zachhuber writes, we observe on the cross a "paradoxical conjunction of opposites: the supreme God is recognised in his abasement; the virtuous one in his exposure to evil; the omnipotent being is found in utter weakness." Zachhuber, "Jesus Christ."

has found or discovered Him as such. It is He Himself who has shown and revealed and made Himself known as such.[7]

Dietrich Bonhoeffer also acknowledges the simultaneous presence of exaltation and humiliation in Jesus Christ's person and work.[8] "We have seen the exalted one, only as the crucified; the sinless one, only as the guilt-laden; the risen one only as the humiliated," he writes. "If it were not so, the *pro nobis* would be destroyed and there would be no faith."[9] As the Son of God gives his ultimate gift as the One who is there for others, as he gives himself away as the greatest gift of reconciliation, he is glorified and exalted already on the cross—and not exclusively in the later moments of his resurrection and ascension.[10] However, the glory that the disciples perceived with their own eyes—both in the transfiguration and the cross—in the moments of revealing and concealing, is always a "mediated glory."[11] For the disciples' not-yet-glorified eyes, there is then no direct access to perceive the divine glory in the Son of God.[12] Although, what they are allowed to see even in their fallen condition presents plenty of goodness and reason for enjoyment.[13] We, too, are invited to perceive Jesus Christ who lives and acts in the dynamic interplay of veiling and unveiling, concealing and revealing.

---

7. CD IV/2:299. "Dieser Hohe ist der in der Niedrigkeit seines Todes Verborgene: der gerade in dieser Verborgenheit wahrhaft Hohe. Und indem er die verschlossene Türe dieses Verborgenseins, seines Todes, von innen aufstößt, offenbart er sich als dieser Hohe. Niemand hat ihn als diesen Hohen entdeckt, enthüllt, aus seiner Verborgenheit herausgeholt. Er selbst hat sich als dieser herausgestellt, offenbar, bekannt gemacht." KD IV/2:333.

8. "Bonhoeffer insists," write James C. Livingston and Francis Schüssler Fiorenza, "that the humiliation and the glorification or exaltation of Jesus Christ must be understood together." Livingston and Schüssler Fiorenza, *Modern Christian Thought*, 117.

9. Bonhoeffer, *Dietrich Bonhoeffer*, 122.

10. "The Humiliated One is pro nobis only as the Exalted One. Only in seeing him as the Risen One, the Exalted One, do we know this incognito God-human. We have the One who was born as a baby as the Ever-Present One, the One laden with sin as the One without sin. So the converse must also be true: we can have the Exalted One only as the Crucified One." DBWE 12:359. See also King, *Beauty*, 169.

11. "The incarnation of God the Son, however, is the *mediated* revelation of the glory of God in the person of Jesus Christ, the indivisible God-man. And thus the glory that no one can see and live has been made perceivable in and through the mediated form of Christ in whom 'the whole fullness of deity dwells bodily' (Col 2:9)." King, *Beauty*, 153.

12. One could argue, of course, that even with glorified eyes, our vision of God remains mediate.

13. This is the point Robert Grosseteste makes and Brendan Case explores his position in more detail in Case, "More Splendid."

Secondly, there is a sense in which radical disciples share in Jesus's simultaneity of humiliation and exaltation. It is significant to note that the three disciples saw not only Jesus clothed in majesty and glory, but Moses and Elijah too "appeared in glory" (Luke 9:31). The promise here is that as Moses and Elijah reflected God's glory, the disciples' too, reflect—imperfectly here—perfectly then—the divine splendor in a similar manner.[14] They do so, however, only when they also share in his humiliation. "Whoever seeks to bear the transfigured image of Jesus," writes Bonhoeffer, "must first have borne the image of the crucified one, defiled in the world."[15] Following the crucified and glorified Christ we share both in his suffering and in his glory at the same time—already here on earth.[16] The apostle Paul, in fact, consistently speaks of our co-glorification with Christ as a consequence of our co-humiliation, our co-suffering (e.g., Rom 8:17; 2 Cor 4:10–11; 2 Tim 2:10–11). It is, in fact, right in the presence of humiliation that the rays of God's glory shine through. "The glory into which apostles and all believers are being transformed is manifested, paradoxically, in cruciform, life-giving activity," Michael J. Gorman writes. "[T]o become the righteousness/justice of God means to share in Christ's gracious self-impoverishment for the benefit of others."[17]

As we have seen earlier, extraordinary acts of love usually go unnoticed in the eyes of this world: their glory is veiled. In this sense, radical disciples embrace the tension of being glorified in obscurity. While on pilgrimage in this life, they are primarily concerned to emulate their Master in his being-for-others, and that happens often in the context of shame and suffering.[18] We already pointed out earlier that only disciples with a recalibrated vision recognize true glory in these obscure acts of love. Plus, it has also been highlighted that emulating Christ in his being-for-others is not to be mistaken with simple activism—frantically trying to do what Jesus did out of one's own resources. This will only lead to exhaustion and burnout. Rather, radical disciples mature as they behold the One in whom exaltation and humiliation dwell in concert. By seeking his face, they are being conformed into

---

14. John of Damascus claims that this was a glory that came "from without," reflecting the glory of God. Boersma, *Seeing God*, 137.

15. DBWE 4:284.

16. "Our goal is to be shaped into the entire *form* of the *incarnate*, the *crucified*, and the *risen one*." DBWE 4:285 (emphasis original).

17. Gorman, "Missional Theosis," 209.

18. "Conformity with Christ is not outwardly displayed in observable splendour," notes Thomas Schmeller, "but in the way of life." ["Nach außen zeigt sich die Angleichung an Christus nicht in wahrnehmbarem Glanz, sondern in der Lebensführung."] Schmeller, *Der zweite Brief*, 228.

his image, and thus empowered to fulfill their mission. "Formation occurs only by being drawn into the form of Jesus Christ," writes Bonhoeffer, "by being conformed to the unique form of the one who became human, was crucified, and is risen."[19] How, then, are we "drawn into," and how does transformation into Christ's image as the glorified and humiliated one take place in the disciple's life?

TRANSFORMATION AND CONTEMPLATION

Theologians past and present have drawn the connection between Jesus's transfiguration and the disciples' transformation.[20] The disciples who witness the transfigured Christ, listen in on his conversation with Moses and Elijah, and hear the voice from the cloud, are drawn into the events. They become active participants as they watch and listen to what is happening around them. The key phrase in this narrative is the one issued from the mysterious cloud, "Listen to him" (Matt 17:5; Mark 9:7; Luke 9:35). We have already explored the importance of listening to Jesus earlier (see chapter 8). In this context, it seems, though, that we are to interpret listening in a broader sense. The auditory goes hand in hand with the visual. However, the disciples do not need to hear the command, "Look at him!" since they cannot take their eyes off him anyway. What they are beholding is simply too mesmerizing. Radical disciples, then, listen *and* look to Jesus. Following the Master is defined by careful attention to his voice and constantly looking at this face. Radical disciples thus study his words as reported in the gospels, and, immersing themselves in the story, they ponder the face of Jesus in his state of humiliation and exaltation. In so doing they are being transformed.

---

19. DBWE 6:93.

20. "[M]any have looked to the transfiguration narrative for an account in which God appeared in such a way as to reveal himself most fully and gloriously in Jesus Christ," writes Boersma, "and in so doing transformed or deified the disciples, drawing them into his beatifying light and thus into his eternal kingdom." Boersma, *Seeing God*, 129–30. Simon S. Lee, too, establishes a clear link between Jesus's transfiguration and the disciples' transformation. "On his second coming, Jesus, who is now the eschatological Son of Man, will vindicate believers who follow him along the same path," writes Lee. "As a part of their vindication, believers are promised that they, too, will experience a transformation in glory similar to Jesus's transfiguration." Lee, *Jesus' Transfiguration*, 213. "For believers, it is now in their current lives that they should be partakers of the divine nature, that is, of Jesus' majesty, power, honor and glory. Similarly to the glory of the Lord for Paul, Jesus' divine nature for 2 Peter is not only the motivating power of the believers' present transformation, but also the very goal of their destiny." Lee, *Jesus' Transfiguration*, 214.

Transformation is linked with contemplation. The apostle Paul describes this vital connection in his Second Letter to the Corinthians: "And we all, with unveiled face, beholding the glory of the Lord, are being transformed into the same image from one degree of glory to another. For this comes from the Lord who is the Spirit" (2 Cor 3:18). Paul contrasts in this passage the old and the new covenant. While the old covenant had some measure of glory, the new covenant by far surpasses the old in glory. To illustrate his point, Paul uses the example of Moses, the mediator of the old covenant (who was, as we recall, also present at the Mount of Transfiguration—surely not a coincidence). After the tragic episode with the golden calf, Moses destroys the first set of stone tablets with God's commandments, and he again goes up on Mount Sinai (Exod 34:4). He spends forty days and nights in God's presence and comes down from the mountain with a new set of stone tablets (Exod 34:28–29). As Moses approaches, the people notice something strange about him. Without being himself aware of it, the skin of his face is shining (Exod 34:29). Like the disciples at Jesus's transfiguration, the people are frightened on account of the shining face and Moses needs to cover it with a veil (Exod 34:33; 2 Cor 3:7). Now why did Moses's face shine? It was certainly not due to any special achievement on his side. The answer presented in the text is that the skin of his face shone because he had been talking with God (Exod 34:29). Simply enjoying intimate fellowship with God on the mountain had left a visible mark on Moses's face. Merely by conversing with God, his external appearance had changed. Paul's argument now is this: if something as glorious as this happened under the old covenant, how much more glory will be revealed to us and in us under the new covenant. By contemplating the face of the friend who is glorified in humiliation, the disciples will experience change—not externally (like Moses)—but since we are now under the new covenant, internally through the Spirit, who is at work in us even, or especially, in suffering.

The principle of the new covenant then is obvious: contemplation leads to profound internal transformation. The Greek word for "transformed" (*metamorphoō*) as a matter of fact refers to a fundamental inward change,[21] and it is the same word that is used to describe Jesus's change of appearance in the transfiguration (*metemorphōthē* in Matt 17:2 and Mark 9:2). Closely observing the glory of Christ in his humiliation and exaltation, radical disciples experience deep character transformation. "Those who behold Christ are being drawn into Christ's image," writes Bonhoeffer, "changed into the likeness of Christ's form. Indeed, they become mirrors

---

21. Bauer et al., *Griechisch-deutsches Wörterbuch*, 1036.

of the divine image."[22] So far, we have referred to contemplation in this context, and before we continue it might be helpful to distinguish it briefly from meditation.[23] According to Kyle Strobel, in the traditional understanding of meditation we focus both on "divine truth" and our "own soul," yet contemplation means setting our mind "on the beauty and glory of God."[24] Meditation, for instance, might include, beyond reflection on the Scriptures, also our consideration of creation and our own feelings. In contrast, contemplation is more narrowly defined, Strobel argues, as it focuses more intentionally on "the pilgrim-anticipation of the beatific-glory we behold in heaven."[25] Contemplation understood along these lines is what we have in mind here. Now both the act of contemplation and the process of transformation happen organically in the disciple. Contemplating the face of Christ is a quiet, almost effortless undertaking—and the transformation that happens as its result comes about in similar, unobtrusive ways.

Transformation, then, is not "achieved" or "produced" by the disciple herself, out of her own strength. Of course, it involves certain spiritual disciplines that disciples develop and implement in their lives by God's grace. However, it is not so much about the act, or the particular form of our contemplation, but about the object that is being contemplated. In his divine self-revelation, God makes himself the "object of human contemplation" (*Gegenstand menschlicher Anschauung*), writes Karl Barth.[26] Contemplation is not so much about our own planning and doing, but about the God who encounters us in the face of Jesus Christ and who, as we look at him, brings about transformation in us.

There is, then, a certain lightness about discipleship—Bonhoeffer speaks about the "simplicity of discipleship."[27] Applied to our discussion of growing fruit of the Spirit earlier, we remember that we cannot force fruit into being ourselves—rather, fruit grows by our abiding in the vine, in Christ. "Fruit is always something full of wonder, something that has been created," Bonhoeffer notes. "It is not something willed into being, but something that has grown organically. The fruit of the Spirit is a gift of which God is the sole source."[28] We also note that the fruit of transformation into the

---

22. DBWE 4:286.
23. Strobel offers a helpful treatment in Strobel, *Glory of God*, 126–36.
24. Strobel, *Glory of God*, 130.
25. Strobel, *Glory of God*, 133.
26. *KD* I/1:333.
27. DBWE 4:287.
28. DBWE 4:266.

image of Christ does not happen instantaneously. Fruit grows over time, yet it definitely grows. Bonhoeffer writes:

> The transformation into the divine image will become ever more profound, and the image of Christ in us will continue to increase in clarity. This is a progression in us from one level of understanding to another and from one degree of clarity to another, toward an ever-increasing perfection in the form of likeness to the image of the Son of God.[29]

An example from the world of psychology may serve to illustrate this point of organic growth over time. Psychologist Robert Zajonc conducted a study in the United States with couples who had been married over twenty-five years.[30] He compared photographs that were taken when they were newlyweds with pictures taken after twenty-five years of marriage. The fascinating result was this: after twenty-five years all couples were rated to look more alike. And the happier the couples were, the more similar they reportedly looked. Simply by the sheer fact of being with each other, the couples grew more alike, sharing facial expressions, laugh lines, and wrinkles around the eyes. A lifetime of conversation, cohabitation, and admiration led to profound transformation. Similarly, radical disciples experience deep character change not by ticking off boxes on a discipleship to-do list, but simply by listening and contemplating the beautiful face of the friend as the Spirit works in them. Transformation through contemplation may work organically, but it does not happen automatically. Radical disciples are keen to develop new skills that create occasions for the spirit of God to perform his work in them.[31]

As we move on to take a closer look at the spiritual disciplines of prayer, Scripture reading, and contemplation, we do so bearing in mind that radical disciples regard this not so much as strategies or techniques but as occasions to meet with their Master and enjoy his company. When referring to contemplation in this context, we adopt what John Coe and Kyle Strobel call "supernatural contemplation," namely, "the contemplation of God [that] is made available to the believer in the Spirit."[32] We thus transition to the next section with Michael Horton's advice in mind, which describes this attitude well: "The issue is not whether we engage in personal disciplines or habits of meditative prayer and reading of Scripture, but whether we do so

---

29. DBWE 4:286.

30. Zajonc et al., "Convergence."

31. I am grateful to Tom Kimber whose consistent focus on contemplation, on silence and solitude, has considerably shaped my thinking here.

32. Coe and Strobel, "Introduction," 6.

in a gospel-driven manner. Is it a technique for personal transformation or is it a saving and sanctifying encounter with the Triune God who has met us in his incarnate Son?"[33]

CONTEMPLATING THE FRIEND'S FACE

In the section "The Day Alone" in *Life Together*, Dietrich Bonhoeffer highlights the importance of silence, solitude, and prayer in the disciple's daily life.[34] As we have seen earlier, Bonhoeffer recognizes the centrality of life in community, yet he stresses, at the same time, the significance of spending time with God alone. In fact, balancing the two is vital and they depend on one another. In Bonhoeffer's words,

> The day together of Christians who live in community is accompanied by each individual's day alone. That is the way it must be. The day together will be unfruitful without the day alone, both for the community and for the individual.[35]

Silence and solitude are essential ingredients of the disciple's spiritual life. The disciple's day is framed by silence before the word in the morning and the evening.[36] It is important to note that Bonhoeffer speaks of silence before the word, that is, silence is not for silence's sake, which can become a "paradise of self-deception."[37] Rather, he argues for a silence that is infused and informed by careful listening to the word of God. The radical disciple sits in silence and lets the word of Christ break into her life. "This is my beloved Son; listen to him" (Mark 9:7). She patiently waits for him and prays with the psalmist, "For God alone, O my soul, wait in silence, for my hope is from him" (Ps 62:5). Bonhoeffer offers, in this context, suggestions that are based on the tradition of *Lectio divina*. In his view, "[t]here are three things for which the Christian needs a regular time alone during the day: *meditation on the Scripture*, *prayer*, and *intercession*. All three should find a place in the *daily period of meditation*."[38]

Meditation was particularly important to Bonhoeffer—and his understanding of the term, it seems, overlaps with what we have so far called contemplation, that is, it is not so much an attention to one's breath, feelings,

---

33. Horton, *Gospel-Driven Life*, 148–49.
34. DBWE 5:81–82.
35. DBWE 5:83.
36. DBWE 5:85.
37. DBWE 5:86.
38. DBWE 5:86 (emphasis original).

or the beauty of creation, but a clear focus on the things of God (and we thus interpret his use of the term meditation in this more narrow sense of contemplation, as defined earlier).

On the question, "Why do I meditate?" Bonhoeffer categorically answers: "Because I am a Christian."[39] Meditation, in his view, is always based on the biblical text. "This time for meditation," he writes, "does not allow us to sink into the void and pit of aloneness [Alleinsein], rather it allows us to be alone [allein] with the Word."[40] It is neither the silence nor the solitude per se that makes an impact on the disciple. Rather, it is the word of God, the voice of the spirit of Christ that the disciple hears and ponders. We are to meditate on a word, a sentence, or a whole passage from Scripture, Bonhoeffer suggests, until "we personally are affected by it."[41] However, he is quick to add, we are not seeking special experiences or insights as such in our meditation.[42] Instead, and that is in his view the "fundamental rule of all meditation," we do "seek God alone."[43]

In silence and solitude, radical disciples contemplate the face of their friend Jesus Christ. The disciple imagines Jesus turning around to her, looking right at her, and hearing him ask, "What are you seeking?" (John 1:38). Their singular intent is this: they want to see the face of their friend. "The life of those who follow proves to be on the right course when nothing comes between them and Christ, not the law, not their own piety, and not the world. The disciples always see only Christ . . . So their vision is simple."[44] In other words, radical disciples pursue what one could call a face reading of the Gospel narratives—a *Lectio faciem*. As they immerse themselves into the various stories, their focus is literally on the face of Christ.[45] "What does his face reflect at a particular moment in the story?" they wonder. "What might Jesus's facial expression have been like when he watched thousands of people being fed from a handful of loaves and fish?" Or, "What was the look on his face when Judas betrayed him, when the disciples fought over who was the greatest, or when he was ridiculed on the cross?" By pursuing a facial contemplation of the biblical text, the disciple becomes even more familiar with Christ in the concrete instances of his glorification and

---

39. Bonhoeffer, *Meditating*, 22.
40. DBWE 5:86–87.
41. DBWE 5:87.
42. DBWE 5:88.
43. DBWE 5:89.
44. DBWE 4:161.
45. Imagining oneself in the gospel story is a key idea of Ignatian spirituality and my reflections in this context are strongly influenced by Ignatius of Loyola; see Fleming, *Ignatian Spirituality*.

humiliation. The direction of Jesus's gaze is also revealing and important to the disciple. We thus ask, "What is Christ looking at?" By inquiring in this way, we are continually in for surprises (as noted earlier, he singled out the poor widow who was invisible to the disciples).

Imagining the face of Christ will take us deeper into his story, and, as recent psychological evidence suggests, it has a significant impact on our experience, even on a physiological level. Psychologists were able to show that imagining facial expressions activates similar brain structures to viewing actual faces with emotional expressions. Whether we indeed see emotional faces or imagine them, there are striking similarities between the neural pathways that are being activated in both cases.[46] "[I]nternally generated emotional events, as the imagery of a happy or angry face," the researchers concluded, "induce comparable early reflexive cortical responses as the direct confrontation with happy or angry faces."[47] A careful contemplation of the face of Christ in the various moments of his story, for instance, as he weeps over Jerusalem (Luke 19:41), or as he asks his disciples whether they want to leave, too (John 6:67), or when he marveled at the faith of the centurion (Luke 7:9), or when he was deeply angered at the stubbornness of the people who did not show compassion with the man with the shriveled hand (Mark 3:5), will evoke a significant response in us in ways beyond what we might have thought possible.

Pursuing a *Lectio faciem*, then, the disciple grows in her knowledge of Christ and becomes even more intimately attached to him. As we follow the King in this way, we see more of Christ, our picture of him becomes richer, with more nuances and more detail. His face becomes more familiar and his actions and words increasingly permeate our inner being. Carefully studying the face of Christ, we are being transformed—which is in fact the key argument of our exercise. We become more like the Master, even in our own perspective; looking at his gaze our vision is being sharpened so that we will be able to see extraordinary instances of glorification in humiliation played out in our own and in our fellow disciples' lives. And as we immerse ourselves into the New Testament stories, we might also ask, "How is Christ looking at me? And how does this change my face?"

CONCLUSION

As we contemplate the face of Christ in his exaltation and humiliation, we are not only being transformed, but we are also granted peace. In the

46. Suess and Rahman, "Mental Imagery."
47. Suess and Rahman, "Mental Imagery," 154.

presence of the transfigured Christ, the disciple Peter felt instantly safe and at home—"it is good that we are here"—so much so that he wanted to make the situation permanent by setting up three tents (Luke 9:33). We have reason to believe that through practicing *Lectio faciem* our faces, too, will reflect some of that poise and serenity. Resting in God's shalom, though, has at the same time an activating component, for radical disciples who enjoy God's peace are, at the same time, called to be peacemakers (Matt 5:9). Jonathan Pennington writes, "The biblical and Christian understanding of flourishing . . . is not just a means for the individual to experience the good but is a universe-sized mission to spread God's *šālôm* (flourishing) or peace throughout his creation."[48] Contemplating the face of Christ, then, brings us peace, yet this peace never leads to apathy but fuels our desire to see all things reconciled under the sovereignty of the King. By contemplating the one who is "there for others," the disciple is likewise transformed into the human being for others.[49] Beholding the face of Jesus Christ in contemplation, we are inspired to befriend the world by loving our neighbor in concrete deeds of mercy.[50] Contemplation, then, rightly understood, always leads to action. Ultimately, of course, our experience and spreading of shalom remains fragmentary in this life. Our vision of Christ remains hazy as we now only see as "in a mirror dimly" (1 Cor 13:12). Walking by faith, not by sight (2 Cor 5:7), we anticipate the fulfillment of the superb promise, "They will see his face" (Rev 22:4). Still placed solidly with our two feet on this earth, we persevere in tensions and strive toward the heavenly Jerusalem, constantly "looking to Jesus, the founder and perfecter of our faith" (Heb 12:2). Longing and praying for the ultimate completion of God's promises in the eschaton, our constant prayer is, "Come, Lord Jesus!" (Rev 22:20).[51]

PERSONAL REFLECTION

Reading the Gospels, where do you detect in Christ's life concrete instances of humiliation and exaltation? How are, in your own life, humiliation and glorification simultaneously present?

48. Pennington, *Sermon on the Mount*, 297.

49. DBWE 8:501 ("Outline for a Book").

50. "What matters is *participating in the reality of God and the world in Jesus Christ today*," writes Bonhoeffer. DBWE 6:55 (emphasis original).

51. Adolf Schlatter notes that the disciples' hope was a very intimate one; they had not merely a "doctrine of the last things," but they longed for Christ's personal return. Schlatter, *History*, 345.

How can you make room in your daily routine for contemplating Christ's face?

Choose a passage from the Gospels and practice the art of facial Gospel reading, *Lectio faciem*. What is the expression of Jesus Christ's face in the particular episode? How does it change throughout the story? How are you affected personally as you contemplate Jesus Christ's face?

Imagine Christ is looking at you. What does his face reveal? And what does he see?

Concluding Remarks

THIS BOOK INVITES CHRISTIAN disciples to embrace a radical form of discipleship. According to the central argument of this book, radical discipleship is an art that requires nurturing and mastering, as our faith is constantly challenged, tested, and refined as we meet various tensions on the way.[1] Christian discipleship is a challenging, complex, and often frustrating enterprise, yet it comes with the promise of a new identity, a new existence with purpose and meaning. Embracing tensions in the three areas of self-denial, cross-bearing, and following, disciples of Christ experience profound transformation: They receive new life through the death of Christ as they constantly shed their decaying old self and put on their new self. They receive a new vision of self and God as they take up their crosses. And they grow up in their relationship with the great friend as they are sent into this world as those who are not of this world, making new friends wherever they go (John 17:14–19; Rom 8:17–23; Phil 3:20–21).

Radical discipleship, then, is about creatively acquiring, through the Holy Spirit, a new posture, new attitudes, and skills to embrace these tensions and to navigate the complex task of following in Christ's footsteps (1 Pet 2:21). The apostle Paul uses the athletic metaphors of running a race and fighting a fight to describe our life of following after Christ (1 Cor 9:24–27; Gal 2:2; 5:7; Phil 2:16).[2] Like the athlete improving on his fitness or the musician refining her technique, it requires tenacity, drive, openness to

---

1. John Koessler also makes the case for discipleship as art, see Koessler, *True Discipleship*. Similarly, Fidelis Ruppert (OSB) encourages his readers to pursue a form of "spiritual art" (*geistliche Kunst*) through the power of the Holy Spirit. Ruppert, *Geistlich Kämpfen lernen*, 49–50.

2. As Medi Ann Volpe put it, "discipleship is about staying in the fight." Volpe, *Rethinking Christian Identity*, 240.

new approaches, readiness for surprises, and the commitment to lifelong learning.[3] This is the underlying meaning of the word "disciple" (*mathētēs* in Greek): a disciple is literally a student, a lifelong apprentice.[4] Radical disciples are therefore eager to discover what St. Benedict called the "instruments of good works" (*instrumenta bonorum operum*), and to put them into practice.[5]

This version of discipleship is radical in the sense that disciples are encouraged to adopt a perhaps confronting, but deeply biblical view of the One who calls them into discipleship. Avoiding lopsided images of Jesus Christ, they follow in the footsteps of their Master who calls them authoritatively into self-denial, cross-bearing, and follow-ship. They walk behind not merely a fine role model, but "the image of the invisible God" in whom "the fullness of God was pleased to dwell" (Col 1:15, 19). Encountering Jesus Christ, nothing stays the same in the disciple; the extent of renewal that takes place in the person of the disciple is radical and comprehensive. Everything is being touched and turned upside down: a new way of thinking, a new volition, a new desire, and a new direction with a new prospect and promise. This newness creates a tension as it is in opposition to the oldness that is—strangely—still attached to the disciple. Embracing this very tension, though, radical disciples experience transformation and growth. Living—and flourishing—as radical disciples, then, means a constant openness to address and inquire what it means to deny oneself, take up one's cross, and to follow Christ.[6]

Another key insight of our reflection was the fact that our own journey of discipleship is intimately linked with Christ's. This has become evident throughout. The Prophet who calls us into self-denial has emptied himself first. The Priest who calls us to cross-bearing has carried his own cross before us. And the King-Friend who invites us to follow him has followed his Father's will for him until the very end, even to the cross. The sacraments provide tangible evidence of our shared journey and offer substantial comfort

---

3. Both the monk in the monastery and the disciple at home face the same task, namely the "acquisition of skills" (*Erwerb von Fertigkeiten*). Ruppert, *Geistlich Kämpfen lernen*, 28.

4. Bauer translates "d. Schüler, d. Jünger," "allg. D. Lehrling, d. Schüler." Bauer et al., *Griechisch-deutsches Wörterbuch*, 985.

5. My insights on and references to St. Benedict here and elsewhere are based on Fidelis Ruppert's excellent book, Ruppert, *Geistlich Kämpfen lernen*. The Latin quote is from Pax CSPB, "Kapitel 4" (my translation).

6. "Faith seeks understanding passionately and relentlessly, or it languishes and eventually dies . . ." writes Daniel Migliore. "Human life ceases to be human not when we do not have all the answers, but when we no longer have the courage to ask the really important questions." Migliore, *Faith Seeking Understanding*, 6.

for us on the way. Baptism signifies our constant dying and rising with Christ as we reject old self impulses and embrace our new self in Christ. The Lord's Supper regularly brings to mind the ultimate cross-bearer who gave his body and blood for us, nourishing us on our journey. In what follows we briefly revisit the three stages of radical discipleship as discussed earlier.

SELF-DENIAL

In the opening section we first turned our attention to *Understanding the Self*. When faced with the call, "Deny yourself," we are first required to develop a solid understanding of the nature of our self. What is the self that we are to deny? Psychologists and theologians agree that our default self is a fragmented self, marred by inconsistencies and self-centeredness. This is the self that follows the "course of this world" (Eph 2:2), is in love with itself, and desperately tries to form its own identity, independent of any reference to God. Turning around ourselves, we ignore God and neighbor and miss out on the purpose for which we have been created. Walking through this diagnosis is a sobering task, but the remedy has much to offer in terms of comfort and encouragement.

In the chapter on *Embracing Newness*, it was thus argued that true purpose, meaning, and fulfillment comes by embracing the new self that is offered as a gift in union with Christ, who in his role as Prophet speaks newness into our being. This new self comes with a profound promise of newness of life that includes the enjoyment of forgiveness and righteousness through Christ. Renewed disciples grow up into real human persons as they are pulled, through the Holy Spirit, away from an exclusive self-love, toward love of God and neighbor. The radical disciple's self derives authenticity, integrity, and stability not through self-fabricated attempts at identity formation, but from her intimate union with Christ. The burden of identity formation has been lifted from us and we simply witness how God makes our person whole as he calls us by name and conforms us into the image of his Son (Rom 8:29). The sacrament of baptism serves as a tangible reminder of our having died and risen to newness together with Christ. Emerging from the waters of baptism, we are now defined by a Christothentic self that is shaped by Christ's own life through the Holy Spirit. It is a self that rests in quiet self-awareness and actively seeks to love God and neighbor. The disciple has experienced a power shift where now the spirit of Christ rules in her thinking and doing. Still, while disciples clearly enjoy newness, they are exposed to the internal conflict between old self and new self. They come to know themselves as susceptible saints. Growing up as disciples means to embrace the dissonance between constant rejection of oldness and constant acceptance of newness. Radical disciples take up this challenge as they seek to flourish in the tension of denying the old and embracing the new in them through Christ again and again.

In the final chapter of this section, *Practicing Self-Denial*, we examined how obedience to this command looks in more practical terms. When calling us to deny ourselves, Jesus Christ does not demand the impossible. The obedience he expects is nourished in us through his Spirit. Radical disciples, then, do not rely on their own strength as they seek to deny any old impulses, traits, and habits, but trust in the Spirit who works in them "both to will and to work for his good pleasure" (Phil 2:13). We carefully consider the newness of our new self, exploring all its precious facets and prospects, reminding ourselves of the many privileges that come with it. Self-denial, then, is about aspiring to a goldilocks posture between rejection of the old self and embrace of the new self. Mindful of potential caricatures of discipleship, where either the new self (the pretentious disciple), or the old self tries to take center stage (the legalistic or depressed disciple), we pursue a position of quiet self-awareness that is content to rest in itself, and focuses on God and the needs of others. In this way, radical disciples mature and grow up as persons with a clear purpose and a sense of fulfillment.

CROSS-BEARING

Bearing the cross is the definitive expression of our discipleship, since we demonstrate here our close relationship with the cross-bearer par excellence. The cross becomes our distinguishing feature.[7] In the first chapter of this section, *Cross-Bearing and Christ's Suffering*, we asked, "What does Jesus mean when he calls us to take up our cross?" We found clues in the significant overlap between the Synoptics' disclosure of Jesus's call to cross-bearing and St. Paul's theology of co-suffering with Christ. It was determined that one first needs to get a clearer understanding of the nature of Jesus's sufferings before it can be ascertained what participation in it means for us. In this first step, then, we looked more carefully at the suffering that the Son of God endured when he clothed himself with humanity, identified with our sin as our perfect substitute, represented us before God, and reconciled us to him. We discovered that here was constant suffering from day one, leading up all the way to the cross. We examined the physical and spiritual suffering that Christ endured and the opposition and persecution

---

7. Suffering with Christ, in Bonhoeffer's view, thus "becomes the identifying mark of a follower of Christ." DBWE 4:89.

he suffered at the hands of the religious elite. Jesus's life was marked by constant testing, and he was exposed to temptation from the beginning of his ministry. Ultimately, the great high priest carried his own cross and gave himself as a sacrifice to God, bearing godforsakenness as the horrid climax of his sufferings. We concluded that in many ways, Jesus's cross is over and beyond our cross and his sufferings remain, to a great extent, inaccessible to us. Our sharing in his sufferings can always only happen in a very limited sense. Still, it is the great high priest who, having carried his own cross, calls us into his fellowship of cross-bearing. There must be some resemblance between Jesus's cross and our little crosses. In a certain way, disciples suffer *with Christ*.[8] We observed, too, that the New Testament documents all witness to the presence of joy, confidence, and even a sentiment of triumph and jubilation when it comes to the cross of Christ. There is a clear tension where joy and suffering are simultaneously present—an experience in which disciples share as they take up their own cross. The Lord's Supper, it was noted, is the sacrament that brings to life the disciple's participation in the sufferings of Christ in the context of a solemn celebration.

In a second step, in the chapter on *Sharing in Christ's Sufferings*, we explored more carefully our own cross in the shadow of Christ's great cross, pointing out parallels and dissimilarities between the two. While only the Son of God lived a perfect life in our place and died his death for our sake, we do continue his representative work through the Spirit. We participate in Christ's representative action by sharing in the suffering of this world. We do not retreat and close our eyes in face of the world's pain and suffering, but we immerse ourselves in it, lament over it and present it to God the Father who promised to restore all things through his Son who resides in us. As fully-embodied beings, we suffer the consequence of the fall in body, mind, and soul and we put our trust in Christ who walked and suffered before us. Like Christ, we suffer physically and spiritually, we endure opposition and persecution, trials and temptations in this world for the sake of the kingdom of God. Knowing that Christ has overcome this world with all its tribulations, we are confident and courageous, sharing in Christ's triumph and his victory on the cross (John 16:33; 1 Cor 15:57). Radical disciples know that even in the darkest night of the soul, Jesus is ever present with them and that they will experience in and through their struggles a breakthrough toward a new vista of God and self. They flourish in the paradoxical tension that joy is present right in the midst of suffering—as Christ himself experienced.

---

8. "The cross is suffering with Christ," Bonhoeffer insists. "Indeed, it is Christ-suffering. Only one who is bound to Christ, as this occurs in discipleship, stands in seriousness under the cross." DBWE 4:87.

Having gained a clearer sense of what sharing in Christ's suffering involves (and what not!), we then moved to the concrete act of taking up the cross.

In the final chapter of this section, *Taking Up the Cross*, we acknowledged first that disciples who give heed to the call to cross-bearing are faced with a formidable tension. Taking up the cross, a figure for torture and death, promises to turn out life-giving in many ways. First, it intensifies the disciple's fellowship with Christ. In their darkest moments, they learn how Christ himself draws near and comforts them. Secondly, by taking up the cross the disciple opens herself for the opportunity for profound transformation. We all have our own stories to share of how dealing with certain challenging episodes in our own biography has shaped and formed us. In hindsight, we might even reflect on some of these episodes with gratitude because we know we have grown in wisdom and maturity (one more reason to look at our present "cotton-wool" culture of "safe spaces" with suspicion). Thirdly, we noted that taking up the cross ultimately means surrender. By surrendering to God, the radical disciple demonstrates that she is not her own, but Christ's, and in this way gains true life and a new vision of God. In the act of surrender, she tastes the new resurrection life in union with Christ with whom she died and rose to new life that comes with a new desire. Having lost her life through surrender, she has gained new life where Christ is at the center and the object of her ultimate desire, prompting her to pray: "I love you O Lord, my strength" (Ps 18:1).

FOLLOWING

Exploring Jesus's invitation to follow him, we first examined the way we follow him *personally*. Christ in his role as King calls disciples individually and bids them to follow after him. With new ears to hear and a new desire to obey, radical disciples welcome the authoritative, effective, and irresistible call to follow their Master, one by one. Letting go of the need for self-determination, possessions, and even certain relationships—if necessary, they experience that, whatever they may have renounced, they will receive it back manifold. Following Jesus Christ, they realize, might be the most demanding and yet, at the same time, the most liberating act, as they flourish in the tension of renouncing independence and finding true life with meaning and purpose. Only loosely attached to their possessions, they discover true prosperity and a reordering of their relationships. This comes with a new sense of freedom; radical disciples are now freed to imitate their great friend's love for God and neighbor. They do so not based on their own strength, but on their intimate union with him. It is not brought about by our (well-meant) motive to obey a master who stands in front or even opposite of us. Rather, it happens by living intimately connected with the Master himself, whom we follow on our journey. Our love finds expression in concrete acts and in circumstances that others might consider ordinary. However, with new eyes to see, disciples perceive and enact spectacular deeds of love in the most ordinary of circumstances.

Broadening our perspective in the subsequent chapter, *Following Together*, we included the communal aspect in our reflections. Radical disciples relish in the friendship that Jesus offers them and they welcome being added to the community of friends. Through the Spirit, who dwells in them, they are enabled and inspired to love their disciple friends and grow up as friends of Christ. As the radical disciple knows herself to be loved by the great friend Jesus, she is, through this love, inspired and enabled to love Christ in turn and extend his love to the other friend. Christian friendship is marked by the presence of deep love for the other in Christ. They regard themselves not only as friends of Jesus individually, but communally, as a fellowship of Jesus's friends who are friends with one another. As they practice the art of spiritual friendship they grow up as disciples, affirming one another, forgiving one another, suffering with one another, and sacrificing themselves for each other. In this way, they grow more closely toward one another and, ultimately, "grow up in every way into him who is the head, into Christ" (Eph 4:15). Radical disciple friends also befriend the world, as they love it "from the Father."[9] Distressed with their surrounding culture of self-centeredness and loneliness, they spread the message of hope and reconciliation in Jesus Christ.

In the concluding chapter, *Seeking the Friend's Face*, we studied the episode of the transfiguration where we observed the mysterious coexistence of exaltation in the moment of majestic splendor and Fatherly affirmation on the one hand, and humiliation in the conversation regarding Jesus's end on the cross on the other hand. We determined that glorification and humiliation are simultaneously present on the mountain, and this applies not only to Christ's person and work, but also to the disciples' lives as they are nourished by the life of their Master through the Spirit. The disciples, here, not only enjoy a glimpse into the Son of God's glory, but they also learn how Jesus's humiliation and glorification are linked with their own story of humiliation and glorification. By following the King-Friend, the disciple lets go of self-determination, possessions, and even relationships. Stepping into the simultaneity of humiliation and exaltation, she finds true fulfillment, prosperity, and a new network of friends who walk with her along

---

9. O'Donovan, *Finding and Seeking*, 75.

the way. In solitude and silence before the word, disciples contemplate the face of Christ in the Gospels (*Lectio faciem*). And as they focus on his face, constantly identifying new facets and features, they grow in their intimate knowledge of him, are being drawn closer to him, and thus experience transformation into his image through the Spirit. The tension remains that their view of Christ remains imperfect in this life, but it is in this tension that they seek to flourish.

CODA

In various places throughout this book, we have touched on the challenges of comparing Christ's threefold office of Prophet, Priest, and King with our own prophetic, priestly, and kingly ministries. While Christ's roles are unique and unrepeatable, there is a sense in which we, by the Holy Spirit and based on the authority of Christ (Matt 28:18), serve the world in a prophetic, priestly, and kingly ministry. And we do so both individually, as disciples called to follow Christ, and, of course, communally, as the group of friends who travel together on the way. In our prophetic ministry (note the lowercase p), we proclaim the costly grace of the gospel; inviting our fellow human beings to use their system two and to explore the full Christ, not a reduced version of him, but a complete One, divine and human, humiliated and exalted, carrying our guilt and rising triumphantly. Our own lives, lived out in our Christothentic selves, bear witness to the precious newness that is offered to everyone who believes in Christ. In our priestly ministry (also with lowercase p) we share the gospel of reconciliation between God and humanity by announcing "the Lord's death until he comes" (1 Cor 11:26). As we take up our little crosses, we are being transformed into a "royal priesthood" (1 Pet 2:9). In this small-scale priesthood we do not mediate between God and humanity, though, but we present this fallen world to God, bringing before him its pain and suffering. We are called to baptize those who respond by faith, not in our own name, but in the name of the triune God, Father, Son, and Holy Spirit (Matt 28:19). As we do so, we invite our new friends into follow-ship that is marked by tensions, by a constant dying and rising with Christ. In our kingly ministry (definitely with lowercase k), as members of the royal household, we witness to the sovereign One who promised, "Behold, I am making all things new" (Rev 21:5). Radical disciples remind their king-friends that Jesus Christ is with them "always, to the end of the age" (Matt 28:20). The focus of our attention rests always on the great friend who walks before us. Contemplating his face in quiet reflection, we grow up into his image until we see him face-to-face.

Bibliography

Abbott, Jo, et al. "The Impact of Loneliness on the Health and Wellbeing of Australians." *InPsych* 40, no. 6 (2018). https://www.psychology.org.au/for-members/publications/inpsych/2018/December-Issue-6/The-impact-of-loneliness-on-the-health-and-wellbei.

Alicke, Mark D., and Olesya Govorun. "The Better-Than-Average Effect." In *The Self in Social Judgement*, edited by Mark Alicke et al., 83–106. New York: Psychology, 2005.

Althaus, Paul. *Die christliche Wahrheit*. Vol. 2. Gütersloh: C. Bertelsmann Verlag, 1948.

Arenson, Kelly E. *Health and Hedonism in Plato and Epicurus*. New York, NY: Bloomsbury Academic, 2019.

Augustinus, Aurelius. *Confessiones/Bekenntnisse Lateinisch/Deutsch*. Ditzingen: Reclam, 2009.

Avila, Teresa of. *The Collected Works of St. Teresa of Avila*. Translated by Kieran Kavanaugh and Otilio Rodriguez. Washington, DC: ICS, 2017.

Baressi, John, and Raymond Martin. "History as Prologue: Western Theories of the Self." In *The Oxford Handbook of the Self*, edited by Shaun Gallagher, 33–56. Oxford: Oxford University Press, 2011.

Barr, James. "Abba Isn't 'Daddy.'" *Journal of Theological Studies* 39 (1988) 28–47.

Barth, Karl. *Der Römerbrief (Zweite Fassung, 1922)*. Karl Barth Gesamtausgabe 47. Edited by Cornelis van der Kooi and Katja Tolstaja. Zürich: Theologischer Verlag, 2010.

Bastian, Brock. *The Other Side of Happiness: Embracing a More Fearless Approach to Living*. London: Penguin, 2018.

Bauckham, Richard. *Jesus and the God of Israel: God Crucified and Other Studies on the New Testament's Christology of Divine Identity*. Grand Rapids, MI: Eerdmans, 2008.

Bauer, Jack J., and Heidi A. Wayment. "The Psychology of the Quiet Ego." In *Transcending Self-Interest: Psychological Explorations of the Quiet Ego*, edited by Heidi A. Wayment and Jack J. Bauer, 7–19. Washington, DC: American Psychological Association, 2008.

Bauer, Walter, et al. *Griechisch-Deutsches Wörterbuch zu den Schriften des Neuen Testaments und der frühchristlichen Literatur*. Edited by Kurt Aland and Barbara Aland. 6., völlig neu bearbeitete Aufl. Berlin: Walter de Gruyter, 1988.

Baum, Caroline. "Our Lock-and-Leave Culture: The Rise of Self-Storage and Clinging to Stuff We Hardly Use." *The Guardian—Australia Edition*, December 17, 2018. https://www.theguardian.com/australia-news/2018/dec/17/our-lock-and-leave-culture-the-rise-of-self-storage-and-clinging-to-stuff-we-hardly-use.

Baumeister, Roy. "The Lowdown on High Self-Esteem." *Los Angeles Times*, January 25, 2005. https://www.latimes.com/archives/la-xpm-2005-jan-25-oe-baumeister25-story.html.

———. "Narcissism as Addiction to Esteem." *Psychological Inquiry* 12, no. 4 (2001) 206–10.

Bautista, Ronn. "Filipino Devotees Nailed to Crosses to Re-Enact Crucifixion." https://www.reuters.com/article/us-religion-easter-philippines-crucifixi/filipino-devotees-nailed-to-crosses-to-re-enact-crucifixion-idUSKCN1RV0U4.

Bavinck, Herman. *Reformed Dogmatics: Holy Spirit, Church, and New Creation*. Vol. 4. Edited by John Bolt. Translated by John Friend. Grand Rapids, MI: Baker Academic, 2008.

Bayer, Hans F. *Das Evangelium des Markus*. Historisch-Theologische Auslegung, Neues Testament. Witten/Giessen: SCM R. Brockhaus/Brunnen, 2008.

Bayer, Oswald. "Luthers 'Simul Iustus Et Peccator.'" *Kerygma und Dogma* 64, no. 4 (2018) 249–64.

———. *Martin Luther's Theology: A Contemporary Interpretation*. Translated by Thomas H. Trapp. Grand Rapids, MI: Eerdmans, 2008.

———. *Theology the Lutheran Way*. Edited by Paul Rorem. Translated by Jeffrey G. Silcock and Mark C. Mattes. Lutheran Quarterly Books. Grand Rapids, MI: Eerdmans, 2007.

BBC. "Christian Persecution 'At Near Genocide Levels.'" *BBC News*, May 3, 2019. https://www.bbc.com/news/uk-48146305.

Becker, Peter. *Seelische Gesundheit und Verhaltenskontrolle*. Göttingen: Hogrefe, 1995.

Beintker, Horst. *Die Überwindung der Anfechtung bei Luther: Eine Studie zu seiner Theologie nach den Operationes in Psalmos 1519–21*. Berlin: Evangelische Verlagsanstalt, 1954.

Benedict XVI. "Deus Caritas Est." http://www.vatican.va/content/benedict-xvi/en/encyclicals/documents/hf_ben-xvi_enc_20051225_deus-caritas-est.html.

Bentham, Jeremy. *An Introduction to the Principles of Morals and Legislation*. Oxford: Clarendon, 1879.

Berkhof, Louis. *Systematic Theology*. Edinburgh: Banner of Truth Trust, 1958.

Bernard, Michael Edwin. *Strength of Self-Acceptance: Theory, Practice, and Research*. New York, NY: Springer, 2013.

Bethge, Eberhard. *Dietrich Bonhoeffer: A Biography*. Minneapolis, MN: Fortress, 2000.

Bird, Michael F. "Justification as Forensic Declaration and Covenant Membership: A *Via Media* Between Reformed and Revisionist Readings of Paul." *Tyndale Bulletin* 57, no. 1 (2006) 109–30.

Bloom, Matt. *Flourishing in Ministry: How to Cultivate Clergy Wellbeing*. London: Rowman & Littlefield, 2019.

Bockmuehl, Markus. *The Epistle to the Philippians*. Black's New Testament Commentaries. Edited by Henry Chadwick. 4th ed. London: A & C Black, 1997.

Bøe, Sverre. *Cross-Bearing in Luke*. Wissenschaftliche Untersuchungen zum Neuen Testament. 2. Reihe. Tübingen: Mohr Siebeck, 2010.

Boersma, Hans. *Seeing God: The Beatific Vision in Christian Tradition*. Grand Rapids, MI: Eerdmans, 2018.

Bonhoeffer, Dietrich. *Dietrich Bonhoeffer: Witness to Jesus Christ*. Minneapolis, MN: Fortress, 1991.
———. *Discipleship*. Translated by Barbara Green and Reinhard Krauss. Fortress, 2001.
———. *Life Together and Prayerbook of the Bible*. Translated by Daniel W. Bloesch and James H. Burtness. Dietrich Bonhoeffer Works. Minneapolis: Fortress, 1996.
———. *Meditating on the Word*. Translated by David McI. Gracie. Lanham, MD: Rowman & Littlefield, 2008.
Bonhoeffer, Dietrich, et al. *A Testament to Freedom: The Essential Writings of Dietrich Bonhoeffer*. Rev. ed. San Francisco, CA: Harper, 1995.
Bonhoeffer, Dietrich, and Maria von Wedemeyer. *Love Letters from Cell 92*. Edited by Ruth-Alice von Bismarck and Ulrich Kabitz. Translated by John Brownjohn. London: Fount/Harper Collins, 1994.
Bovon, François. *Das Evangelium nach Lukas*. Evangelisch-Katholischer Kommentar zum Neuen Testament. Vol. 3 (1. Teilband). Edited by Rudolf Schnackenburg et al. Zürich: Benziger Verlag AG, 1989.
Brady, Sheryl. *You Have It In You! Empowered to Do the Impossible*. New York, NY: Howard, 2012.
Brakke, David. *The Gnostics: Myth, Ritual, and Diversity in Early Christianity*. Cambridge, MA: Harvard University Press, 2010.
Brandtstädter, Jochen, and Richard M. Lerner. *Action and Self-Development: Theory and Research through the Life Span*. Thousand Oaks, CA: Sage, 1999.
Bräutigam, Michael. "Good Will Hunting: Adolf Schlatter on Organic Volitional Sanctification." *Journal of the Evangelical Theological Society* 55, no. 1 (2012) 125–43.
———. *Union with Christ: Adolf Schlatter's Relational Christology*. Eugene, OR: Pickwick, 2015.
Bray, Gerald Lewis. *God Has Spoken: A History of Christian Theology*. Wheaton, IL: Crossway, 2014.
Breckler, Steven J., and Anthony G. Greenwald. "Motivational Facets of the Self." In *Handbook of Motivation and Cognition: Foundations of Social Behavior*, edited by Richard M. Sorrentino and E. Tory Higgins, 145–64. New York, NY: Guilford, 1986.
Brock, Rita Nakashima. "And a Little Child Will Lead Us: Christology and Child Abuse." In *Christianity, Patriarchy, and Abuse: A Feminist Critique*, edited by Joanne Carlson Brown and Carole R. Bohn, 42–61. Cleveland, OH: Pilgrim, 1989.
Brooks, David. *The Second Mountain: The Quest for a Moral Life*. New York, NY: Random House, 2019.
Bruine de Bruin, Wändi, et al. "Age Differences in Reported Social Networks and Well-Being." *Psychology and Aging* 35, no. 2 (2020) 159–68.
Bultmann, Rudolf. *Der Zweite Brief an die Korinther*. Kritisch-Exegetischer Kommentar über das Neue Testament (Begründet von H.A.W. Meyer). Edited by Ferdinand Hahn. Göttingen: Vandenhoeck und Ruprecht, 1976.
———. "Neues Testament und Mythologie: Das Problem der Entmythologisierung der Neutestamentlichen Verkündigung." In *Kerygma und Mythos: Ein theologisches Gespräch*, edited by Hans-Werner Bartsch, 15–48. Hamburg-Bergstedt: Herbert Reich-Evangelischer Verlag 1960.
Burkholder, Benjamin. "Violence, Atonement, and Retributive Justice: Bonhoeffer as a Test Case." *Modern Theology* 33, no. 3 (2017) 395–413.
Burns, Paul C. "Augustine of Hippo: The Christian Life, Then and Now." In *Sources of the Christian Self: A Cultural History of Christian Identity*, edited by James M. Houston and Jens Zimmermann, 209–22. Grand Rapids, MI: Eerdmans, 2018.

Cacioppo, John T., and William Patrick. *Loneliness: Human Nature and the Need for Social Connection*. New York, NY: Norton, 2008.

Cacioppo, Stephanie et al. "Loneliness: Clinical Import and Interventions." *Perspectives on Psychological Science* 10, no. 2 (2015) 238–49.

Calhoun, Lawrence G., and Richard G. Tedeschi. *Posttraumatic Growth in Clinical Practice*. New York, NY: Routledge, 2013.

Calvin, John. *A Harmony of the Gospels: Matthew, Mark and Luke*. Calvin's New Testament Commentaries. Vol. 2. Edited by David W. Torrance and Thomas F. Torrance. Translated by T. H. L. Parker. Edinburgh: Saint Andrew, 1972.

Campbell, Bradley, and Jason Manning. *The Rise of Victimhood Culture: Microaggressions, Safe Spaces, and the New Culture Wars*. New York: Palgrave Macmillan, 2018.

Campbell, Murray. "Did Jesus Empty Himself of His Divine Powers?" *MurrayCampbell.Net: Ideas About and for Melbourne*, October 1, 2018. https://murraycampbell.net/2018/10/01/did-jesus-empty-himself-of-his-divine-powers/.

Campi, Emidio. "The Reformation in Zurich." In *A Companion to the Swiss Reformation*, edited by Amy Nelson Burnett and Emidio Campi, 59–125. Brill's Companions to the Christian Tradition. Leiden: Brill, 2016.

Carlson Brown, Joanne, and Rebecca Parker. "For God So Loved the World?" In *Christianity, Patriarchy, and Abuse: A Feminist Critique*, edited by Joanne Carlson Brown and Carole R. Bohn, 1–30. Cleveland, OH: Pilgrim, 1989.

Case, Brendan. "'More Splendid Than the Sun': Christ's Flesh among the Reasons for the Incarnation." *Modern Theology* 36, no. 4 (2020) 754–77.

Casey, Michael. *Sacred Reading: The Ancient Art of Lectio Divina*. Liguori, MO: Triumph, 1996.

Chapman, David W. *Ancient Jewish and Christian Perceptions of Crucifixion*. Grand Rapids, MI: Baker Academic, 2010.

Cialdini, R. B., et al. "Basking in Reflected Glory: Three (Football) Field Studies." *Journal of Personality and Social Psychology* 34 (1976) 366–75.

Coe, John H., and Kyle C. Strobel. "Introduction: Retrieving the Heart of the Christian Faith." In *Embracing Contemplation: Reclaiming a Christian Spiritual Practice*, edited by John H. Coe and Kyle C. Strobel, 1–15. Downers Grove, IL: IVP Academic, 2019.

Cohen, Sheldon, and Thomas A. Wills. "Stress, Social Support, and the Buffering Hypothesis." *Psychological Bulletin* 98, no. 2 (1985) 310–57.

Cohen, Sheldon. et al. "Social Ties and Susceptibility to the Common Cold." *JAMA* 277, no. 24 (1997) 1940–44.

Conzen, Peter. *Erik H. Erikson: Grundpositionen seines Werkes*. Stuttgart: Kohlhammer, 2010.

Coogan, Michael David, and Vasudha Narayanan. *Eastern Religions: Origins, Beliefs, Practices, Holy Texts, Sacred Places*. Oxford: Oxford University Press, 2005.

Cortez, Marc. *Christological Anthropology in Historical Perspective: Ancient and Contemporary Approaches to Theological Anthropology*. Grand Rapids, MI: Zondervan, 2016.

Crisp, Oliver D. "On the Vicarious Humanity of Christ." *International Journal of Systematic Theology* 21, no. 3 (2019) 235–50.

———. "Was Christ Sinless or Impeccable?" In *God Incarnate: Explorations in Christology*, 122–36. London: T. & T. Clark, 2009.

Danz, Christian, and Jan-Heiner Tuck, eds. *Martin Luther im Widerstreit der Konfessionen: Historische und theologische Perspektiven* Freiburg i. Br.: Herder, 2017.

Dawn, Marva J. *Being Well When We're Ill: Wholeness and Hope in Spite of Infirmity*. Minneapolis, MN: Augsburg, 2008.

———. *Reaching Out Without Dumbing Down: A Theology of Worship for the Turn-of-the-Century Culture*. Grand Rapids, MI: Eerdmans, 1995.

De Gruchy, John, *Dietrich Bonhoeffer: Witness to Jesus Christ*. Minneapolis, MN: Fortress, 1991.

De Ste. Croix, Geoffrey E. M., et al. *Christian Persecution, Martyrdom, and Orthodoxy*. Oxford: Oxford University Press, 2006.

DeGroat, Chuck. *Wholeheartedness: Busyness, Exhaustion, and Healing the Divided Self*. Grand Rapids, MI: Eerdmans, 2016.

Denworth, Lydia. *Friendship: The Evolution, Biology, and Extraordinary Power of Life's Fundamental Bond*. New York, NY: W. W. Norton & Company, 2020.

Detweiler, Craig. *Selfies: Searching for the Image of God in a Digital Age*. Grand Rapids, MI: Brazos 2018.

DeVine, Mark. *Shalom Yesterday, Today, and Forever: Embracing All Three Dimensions of Creation and Redemption*. Eugene, OR: Wipf & Stock, 2019.

Dieter, Melvin Easterday. *The Holiness Revival of the Nineteenth Century*. Studies in Evangelicalism. 2nd ed. Lanham, MD: Scarecrow, 1996.

Dietrich, Martin O. "Introduction to Luther's 'Comfort When Facing Grave Temptations' (1521)." In *Devotional Writings I*, edited by Martin O. Dietrich, 181–82. Luther's Works Philadelphia, PA: Fortress, 1969.

Dingel, Irene, ed. *Die Bekenntnisschriften der Evangelisch-Lutherischen Kirche*. Göttingen: Vandenhoeck & Ruprecht, 2014.

Dixon, Sandra Lee. *Augustine: The Scattered and Gathered Self*. St. Louis, MO: Chalice, 1999.

Dschulnigg, Peter. *Das Markusevangelium*, Theologischer Kommentar Zum Neuen Testament. Stuttgart: Verlag W. Kohlhammer, 2007.

Dunn, James D. G. *Romans 1–8*. Word Biblical Commentary. Vol. 38a. Edited by David A. Hubbard and Glen W. Barker. Dallas, TX: Word, 1988.

Dunning, David. *Self-Insight: Roadblocks and Detours on the Path to Knowing Thyself*. Essays in Social Psychology. New York, NY: Psychology, 2005.

Dunning, David, et al. "Flawed Self-Assessment: Implications for Health, Education, and the Workplace." *Psychol Sci Public Interest* 5, no. 3 (December 2004) 69–106.

———. "Why People Fail to Recognize Their Own Incompetence." *Current Directions in Psychological Science* 12, no. 3 (2003) 83–87.

Edgar, Brian. *God Is Friendship: A Theology of Spirituality, Community, and Society*. Wilmore, KY: Seedbed, 2013.

Edwards, James R. *The Gospel According to Mark*. The Pillar New Testament Commentary. Grand Rapids, MI: Eerdmans, 2002.

Elliott, Matthew. *Faithful Feelings: Emotion in the New Testament*. Leicester: Inter-Varsity Press, 2005.

Ellis, Albert, et al. *Personality Theories: Critical Perspectives*. Los Angeles, CA: SAGE, 2009.

Elliston, Clark J. *Dietrich Bonhoeffer and the Ethical Self: Christology, Ethics, and Formation*. Minneapolis, MN: Fortress 2016.

Elshtain, Jean Bethke. *Who Are We?: Critical Reflections and Hopeful Possibilities*. Grand Rapids, MI: W. B. Eerdmans, 2000.

Evans, C. Stephen. *Exploring Kenotic Christology: The Self-Emptying of God*. Oxford: Oxford University Press, 2006.

Fava, Maurizio. "Depression With Physical Symptoms: Treating to Remission." *The Journal of Clinical Psychiatry* 64, no. S7 (2003) 24–28.

Ferguson, Niall. *Civilization: The West and the Test*. New York, NY: Penguin, 2011.

Fitzmyer, Joseph A. *The Gospel According to Luke (I–IX): Introduction, Translation, and Notes*. The Anchor Bible. Vol. 1 of 2. Edited by William Foxwell Albright and David Noel Freedman. Garden City, NY: Doubleday, 1981.

Fleming, David L. *What Is Ignatian Spirituality?* Chicago, IL: Loyola, 2008.

Focant, Camille. *L'évangile Selon Marc*. Commentaire Biblique: Nouveau Testament. Vol. 2. Paris: Les Editions du Cerf, 2004.

Ford, David. *The Future of Christian Theology*. Blackwell Manifestos. Oxford: Wiley-Blackwell, 2011.

———. *Self and Salvation: Being Transformed*. Cambridge Studies in Christian Doctrine. Cambridge: Cambridge University Press, 1999.

Frame, John M. *Systematic Theology: An Introduction to Christian Belief*. Phillipsburg, NJ: P&R 2013.

Frank, Karl Suso. "Nachfolge Jesu (II. Alte Kirche und Mittelalter)." In *Theologische Realenzyklopädie*, edited by Gerhard Müller, 686–91. Berlin: Walter de Gruyter, 1994.

Frankl, Viktor E. *Man's Search for Meaning*. London: Rider, 2004.

Freud, Sigmund. *Eine Schwierigkeit der Psychoanalyse (1917)*. Gesammelte Werke: Chronologisch geordnet (Werke aus den Jahren 1917–1920). Vol. 12. Edited by Anna Freud. Frankfurt a. M.: Fischer, 1946.

Fromm, Erich. *Authentisch leben*. Freiburg im Breisgau: Herder, 2017.

Gallagher, Robert L. "'Me and God, We'd Be Mates': Toward an Aussie Contextualized Gospel." *International Bulletin of Missionary Research* 30, no. 3 (2006) 127–32.

Gathercole, Simon J. *Defending Substitution: An Essay on Atonement in Paul*. Acadia Studies in Bible and Theology. Grand Rapids, MI: Baker Academic, 2015.

Gorman, Michael J. "Paul's Corporate, Cruciform, Missional Theosis in 2 Corinthians." In *"In Christ" in Paul: Explorations in Paul's Theology of Union and Participation*, edited by Michael J. Thate et al., 181–210. Tübingen: Mohr Siebeck, 2018.

Gräßer, Erich. *An die Hebräer*. Evangelisch-Katholischer Kommentar zum Neuen Testament. Edited by Rudolf Schnackenburg et al. Vol. 1 of 3. Teilband (Hebr 1–6) Zürich: Benziger, 1990.

Greene-McCreight, Kathryn. *Darkness Is My Only Companion: A Christian Response to Mental Illness*. 2nd ed. Grand Rapids, MI: Brazos, 2015.

Greenwald, Anthony G. "Self-Knowledge and Self-Deception." In *Self-Deception: An Adaptive Mechanism?*, edited by Joan S. Lockard and Delroy L. Paulhus, 113–31. Englewood Cliffs, NJ: Prentice Hall, 1988.

———. "Self-Knowledge and Self-Deception: Further Consideration." In *The Mythomanias: The Nature of Deception and Self-Deception*, edited by Michael S. Myslobodsky, 51–71. Mahwah, NJ: Lawrence Erlbaum, 1997.

Greggs, Tom. *Dogmatic Ecclesiology: The Priestly Catholicity of the Church*. Vol. 1. Grand Rapids, MI: Baker Academic, 2019.

Grenz, Stanley J. *The Social God and the Relational Self: A Trinitarian Theology of the Imago Dei*. Louisville, KY: Westminster John Knox, 2001.

Hahn, Ferdinand. *Theologie des Neuen Testaments (Band 1: Die Vielfalt des Neuen Testaments)*. 3rd ed. Vol. 1 of 2. Tübingen: Mohr Siebeck, 2011.

Hanna, Philippa. *Amazing You: 365 Devotions for Dreamers*. Savage, MN: BroadStreet, 2018.

Harries, Richard. *The Passion in Art*. Ashgate Studies in Theology, Imagination, and the Arts. Aldershot, England: Ashgate, 2004.

Harris, Peter. "Sufficient Grounds for Optimism?: The Relationship Between Perceived Controllability and Optimistic Bias." *Journal of Social and Clinical Psychology* 15, no. 1 (1996) 9–52.

Harvey, John D. *A Commentary on Romans*. Grand Rapids, MI: Kregel, 2019.

Heider, Fritz. *The Psychology of Interpersonal Relations*. New York, NY: Wiley, 1958.

Hendrix, Michael. "Lonely America." *National Review*, March 29, 2018. https://www.nationalreview.com/magazine/2018/04/16/lonely-america/.

Hendrix, Scott H. *Martin Luther: Visionary Reformer*. New Haven, CT: Yale University Press, 2015.

Hengel, Martin. *Crucifixion in the Ancient World and the Folly of the Message of the Cross*. London: SCM, 1977.

Hewstone, Miles, et al. *An Introduction to Social Psychology*. 5th ed. Chichester, West Sussex: BPS Blackwell, 2015.

Higgins, E. T. "Self-Discrepancy: A Theory Relating Self and Affect." *Psychological Review* 94, no. 3 (July 1987) 319–40.

Holl, Karl. "Was verstand Luther unter Religion? (1917)." In *Gesammelte Aufsätze zur Kirchengeschichte*, 1–110. Tübingen: Mohr Siebeck, 1932.

———. *What Did Luther Understand by Religion?* Translated by Fred W. Meuser and Walter R. Wietzke. Philadelphia, PA: Fortress, 1977.

Holt-Lunstad, Julianne. et al. "Loneliness and Social Isolation as Risk Factors for Mortality: A Meta-Analytic Review." *Perspectives on Psychological Science* 10, no. 2 (2015) 227–37.

Horton, Michael Scott. *The Christian Faith: A Systematic Theology for Pilgrims on the Way*. Grand Rapids, MI: Zondervan, 2011.

———. *Christless Christianity: The Alternative Gospel of the American Church*. Grand Rapids, MI: Baker, 2008.

———. *The Gospel-Driven Life: Being Good News People in a Bad News World*. Grand Rapids, MI: Baker 2009.

———. *Ordinary: Sustainable Faith in a Radical, Restless World*. Grand Rapids, MI: Zondervan, 2014.

Hovland, C. Warren. "Anfechtung in Luther's Biblical Exegesis." In *Reformation Studies: Essays in Honor of Roland H. Bainton*, edited by Franklin H. Littell, 46–60. Richmond: John Knox, 1962.

Hurtado, Larry W. *How on Earth Did Jesus Become a God?: Historical Questions About Earliest Devotion to Jesus*. Grand Rapids, MI: Eerdmans, 2005.

———. *One God, One Lord: Early Christian Devotion and Ancient Jewish Monotheism*. Cornerstones Series. 3rd ed. London: Bloomsbury T. & T. Clark, 2015.

Hwang, Tzung-Jeng, et al. "Loneliness and Social Isolation During the Covid-19 Pandemic." *International Psychogeriatrics* 26 (2020) 1–4.

Idleman, Kyle. *Not a Fan: Becoming a Completely Committed Follower of Jesus*. Updated and expanded ed. Grand Rapids, MI: Zondervan, 2016.

Jacoby, Matthew. *Deeper Places: Experiencing God in the Psalms*. Grand Rapids, MI: Baker, 2013.

Jebb, Andrew T., et al. "Happiness, Income Satiation and Turning Points around the World." *Nature Human Behaviour* 2, no. 1 (2018) 33–38.

Jeffery, Steve, et al. *Pierced for Our Transgressions: Rediscovering the Glory of Penal Substitution*. Wheaton, IL: Crossway 2007.

Jenson, Matt. *The Gravity of Sin: Augustine, Luther, and Barth on Homo Incurvatus in Se*. London: T. & T. Clark, 2006.

Johnson, Bill. *Experience the Impossible: Simple Ways to Unleash Heaven's Power on Earth*. Bloomington, MN: Chosen, 2014.

———. *When Heaven Invades Earth: A Practical Guide to a Life of Miracles*. Shippensburg: Treasure House, 2003.

Kahn, Robert L., and Toni C. Antonucci. "Convoys over the Life-Course: Attachment, Roles and Social Support." In *Life-Span Development and Behavior*, edited by Paul B. Baltes and Orville G. Brim, 254–83. New York, NY: Academic, 1980.

Kahneman, Daniel. *Thinking, Fast and Slow*. London: Penguin, 2011.

Kahneman, Daniel, and Angus Deaton. "High Income Improves Evaluation of Life but Not Emotional Well-Being." *PNAS* 21, no. 38 (2010) 16489–493.

Kahneman, Daniel, and Amos Tversky. "Availability: A Heuristic for Judging Frequency and Probability." *Cognitive Psychology* 5, no. 2 (1973) 207–32.

Kai, Lisa. *Perfectly You: Get Set Free from Insecurity and Become Exactly Who God Created You to Be*. New Kensington, PA: Whitaker House, 2017.

Kant, Immanuel. "Beantwortung der Frage: Was ist Aufklärung?" *Berlinische Monatsschrift* 12 (1784) 481–94.

———. *Critique of Pure Reason: A Revised and Expanded Translation Based on Meiklejohn*. Edited by Vasilis Politis. London: Everyman, 1993.

———. *Kritik der reinen Vernuft*. Hamburg: Felix Meiner, 1956.

Kapic, Kelly M. *Embodied Hope: A Theological Meditation on Pain and Suffering*. Downers Grove, IL: IVP, 2017.

Käufer, Stephan. "Jaspers, Limit-Situations, and the Methodological Function of Authenticity." In *Heidegger, Authenticity, and the Self: Themes from Division Two of Being and Time*, edited by Denis McManus, 95–115. London: Routledge, Taylor & Francis Group, 2015.

Keener, Craig S. *Galatians*. New Cambridge Bible Commentary. Cambridge: Cambridge University Press, 2018.

Keller, Timothy. *Blessed Self-Forgetfulness (1 Corinthians 3:21—4:7)*. Leyland: 10Publishing, 2002.

———. *The Freedom of Self-Forgetfulness*. Leyland: 10Publishing, 2012.

———. *Walking With God Through Pain and Suffering*. New York, NY: Dutton, 2013.

Kierkegaard, Søren. *Papers and Journals: A Selection*. Penguin Classics. London: Penguin, 1996.

———. *The Point of View*. Kierkegaard's Writings. Edited by Howard V. Hong and Edna H. Hong. Princeton, NJ: Princeton University Press, 1998.

Kilby, Karen. "Perichoresis and Projection: Problems with Social Doctrines of the Trinity." *New Blackfriars* 81, no. 956 (2000) 432–45.

King, Jonathan. *The Beauty of the Lord: Theology as Aesthetics*. Studies in Historical and Systematic Theology. Bellingham, WA: Lexham, 2018.

Klein, Hans. *Das Lukasevangelium*. Kritisch-Exegetischer Kommentar über das Neue Testament. 10th ed. Vol. 1 of 3. Göttingen: Vandenhoeck & Ruprecht, 2005.

Koessler, John. *True Discipleship: A Companion Guide: The Art of Following Jesus*. Chicago, IL: Moody, 2003.

Kolb, Robert. "Niebuhr's 'Christ and Culture in Paradox' Revisited." *Lutheran Quarterly* 10, no. 3 (1996) 259–79.

Konersmann, Ralf. *Die Unruhe der Welt*. S. Fischer Wissenschaft. Frankfurt am Main: S. Fischer, 2015. doi:9783100383006.

Köstenberger, Andreas J. *John*. Baker Exegetical Commentary on the New Testament. Grand Rapids, MI: Baker Academic, 2004.
Lampe, Kurt. *The Birth of Hedonism: The Cyrenaic Philosophers and Pleasure as a Way of Life*. Princeton, NJ: Princeton University Press, 2015.
Lang, Friedrich. *Die Briefe an die Korinther*. Das Neue Testament Deutsch—Neues Göttinger Bibelwerk. Edited by Peter Stuhlmacher and Hans Weder. Vol. 7. Göttingen: Vandenhoeck & Ruprecht, 1994.
Langer, Ellen J. "The Illusion of Control." *Journal of Personality and Social Psychology* 32, no. 2 (1975) 311–28.
Langer, Ellen J., and Jane Roth. "Heads I Win, Tails It's Chance: The Illusion of Control as a Function of the Sequence of Outcomes in a Purely Chance Task." *Journal of Personality and Social Psychology* 32, no. 6 (1975) 951–55.
Law, David R. "Kenotic Christology." In *The Blackwell Companion to Nineteenth-Century Theology*, edited by David Fergusson, 251–79. Chichester: Wiley-Blackwell.
Lawrence, Joel. *Bonhoeffer: A Guide for the Perplexed*. Guides for the Perplexed. London: T. & T. Clark, 2010.
Lecky, Prescott, and John F. A. Taylor. *Self-Consistency: A Theory of Personality*. New York, NY: Island, 1945.
Lee, Simon S. *Jesus' Transfiguration and the Believers' Transformation: A Study of the Transfiguration and Its Development in Early Christian Writings*. Wissenschaftliche Untersuchungen zum Neuen Testament 2. Reihe. Tübingen: Mohr Siebeck, 2009.
Lészai, Lehel. *Discipleship in the Synoptics*. Leipzig: Evangelische Verlagsanstalt, 2017.
Lewis, C. S. *Prince Caspian: The Return to Narnia*. The Chronicles of Narnia. London: The Folio Society, 1996.
Lewis, Clive Staples. *The Four Loves*. London: Fount Paperbacks, 1977.
———. *The Screwtape Letters*. London: Font, 1977.
Liebendörfer, Bernd. *Der Nachfolge-Gedanke Dietrich Bonhoeffers und seine Potentiale in der Gegenwart*. Stuttgart: Kohlhammer, 2016.
Lippmann, Eric. *Identität im Zeitalter des Chamäleons: Flexibel sein und Farbe bekennen*. 3rd ed. Göttingen: Vandenhoeck & Ruprecht, 2018.
Livingston, James C., and Francis Schüssler Fiorenza. *Modern Christian Thought*. Vol. 2. Rev. ed. Minneapolis, MN: Fortress, 2006.
Lloyd-Jones, D. Martyn. *Spiritual Depression: Its Causes and Cure*. Grand Rapids, MI: Eerdmans, 2003.
Loades, Maria Elizabeth, et al. "Rapid Systematic Review: The Impact of Social Isolation and Loneliness on the Mental Health of Children and Adolescents in the Context of Covid-19." *Journal of the American Academy of Child and Adolescent Psychiatry* 59, no. 11 (2020) 1218–39.
Loewenich, Walther von. *Luther's Theology of the Cross*. Translated by Herbert J. A. Bouman. Belfast: Christian Journals 1976.
Lundgaard, Kris. *Through the Looking Glass: Reflections on Christ That Change Us*. Phillipsburg, NJ: P&R, 2000.
Luther, Martin. *Der Galaterbrief*. D. Martin Luthers Epistel-Auslegung. Edited by Hermann Kleinknecht. 2nd ed. Vol. 4. Göttingen: Vandenhoeck & Ruprecht, 1987.
———. *Letters of Spiritual Counsel*. Translated by Theodore G. Tappert. Vancouver: Regent College, 2003.
———. *Luther's Correspondence and Other Contemporary Letters*. Translated and edited by Preserved Smith and Charles M. Jacobs. Philadelphia, PA: Lutheran Publication Society, 1918.

———. *Zweiter Teil: Das Matthäus-Evangelium (Kap. 3–25)*. D. Martin Luthers Evangelien-Auslegung. Edited by Erwin Mühlhaupt. 4th ed. Göttingen: Vandenhoeck & Ruprecht, 1973.

Luz, Ulrich. *Das Evangelium nach Matthäus*. Evangelisch-Katholischer Kommentar zum Neuen Testament. Edited by Rudolf Schnackenburg, et al. Vol. 1 (2. Teilband, Mt 8–17). Zürich und Braunschweig: Benziger Verlag AG, 1990.

———. "Nachfolge Jesu (I. Neues Testament)." In *Theologische Realenzyklopädie*, edited by Gerhard Müller, 678–86. Berlin: Walter de Gruyter, 1994.

Maaz, Hans-Joachim. *Die narzisstische Gesellschaft: Ein Psychogramm*. München: C. H. Beck, 2012.

Macaskill, Grant. *Living in Union with Christ: Paul's Gospel and Christian Moral Identity*. Grand Rapids, MI: BakerAcademic, 2019.

MacCulloch, Diarmaid. *Silence: A Christian History*. New York, NY: Viking, 2013.

Macleod, Donald. *Christ Crucified: Understanding the Atonement*. Downers Grove, IL: InterVarsity 2014.

———. *The Person of Christ*. Contours of Christian Theology. Downers Grove, IL: InterVarsity, 1998.

Macvean, Mary. "For Many People, Gathering Possessions is Just the Stuff of Life." *Los Angeles Times*, March 21, 2014. https://www.latimes.com/health/la-xpm-2014-mar-21-la-he-keeping-stuff-20140322-story.html.

Mann, Thomas. *Buddenbrooks*. Translated by H. T. Lowe-Porter. New York, NY: Vintage International, 1992.

———. *Die Buddenbrooks*. Frankfurt am Main: Fischer Taschenbuch Verlag, 2007.

Markus, Hazel, and Zivi Kunda. "Stability and Malleability of the Self-Concept." *Journal of Personality and Social Psychology* 51, no. 4 (October 1986) 858–66.

Markus, Hazel, and Paula Nurius. "Possible Selves." *American Psychologist* 41, no. 9 (1986) 954–69.

Markus, Hazel, and Elissa Wurf. "The Dynamic Self-Concept: A Social Psychological Perspective." *Annual Review of Psychology* 38 (1987) 299–337.

McCall, Thomas H. *Against God and Nature: The Doctrine of Sin*. Foundations of Evangelical Theology Series. Wheaton, IL: Crossway, 2019.

McCormack, Bruce. "Kenoticism in Modern Christology." In *The Oxford Handbook of Christology*, edited by Francesca Aran Murphy, 444–57. Oxford: Oxford University Press, 2015.

McGrath, Alister E. *Iustitia Dei: A History of the Christian Doctrine of Justification*. 2nd ed. Cambridge: Cambridge University Press, 1998.

———. *The Making of Modern German Christology 1750–1990*. 2nd ed. Eugene, OR: Wipf & Stock, 1994.

McKinley, John E. *Tempted for Us: Theological Models and the Practical Relevance of Christ's Impeccability and Temptation*. Colorado Springs, CO: Paternoster, 2009.

McKirdy, Euan. "The Crux of the Matter: The Filipinos Crucified on Good Friday." https://edition.cnn.com/2016/03/25/asia/philippines-easter-good-friday-crucifixion/index.html.

McLoughlin, William Gerald, Jr. *Modern Revivalism: Charles Grandison Finney to Billy Graham*. Reprint ed. Eugene, OR: Wipf & Stock, 2005.

Melanchthon, Philipp. *Loci Communes: 1521; Lateinisch und Deutsch*. Translated by Horst Georg Pöhlmann. Gütersloh: Mohn, 1993.

Migliore, Daniel L. *Faith Seeking Understanding: An Introduction to Christian Theology*. 3rd ed. Grand Rapids, MI: Eerdmans, 2014.

Moltmann, Jürgen. *Kirche in der Kraft des Geistes: Ein Beitrag zur messianischen Ekklesiologie*. Gütersloh: Gütersloher Verlagshaus, 1975.

———. *The Trinity and the Kingdom of God*. Translated by Margret Kohl. London: SCM, 1981.

Moo, Douglas J. *Galatians*. Baker Exegetical Commentary on the New Testament. Grand Rapids, MI: Baker Academic, 2013.

Moore, Christopher. *Socrates and Self-Knowledge*. Cambridge: Cambridge University Press, 2015.

Mor, Nilly, and Jennifer Winquist. "Self-Focused Attention and Negative Affect: A Meta-Analysis." *Psychological Bulletin* 128, no. 4 (2002) 638–62.

Moreland, James Porter. "About Love Your God With All Your Mind." http://www.jpmoreland.com/books/with-all-your-mind/.

———. *Love Your God with All Your Mind: The Role of Reason in the Life of the Soul*. Rev. ed. Colorado Springs, CO: NavPress, 2012.

Morris, Leon. *The Gospel According to Matthew*. The Pillar New Testament Commentary. Edited by D. A. Carson. Grand Rapids, MI: Eerdmans 1992.

Mounstephen, Philip. "Bishop of Truro's Independent Review for the Foreign Secretary of FCO Support for Persecuted Christians: Final Report and Recommendations." July 4, 2019. https://christianpersecutionreview.org.uk/report/.

Mueller, John H. "Self-Awareness and Access to Material Rated as Self-Descriptive or Nondescriptive." *Bulletin of the Psychonomic Society* 19, no. 6 (1982) 323–26.

Müller, Jac J. *The Epistles of Paul to the Philippians and to Philemon*. The New International Commentary on the New Testament. Grand Rapids, MI: Eerdmans, 1955.

Muller, Robert T. "What Can Minimalism Do for Mental Health?" https://www.psychologytoday.com/au/blog/talking-about-trauma/201902/what-can-minimalism-do-mental-health.

Mummendey, Hans Dieter. *Psychologie des "Selbst": Theorien, Methoden und Ergebnisse der Selbstkonzeptforschung*. Göttingen: Hogrefe, 2006.

Myers, David G. *The Inflated Self: Human Illusions and the Biblical Call to Hope*. New York, NY: Seabury, 1980.

National Institutes of Health. "Opioid Overdose Crisis." *National Institute on Drug Abuse*, March 11, 2021. https://nida.nih.gov/research-topics/opioids/opioid-overdose-crisis.

Nehamas, Alexander. *On Friendship*. New York: Basic, 2016.

Nelson, Peter K. "Discipleship Dissonance: Toward a Theology of Imperfection Amidst the Pursuit of Holiness." *Journal of Spiritual Formation and Soul Care* 4, no. 1 (2011) 63–92.

Newbigin, Lesslie. *Foolishness to the Greeks: The Gospel and Western Culture*. Grand Rapids, MI: Eerdmans, 1986.

Nickerson, Raymond S. "Confirmation Bias: A Ubiquitous Phenomenon in Many Guises." *Review of General Psychology* 2, no. 2 (1998) 175–220.

Niebuhr, H. Richard. *Christ and Culture*. New York, NY: Harper, 1951.

Nisbett, Richard E., and Timothy D. Wilson. "The Halo Effect: Evidence for Unconscious Alteration of Judgments." *Journal of Personality and Social Psychology* 35, no. 4 (1977) 250–56.

Nolen-Hoeksema, Susan. "The Role of Rumination in Depressive Disorders and Mixed Anxiety/Depressive Symptoms." *Journal of Abnormal Psychology* 109, no. 3 (2000) 504–11.

Noll, Mark A. *The Scandal of the Evangelical Mind*. Grand Rapids, MI: Eerdmans, 1994.

Nolland, John. *Luke 9:21—18:34*. Word Biblical Commentary. Edited by Ralph P. Martin. Vol. 35b. Nashville, TN: Thomas Nelson, 1993.

Norwich, Julian of. *Revelations of Divine Love: The Short Text and the Long Text*. New York, NY: Oxford University Press, 2015.

Nuttin, Jozef M. "Narcissism Beyond Gestalt and Awareness: The Name Letter Effect." *European Journal of Social Psychology* 15, no. 3 (1985) 353–61.

Oberman, Heiko Augustinus. *Luther: Man Between God and the Devil*. New Haven, CT: Yale University Press, 1989.

O'Donovan, Oliver. *Entering into Rest*. Ethics as Theology. Vol. 3. Grand Rapids, MI: Eerdmans, 2017.

———. *Finding and Seeking*. Ethics as Theology. Vol. 2. Grand Rapids, MI: Eerdmans, 2014.

Ohrnberger, Julius, et al. "The Relationship Between Physical and Mental Health: A Mediation Analysis." *Social Science and Medicine* 195 (2017) 42–49.

Olson, J. K. *Irreplaceable You: Bravely Living in the Skin You're In*. Franklin, TN: Worthy, 2017.

Open Doors. "Christian Persecution." https://www.opendoorsusa.org/christian-persecution/.

Opitz, Peter, and Ernst Saxer, eds. *Zwingli lesen: Zentrale Texte des Zürcher Reformators in heutigem Deutsch*. 2nd ed. Zürich: Theologischer Verlag Zürich, 2019.

Osteen, Joel. *Become a Better You: 7 Keys to Improving Your Life Every Day*. Anniversary ed. New York, NY: Howard, 2017.

———. *You Can, You Will: 8 Undeniable Qualities of a Winner*. New York, NY: Faith Words, 2014.

———. *Your Best Life Now: 7 Steps to Living at Your Full Potential*. Rev. and expanded ed. New York, NY: FaithWords, 2015.

Osteen, Victoria. *Exceptional You!: 7 Ways to Live Encouraged, Empowered, and Intentional*. New York, NY: Faith Words, 2019.

Otten, Willemien. *Augustine Our Contemporary: Examining the Self in Past and Present*. Notre Dame, IN: University of Notre Dame Press, 2018.

Owen, John, et al. *Overcoming Sin and Temptation*. Wheaton, IL: Crossway, 2006.

Oyserman, Daphna, et al. "Self, Self-Concept, and Identity." In *Handbook of Self and Identity*, edited by Markus R. Leary and June Price Tangney, 69–104. New York, NY: Guilford, 2012.

Pannenberg, Wolfhart. "Identität und Wiedergeburt." In *Identität*, edited by Odo Marquard and Karlheinz Stierle, 607–11. München: Wilhelm Fink, 1996.

Pax CSPB. "Kapitel 4—Die Werkzeuge der geistlichen Kunst." http://benediktiner.benediktiner.de/index.php/die-geistliche-kunst-2/die-werkeuge-der-geistlichen-kunst.html.

———. "Kapitel 33—Eigenbesitz des Mönches: Regula Benedicti—Kapitel 33.3." http://www.benediktiner.de/index.php/zur-organisation-des-klosters-2/eigenbesitz-des-moenches-rb.html.

———. "Regula Benedicti—Kapitel 58.26/27." http://www.benediktiner.de/index.php/die-aufnahme-ordnung-2/aufnahmeordnung-von-bruedern-rb.html.

Peale, Norman Vincent. *You Can If You Think You Can*. Palmer, AK: Fireside, 1987.

Pennington, Jonathan T. *The Sermon on the Mount and Human Flourishing: A Theological Commentary*. Grand Rapids, MI: Baker Academic, 2017.

Peppiatt, Lucy. *The Disciple: On Becoming Truly Human*. Eugene, OR: Cascade, 2012.
Peterson, Eugene H. *A Long Obedience in the Same Direction: Discipleship in an Instant Society*. Downers Grove, IL: IVP, 2019.
———. *Practice Resurrection: A Conversation on Growing Up in Christ*. London: Hodder & Stoughton, 2011.
Peterson, Jordan B. *12 Rules for Life: An Antidote to Chaos*. Toronto: Random House Canada, 2018.
Piper, John. *The Dangerous Duty of Delight*. Sisters, OR: Multnomah, 2001.
———. *The Hidden Smile of God: The Fruit of Affliction in the Lives of John Bunyan, William Cowper, and David Brainerd*. The Swans Are Not Silent. Wheaton, IL: Crossway, 2001.
Placher, William C. *The Domestication of Transcendence: How Modern Thinking About God Went Wrong*. Louisville, KY: Westminster John Knox, 1996.
Plantinga, Cornelius. *Not the Way It's Supposed to Be: A Breviary of Sin*. Grand Rapids, MI: Eerdmans, 1995.
Plasger, Georg, and Heinz-Günther Stobbe, eds. *Gewalt gegen Christen: Formen, Gründe, Hintergründe*. Leipzig: Evangelische Verlagsanstalt, 2014.
Podmore, Simon D. *Struggling with God: Kierkegaard and the Temptation of Spiritual Trial*. Cambridge: James Clarke & Co, 2013.
Precht, Richard David. *Who Am I? And If So, How Many? A Philosophical Journey*. Translated by Shelley Frisch. New York, NY: Spiegel & Grau, 2011.
Purves, Andrew. *The Crucifixion of Ministry: Surrendering Our Ambitions to the Service of Christ*. Downers Grove, IL: IVP, 2007.
———. *Reconstructing Pastoral Theology: A Christological Foundation*. Louisville, KY: Westminster John Knox, 2004.
Reddie, Mark. "Australia on Brink of Prescription Painkiller Epidemic, Doctors Say." *ABC News*, May 13, 2018. https://www.abc.net.au/news/2018-15-13/australia-on-brink-of-prescription-painkiller-epidemic/9753506.
Reimer, David J. "Biblical Perspectives on Consumerism." *Scottish Bulletin of Evangelical Theology* 35, no. 1 (2017) 4–18.
Richards, Blake A., and Paul W. Frankland. "The Persistence and Transience of Memory." *Neuron* 94, no. 6 (2017) 1071–84.
Riches, John K. "Nachfolge Jesu (Iii. Von der Reformation bis zur Gegenwart)." In *Theologische Realenzyklopädie*, edited by Gerhard Müller, 691–701. Berlin: Walter de Gruyter, 1994.
Richmond, James. *Ritschl, a Reappraisal: A Study in Systematic Theology*. London: Collins, 1978.
Rievaulx, Aelred of. *Spiritual Friendship*. Translated by Mary Eugenia Laker. Kalamazoo, MI: Cistercian, 1977.
Ritschl, Albrecht. *The Christian Doctrine of Justification and Reconciliation*. Translated by Hugh R. Mackintosh and A. B. Macaulay. Edinburgh: T. & T. Clark, 1900.
Rittgers, Ronald K. *The Reformation of Suffering: Pastoral Theology and Lay Piety in Late Medieval and Early Modern Germany*. Oxford Studies in Historical Theology. Oxford: Oxford University Press, 2012.
Roelofs, Jeffrey, et al. "Effects of Neuroticism on Depression and Anxiety: Rumination as a Possible Mediator." *Personality and Individual Differences* 44, no. 3 (2008) 576–86.
Rosner, Brian S., and Jonathan Lunde. *Known by God: A Biblical Theology of Personal Identity*. Biblical Theology for Life. Grand Rapids, MI: Zondervan, 2017.

Ross, Michael, and Michael Conway. "Remembering One's Own Past: The Construction of Personal Histories." In *Handbook of Motivation and Cognition: Foundations of Social Behavior*, edited by Richard M. Sorrentino and E. Tory Higgins, 122–44. New York: Guilford, 1986.

Rothbaum, Fred, et al. "Changing the World and Changing the Self: A Two-Process Model of Perceived Control." *Journal of Personality and Social Psychology* 42, no. 1 (1982) 5–37.

Ruppert, Fidelis. *Geistlich Kämpfen lernen: Benediktinische Lebenskunst für den Alltag*. 2nd ed. Münsterschwarzach: Vier-Türme GmbH Verlag, 2012.

Saunders, Anna, and Debbie Pinfold, eds. *Remembering and Rethinking the GDR: Multiple Perspectives and Plural Authenticities*. Palgrave Macmillan Memory Studies. Houndmills: Palgrave Macmillan, 2013.

Schaff, Philip, ed. *The Greek and Latin Creeds with Translations*. 6th ed. Vol. 2. The Creeds of Christendom: With a History and Critical Notes. Grand Rapids, MI: Baker, 1996.

Schäufele, Wolf-Dietrich. "Luther as Church Father." In *Martin Luther: A Christian Between Reforms and Modernity (1517–2017)*, edited by Alberto Melloni, 109–22. Boston, MA: Walter de Gruyter, 2017.

Schlatter, Adolf. *Aus meiner Sprechstunde*. Third ed. Bethel: Verlagshandlung der Anstalt Bethel, 1952.

———. "Christi Versöhnen und Christi Vergeben." In *Der Einzige und Wir Anderen*, 188–207. Velbert: Freizeiten-Verlag, 1929.

———. *Das christliche Dogma*. 2nd ed. Stuttgart: Calwer, 1923.

———. *Das Evangelium des Lukas: Aus seinen Quellen erklärt*. Stuttgart: Calwer Vereinsbuchhandlung, 1931.

———. "Der Dienst des Christen in der älteren Dogmatik." *Beiträge zur Förderung Christlicher Theologie* 1 (1897).

———. *Der Evangelist Matthäus: Seine Sprache, sein Ziel, seine Selbständigkeit*. Stuttgart: Calwer Vereinsbuchhandlung, 1929.

———. *Der Glaube im Neuen Testament*. 6th ed. Stuttgart: Calwer, 1982.

———. "Der Wert und Unwert Unseres Wissens." *Monatsschrift für Pastoraltheologie* 28 (1932) 259–65.

———. *Die Dienstpflicht des Christen in der apostolischen Gemeinde*. Stuttgart: Quell-Verlag der Ev. Gesellschaft, 1929.

———. *The History of the Christ: The Foundation of New Testament Theology*. Translated by Andreas J. Köstenberger. Grand Rapids, MI: Baker, 1997.

———. "Jesu Gottheit und das Kreuz." *Beiträge zur Förderung christlicher Theologie* 5, no. 5 (1913).

———. *Markus: Der Evangelist für die Griechen*. Stuttgart: Calwer Vereinsbuchhandlung, 1935.

———. "Noch ein Wort über den Christlichen Dienst." *Beiträge zur Förderung christlicher Theologie* 9, no. 6 (1905) 47–83.

Schlingensiepen, Ferdinand. *Dietrich Bonhoeffer, 1906–1945: Martyr, Thinker, Man of Resistance*. Translated by Isabel Best. London: T. & T. Clark, 2010.

Schmeller, Thomas. *Der Zweite Brief an die Korinther (Teilband 1, 2Kor 1,1–7,4)*. Evangelisch-Katholischer Kommentar zum Neuen Testament. Edited by Ulrich Luz et al. 2 vols. Neukirchen-Vluyn: Neukirchener Theologie, 2010.

Schmitz, Florian. *"Nachfolge": Zur Theologie Dietrich Bonhoeffers.* Forschungen zur Systematischen und Ökumenischen Theologie. Göttingen; Bristol, CT: Vandenhoeck & Ruprecht, 2013.

Schrage, Wolfgang. *Der Erste Brief an die Korinther (1. Teilband, 1Kor 1,1–6-6,11).* Evangelisch-Katholischer Kommentar zum Neuen Testament. Edited by Rudolf Schnackenburg et al. Zürich: Benziger, 1991.

Schreiner, Thomas R. *Romans.* Baker Exegetical Commentary on the New Testament. Grand Rapids, MI: Baker 1998.

Schürmann, Heinz. *Das Lukasevangelium (Erster Teil).* Herders Theologischer Kommentar zum Neuen Testament. Edited by Alfred Wikenhauser et al. Freiburg: Herder, 1984.

Schwarz, Norbert, et al. "Ease of Retrieval as Information: Another Look at the Availability Heuristic." *Journal of Personality and Social Psychology* 61, no. 2 (1991) 195–202.

Schwöbel, Christoph. "Christology and Trinitarian Thought." In *Trinitarian Theology Today*, edited by Christoph Schwöbel, 113–46. Edinburgh: T. & T. Clark, 1995.

Seltzer, Leon F. "Self-Absorption: The Root of All (Psychological) Evil?" Psychology Today. https://www.psychologytoday.com/au/blog/evolution-the-self/201608/self-absorption-the-root-all-psychological-evil.

Shakespeare, William. *Hamlet: Text of the Play, the Actors' Gallery, Contexts, Criticism, Afterlives, Resources.* A Norton Critical Ed. New York. NY: W. W. Norton & Co., 2011.

Silva, Moisés. *Philippians.* Baker Exegetical Commentary on the New Testament. 2nd ed. Grand Rapids, MI: Baker Academic, 2005.

Smith, Christian, and Melinda Lundquist Denton. *Soul Searching: The Religious and Spiritual Lives of American Teenagers.* New York: Oxford University Press, 2005.

Smith, David Oliver. *Matthew, Mark, Luke, and Paul: The Influence of the Epistles on the Synoptic Gospels.* Eugene, OR: Wipf & Stock, 2011.

Snodgrass, Klyne R. *Who God Says You Are: A Christian Understanding of Identity.* Grand Rapids, MI: Eerdmans, 2018.

Soulen, R. Kendall. *The Divine Name(s) and the Holy Trinity.* Louisville, KY: Westminster John Knox 2011.

Spurgeon, Charles Haddon. *Lectures to My Students.* Grand Rapids, MI: Zondervan, 1979.

Spurrier, William A. *A Guide to the Christian Faith.* New York: Scribner, 1952.

Stöhr, Martin. "Bonhoeffer Antworten—Nicht Feiern!" *Junge Kirche* 56, no. 4 (1995) 194.

Stolz, Jörg, et al. *Religion und Spiritualität in der Ich-Gesellschaft: Vier Gestalten des (Un) Glaubens.* Beiträge zur Pastoralsoziologie (Spi-Reihe). Zürich: Edition NZN bei TVZ, 2014.

Storr, Will. *Selfie: How We Became So Self-Obsessed and What It's Doing to Us.* London: Picador, 2017.

Stott, John R. W. *The Cross of Christ.* 2nd ed. Downers Grove, IL: IVP, 1989.

———. *The Radical Disciple: Wholehearted Christian Living.* Downers Grove, IL: IVP 2010.

———. *Your Mind Matters: The Place of the Mind in the Christian Life.* London: InterVarsity, 1973.

Strobel, Kyle. *Formed for the Glory of God: Learning from the Spiritual Practices of Jonathan Edwards.* Downers Grove, IL: IVP, 2013.

Stuhlmacher, Peter. *Der Brief an die Römer.* Das Neue Testament Deutsch—Neues Göttinger Bibelwerk. Edited by Peter Stuhlmacher and Hans Weder. Vol. 6. Göttingen: Vandenhoeck & Ruprecht, 1998.

Suess, Franziska, and Rasha Abdel Rahman. "Mental Imagery of Emotions: Electrophysiological Evidence." *NeuroImage* 114 (2015) 147–57.

Swaminathan, Nikhil. "Why Does the Brain Need So Much Power?" *Scientific American*, 2008. https://www.scientificamerican.com/article/why-does-the-brain-need-s/.

Sweeney, Tanya. "Happy 60th birthday to Madonna, the Queen of Reinvention." *The Independent* (Ireland), August 12, 2018. https://www.independent.ie/entertainment/music/happy-60th-birthday-to-madonna-the-queen-of-reinvention-how-she-continues-to-pave-the-way-for-women-everywhere-37201633.html.

Talaifar, Sanaz, and William Swann. "Self and Identity." *Oxford Research Encyclopedia of Psychology* (2018). Oxford Research Encyclopedias. https://oxfordre.com/view/10.1093/acrefore/9780190236557.001.0001/acrefore-9780190236557-e-242.

Talbert, Charles H. *Romans.* Smyth & Helwys Bible Commentary. Macon, GA: Smyth & Helwys, 2002.

Tauler, Johann. *Von der Nachfolge des armen Lebens Jesu Christi.* Regensburg: Verlag von Georg Joseph Manz, 1855.

Taylor, Shelley E. *Positive Illusions: Creative Self-Deception and the Healthy Mind.* New York, NY: Basic, 1989.

———. *The Tending Instinct: How Nurturing Is Essential to Who We Are and How We Live.* New York, NY: Holt, 2002.

Taylor, Shelley E., et al. "Biobehavioral Responses to Stress in Females: Tend-and-Befriend, Not Fight-or-Flight." *Psychological Review* 107, no. 3 (2000) 411–29.

———. "Psychological Resources, Positive Illusions, and Health." *American Psychologist* 55, no. 1 (Jan 2000) 99–109.

Taylor, Shelley E., and Jonathon D. Brown. "Illusion and Well-Being: A Social Psychological Perspective on Mental Health." *Psychological Bulletin* 103, no. 2 (1988) 193–210.

Taylor, Shelley E., and Marci Lobel. "Social Comparison Activity Under Threat: Downward Evaluation and Upward Contacts." *Psychological Review* 96, no. 4 (1989) 569–75.

Tedeschi, Richard G., and Bret A. Moore. *The Posttraumatic Growth Workbook: Coming through Trauma Wiser, Stronger, and More Resilient.* Oakland, CA: New Harbinger, 2016.

Thielman, Frank. *Romans.* Zondervan Exegetical Commentary on the New Testament. Grand Rapids, MI: Zondervan, 2018.

Tierney, John, and Roy F. Baumeister. *The Power of Bad: How the Negativity Effect Rules Us and How We Can Rule It.* New York, NY: Allen Lane, 2019.

Tietz, Christiane. *Theologian of Resistance: The Life and Thought of Dietrich Bonhoeffer.* Translated by Victoria Barnett. Minneapolis, MN: Fortress 2016.

Trivedi, Madhukar H. "The Link Between Depression and Physical Symptoms." *Primary Care Companion to the Journal of Clinical Psychiatry* 6, no. S1 (2004) 12–16.

Trueman, Carl R. *The Real Scandal of the Evangelical Mind.* Chicago, IL: Moody, 2011.

Turner, Léon. *Theology, Psychology, and the Plural Self.* Ashgate Science and Religion Series. Burlington, VT: Ashgate, 2008.

Twenge, Jean M., and W. Keith Campbell. *The Narcissism Epidemic: Living in the Age of Entitlement.* New York, NY: Atria, 2013.

Valentine, Leigh. *Successfully You: Reversing Your Misfortune*. Shippensburg, PA: Destiny Image, 2008.
Vandermeersch, Patrick. "Self-Flagellation in the Early Modern Era." In *The Sense of Suffering: Constructions of Physical Pain in Early Modern Culture*, edited by Jan Frans van Dijkhuizen and Karl A. E. Enenkel, 253–66. Leiden: Brill, 2009.
Vassilopoulos, Stephanos P. "Social Anxiety and Ruminative Self-Focus." *Journal of Anxiety Disorders* 22, no. 5 (2008) 860–67.
Vlastuin, Willem van. *Be Renewed: A Theology of Personal Renewal*. Reformed Historical Theology. Edited by Herman J. Selderhuis. Vol. 26. Göttingen: Vandenhoeck & Ruprecht, 2014.
Volf, Miroslav. *After Our Likeness: The Church as the Image of the Trinity*. Sacra Doctrina. Grand Rapids, MI: Eerdmans, 1998.
Volpe, Medi Ann. *Rethinking Christian Identity: Doctrine and Discipleship*. Malden, MA: J. Wiley, 2013.
Voorwinde, Stephen. *Jesus' Emotions in the Gospels*. London: T. & T. Clark, 2011.
Wahlde, Urban C., von. *Gnosticism, Docetism, and the Judaisms of the First Century: The Search for the Wider Context of the Johannine Literature and Why It Matters*. London: Bloomsbury T. & T. Clark, 2015.
Warfield, Benjamin B. "On the Emotional Life of Our Lord (1912)." In *The Person and Work of Christ*, 93–145. Philadelphia, PA: Presbyterian and Reformed, 1950.
Watkins, Ed, and John D. Teasdale. "Adaptive and Maladaptive Self-Focus in Depression." *Journal of Affective Disorders* 82, no. 1 (2004) 1–8.
Webber, Rebecca. "Reinvent Yourself." *PsychologyToday*, May 6, 2014. https://www.psychologytoday.com/us/articles/201405/reinvent-yourself.
Webster, John. "Discipleship and Calling." *Scottish Bulletin of Evangelical Theology* 23, no. 2 (2005) 133–47.
———. "Discipleship and Obedience." *Scottish Bulletin of Evangelical Theology* 24, no. 1 (2006) 4–18.
Weder, Hans. "Der Lebensraum des Zweifels." In *Anfechtung*, edited by Stefan Berg Pierre Bühler et al. Hermeneutische Untersuchungen zur Theologie, 17–32. Tübingen: Mohr Siebeck, 2016.
Wiener, Gary, ed. *Microaggressions, Safe Spaces, and Trigger Warnings*. Current Controversies. New York: Greenhaven, 2018.
Weinhardt, Joachim. *Wilhelm Herrmanns Stellung in der rischlschen Schule*. Tübingen: J. C. B. Mohr, 1996.
Weinstein, Neil D. "Unrealistic Optimism About Future Life Events." *Journal of Personality and Social Psychology* 39, no. 5 (1980) 806–20.
Welker, Michael. "Barth's 'Tambacher Vortrag' und Bonhoeffers 'Tiefe Diesseitigkeit': Bahnbrechende Impulse für Kirche und Gesellschaft noch heute." *Evangelische Theologie* 79, no. 4 (2019) 246–57.
———. *Quests for Freedom: Biblical, Historical, Contemporary*. 2nd ed. Eugene, OR: Cascade, 2019.
———. "Selbst-Säkularisierung und Selbst-Banalisierung: Verfallen die Christlichen Kirchen im 21. Jahrhundert?" *Brennpunkt Gemeinde* 1 (2001) 15–21.
Wells, David F. *Above All Earthly Pow'rs: Christ in a Postmodern World*. Grand Rapids, MI: Eerdmans 2005.
Wellum, Stephen J. "Heaven in Paul's Letters." In *Heaven*, edited by Christopher W. Morgan and Robert A. Patterson, 83–109. Wheaton, IL: Crossway, 2014.

Wengst, Klaus. *Das Johannesevangelium.* Theologischer Kommentar zum Neuen Testament. Edited by Ekkehard W. Stegemann et al. Stuttgart: Kohlhammer, 2019.

Wilhite, David E. *The Gospel According to Heretics: Discovering Orthodoxy through Early Christological Conflicts.* Grand Rapids, MI: Baker Academic, 2015.

Willard, Dallas. *Renovation of the Heart: Putting on the Character of Christ.* Leicester: Inter-Varsity, 2002.

Williams, Rowan. *Being Disciples: Essentials of the Christian Life.* London: SPCK, 2016.

Wills, Thomas A. "Downward Comparison Principles in Social Psychology." *Psychological Bulletin* 90, no. 2 (1981) 245–71.

Wilson, John Elbert. *Introduction to Modern Theology: Trajectories in the German Tradition.* Louisville, KY: Westminster John Knox 2007.

Wilson, Timothy D. *Strangers to Ourselves: Discovering the Adaptive Unconscious.* Cambridge, MA: Belknap, 2002.

Wirth, Mathias. *Distanz des Gehorsams: Theorie, Ethik und Kritik einer Tugend.* Religion in Philosophy and Theology. Tübingen: Mohr Siebeck, 2016.

Wirtz, Markus Antonius, and Janina Strohmer. *Dorsch: Lexikon der Psychologie.* 18th ed. Bern: Hogrefe, 2017.

Witherington, Ben. *Matthew.* Smyth and Helwys Bible Commentary. Macon, GA: Smyth & Helwys 2006.

Witten, Marsha Grace. *All Is Forgiven: The Secular Message in American Protestantism.* Princeton, NJ: Princeton University Press, 1993.

Wortley, John. *The "Anonymous" Sayings of the Desert Fathers: A Select Edition and Complete English Translation.* New York, NY: Cambridge University Press, 2013.

Wright, N. T. *Pauline Perspectives: Essays on Paul, 1978–2013.* London: SPCK, 2013.

Yeginsu, Ceylan. "U. K. Appoints a Minister for Loneliness." *New York Times,* January 17, 2018. https://www.nytimes.com/2018/01/17/world/europe/uk-britain-loneliness.html.

Zachhuber, Johannes. "Jesus Christ in Martin Luther's Theology." In *The Oxford Research Encyclopedia of Martin Luther.* http://religion.oxfordre.com/view/10.1093/acrefore/9780199340378.001.0001/acrefore-9780199340378-e-327?rskey=EUuQ2C&result=2.

Zachman, Randall C. "'Deny Yourself and Take up Your Cross': John Calvin on the Christian Life." *International Journal of Systematic Theology* 11, no. 4 (2009) 466–82.

Zajonc, Robert B., et al. "Convergence in the Physical Appearance of Spouses." *Motivation and Emotion* 11, no. 4 (1987) 335–48.

Zimmermann, Jens. "Dietrich Bonhoeffer: The Question of Christian Identity." In *Sources of the Christian Self: A Cultural History of Christian Identity,* edited by James M. Houston and Jens Zimmermann. Grand Rapids, MI: Eerdmans, 2018.

Subject Index

Adam
    being in, 49, 51, 55
    old Adam, 55, 55nn36–37, 57, 72
    temptation of, 108
affirmation in spiritual friendship,
    169–70
Althaus, Paul, 54, 56n39, 56n43, 58n48
Anfechtung, 105, 109
antinomianism, 12, 72
Antonucci, Toni, 167
Apology to the Augsburg Confession,
    171–72
Arianism, 18–19
Asian cultures, 39n44
Athanasian Creed, 16
atonement, 24–25, 93–94, 94n71
Augustine of Hippo, 35
Australia, 14, 80, 142, 157
authenticity, 3, 44–45, 44n86, 53
authoritative call, 21, 135, 137–38
autobiography genre, 39n44
autonomy, 139
availability heuristic, 10n8

baptism, 47–50, 56, 95, 199
Barnabas, 168
Barr, James, 14n31
Barth, Karl
    being in Adam, 55
    and contemplation, 189
    on discipleship, 7, 147–48, 149n68

    encountering Christ, 26
    exaltation and humiliation, 184–85
    and following, 135–36, 138, 139,
        140, 140n21
    God as wholly other, 17n46
    and grace, 151
    and obedience, 146n53
    and relationships, 144
    and renunciation, 141n29
    and self-knowledge, 68, 68n29
    and surrender, 126
    and temptation, 94, 108
Bastian, Brock, 14n30, 80–81
Bauckham, Richard, 22
Bauer, Jack J., 74
Baumeister, Roy F., 39, 41–43
Bayer, Hans F., 67, 83
Bayer, Oswald, 7–8n21, 55n37
bearing fruit, 124
Becker, Peter, 74
befriending the world, 176–80
Being Disciples (Williams), 169
Beintker, Horst, 109n55
Benedict XVI (pope), 163
Bentham, Jeremy, 80n4
Bethge, Eberhard, 26, 45n87, 112,
    168–69
better-than-average effect, 40
biblical witness, 42
Bird, Michael F., 50n15
Bloom, Matt, 74n56, 75

SUBJECT INDEX

Bockmuehl, Markus, 22, 22n70
Bøe, Sverre, 83, 83n25, 84n26, 104, 126n39
Boersma, Hans, 183n2, 187n20
Bonhoeffer, Dietrich
   atonement, 93–94n71
   baptism, 49, 56
   bearing the suffering of the world, 98–99
   befriending the world, 177–80, 178n104
   being extraordinary, 155n89
   being in Adam, 51n18
   call to discipleship, 135–36, 135n3, 138, 148, 151n75
   cheap grace, 5n14, 12, 12n22
   Christothentic identity, 52
   communal self-denial, 71n41
   Confessing Church movement, 114–15
   confession, 172–73
   costly grace, 54
   death of old self, 139, 139n20
   on discipleship, 6–7, 64–65, 69, 149
   discipline, 61n2
   fellowship of the disciples, 113
   fellowship through suffering, 118n15, 119–20, 120n21, 174n87, 175
   forgiveness, 170n60, 171, 171n62
   God acting for us (*pro nobis*), 88, 88n46
   godforsakenness, 109, 109n52, 112
   inspired love for others, 161–62
   on Jesus Christ, 17, 17n47, 18, 183, 185–87, 185n8, 188
   Jesus's humanity, 87, 87n43
   and Kierkegaard, 138n15
   letting go of intimate relationships, 145
   on love, 75
   loving God and neighbor, 152–56, 152n79
   on obedience, 65n16, 146n53
   opposition and persecution, 91
   physical suffering, 90n56
   pious self, 67
   on possessions, 142–44
   relationship with Jesus Christ, 68n27
   righteousness, 50–51, 50n13, 51n19
   sacrifice, 93
   sanctification, 168n52
   self-centeredness, 44, 45n87
   self-denial and cross-bearing, 84
   self-understanding, 38
   shapes of the cross, 115–16
   shaping in friendship, 168–69
   silence and contemplation, 191–92
   simplicity of discipleship, 189–90
   suffering, 100, 102, 103–4
   temptations, 105n41, 106–8, 107n46, 107n47, 119n17
   this-worldliness of life, 26, 26n87
   thriving in tensions, 2n4
   uniqueness of Jesus's cross, 93–94
   unresolved contradictions, 59
Bovon, François, 4, 4n12, 66n22
Brandtstädter, Jochen, 33
Brock, Rita Nakashima, 24n81
Brooks, David, 3n9, 33, 43, 154, 155, 158
brotherly love, 164–65
The Buddenbrooks (Mann), 71
Bultmann, Rudolf, 20, 127, 127n43

Cacioppo, John, 157
Calvin, John, 43, 74n55, 86, 122n27
Campbell, Keith, 43
Campbell, Murray, 21n68
Case, Brendan, 185n13
Casey, Michael, 16, 16n39, 134n1, 151
Chalcedonian Creed, 18
cheap grace, 5n14, 12, 12n22, 27, 64, 72
Christ and Culture (Niebuhr), 12
Christian self-help books, 32
Christian views on friendship. *See* spiritual friendship
Christless Christianity (Horton), 25n84
Christlikeness, 123
Christologies, 17–18, 20–21n65, 21, 22n70
Christospection, 69
Christothentic identity, 51–54, 138, 199
church as Christ's body, 99, 178
Church Dogmatics (Barth), 7
Cialdini, Robert, 40
Coe, John, 190

cognitive development, 122
Cohen, Sheldon, 173–74
comfort, 121
commitment, 125, 167
community of disciples, 98–99, 160, 170, 174, 177–78
Confessing Church movement, 114
confession in spiritual friendship, 171–73
confirmation bias, 41
consider *(logizomai)*, 69n34
constant demolition and renewal, 54–56, 62
consumerism, 141–44
contemplation, 187–95, 204
contemporary Christianity, 7, 14
contemporary disciples, 4, 179
contradictions, 59, 112
Cortez, Marc, 58n48
costly discipleship, 13, 31, 133, 138, 183
costly grace, 5, 12, 25, 50, 54, 204
The Cost of Discipleship (Bonhoeffer), 7
co-suffering, Paul's theology of, 174, 186, 200
COVID-19 pandemic, 80, 157, 175–76, 179
creative self-talk, 70
cross-bearing, 1–4, 6, 79–96, 200–202
    Bøe on, 83n23–25
    Christ's sufferings, 85–93
    embracing tensions, 5
    fellowship through suffering, 118–21
    reflections on, 128–29
    shapes of the cross, 115–18
    sharing in Christ's sufferings, 102–4
    and surrender, 126n39
    transformation through suffering, 121–25
    uniqueness of Jesus's cross, 93–95
    what is the cross, 82–85
crucifixion, 83, 104, 184
cultural acceleration, 33
cultural conservatism, 12
culture surrounding disciples, 1, 12

Dawn, Marva, 13, 16n41
deadness, 55–56
Deaton, Angus, 143
DeGroat, Chuck, 144

de Gruchy, John, 88n46
demolition, 54–55, 62, 65
Denton, Melinda Lundquist, 13
denying oneself, 1–4, 5, 31–76, 199–200
    and Brown, 66n22
    Christothentic identity, 51–54
    cross-bearing, 84
    and Dschulnigg, 66n19
    identity confusion, 32–34
    inconsistent self, 34–39
    new self/newness, 47–51
    obedience, 63–65
    old and new self tension, 54–57
    putting off oldness, 65–68
    putting on newness, 68–71
    self-awareness, 71–75
    self-centeredness, 39–45
    self-understanding, 31–32
    thriving in dissonance, 57–59
depressed disciple, 72–73, 100
desert fathers, 42n65, 123, 124n35
desire through surrender, 125–26, 202
Detweiler, Craig, 42–44
Deus Caritas Est (Benedict XVI), 163
development, 121–22
Diet of Worms, 103
Dietrich, Martin O., 105n38
discernment and deliberation, 148
discipleship. *See* radical discipleship
Discipleship (Bonhoeffer), 64
discipline, 61, 61n2, 124
dissonance of old and new, 57–59, 200
"Distance of Obedience" *(Distanz des Gehorsams)* (Wirth), 64
distressed disciples, 95
divine revelation, 19
divinity of Christ, 17–23, 24, 93n68. *See also* transfiguration account
Docetism, 18
domestication of God, 13–14, 64
Dorotheus of Gaza, 66
Dschulnigg, Peter, 66n19
Dunn, James, 68n28
Dunning, David, 38
dynamic self-concept, 36

Edgar, Brian, 158–59, 161n20, 165n42, 166n44, 168, 171n64

SUBJECT INDEX

election and discipleship, 136–37
Elijah, 182, 185–86, 187
Elshtain, Jean Bethke, 69n32
embodied suffering, 101
embracing tensions, 4, 5, 9–28, 112, 141, 180, 186, 197–99
emotional love, 162
encountering Christ, 26, 198
equilibrium, 71–72
Erikson, Erik H., 121–22
evangelicals, 11–12
evil and suffering, 106–7
exaltation and humiliation, 183, 184–86, 187, 193–94, 203–4
expansion in spiritual friendships, 163–64

face of Christ, 6, 134, 182–95, 204
fellowship through suffering, 112, 118–21, 174, 201–2
Ferguson, Niall, 1n2
Fiorenza, Francis Schüssler, 185n8
Fitzmyer, Joseph A., 82n17
Focant, Camille, 83
following, 1–4, 6–7, 133–56, 157–81, 197–98, 202–4
    befriending the world, 176–80
    call to discipleship, 134–39
    christological paradoxes, 17
    costly discipleship, 31
    cross-bearing, 79, 81–82
    denying oneself, 67
    identity formation, 34
    and imitation, 148–52
    immediacy and deliberation, 146–48
    intimacy, 144–46
    Jesus's divinity, 21–23
    letting go and flourishing, 139–46
    loving God and neighbor, 152–55
    obedience, 63–65
    possessions, 141–44
    self-determination to freedom, 139–41
    and sin, 24
    spiritual friendship, 159–76
Forbes, Greg, 122n30, 141n28
Ford, David F., 33n7
forgetting, 69. *See also* self-forgetfulness

forgiveness and righteousness, 47, 50–51, 69, 73, 199. *See also* self-forgiveness
forgiveness in spiritual friendship, 170–71
Frankl, Victor, 81
Freud, Sigmund, 36, 121
friends first policy, 174–75
friendship
    defined, 158–59
    holy friendships, 166n44
    and obedience, 64
    O'Donovan on, 158–59, 160, 161, 161n21, 163, 164, 165, 165n39, 167, 167n48, 168n54
    reordering of, 165
    See also spiritual friendship
Fromm, Erich, 44
fruitfulness in spiritual friendship, 165–67
fruit of the Spirit, 165–67, 165n42, 168–69, 170, 189–90

Gallagher, Robert, 14
gender, 33
genuine worship, 16n41
Gerhard, Johann, 4n13
German Christians, 114
German homegroup movement, 172n71
Germany, 114–15
Gethsemane, 85, 90
gift from God, 47–49
glorification and humiliation, 183–84, 188, 192–93, 194, 203
glorified friend, 183–87
Gnosticism, 18
God, domestication of, 13–17
godforsakenness, 92–93, 93n68, 94, 105, 109–12, 201
Gorman, Michael, 89, 186
gospel/Gospels, 12–13, 23–28, 69, 73, 117, 162n30, 187, 192, 194–95, 204
Gospel of John, 94, 138, 184
grace
    Barth on, 151
    cheap grace, 5n14, 12, 12n22, 27, 64, 72

costly grace, 5, 12, 25, 50, 54
    forgiveness through, 170–71
    grace-empowered love of God and neighbor, 152–53
    intimation by, 151, 156
    Schlatter on, 151
Greco-Roman world, 18, 161
Greene-McCreight, Kathryn, 121, 125
Greenwald, Anthony, 41
Greggs, Tom, 170n59, 178
Grenz, Stanley, 38
grief, 89–90. *See also* suffering(s)
Grosseteste, Robert, 185n13

Hahn, Ferdinand, 145n51, 147
Harvey, John D., 57n45
hedonism, 80, 80n4
Heidegger, Martin, 44n85
Heider, Fritz, 35
Hendrix, Michael, 158
Hess, Johann, 176
Hewstone, Miles, 40n56
Higgins, Edward Tory, 37
Hingabe, 125–26
Holl, Karl, 56n41, 109
holy friendships, 166n44
Holy Spirit
    costly gospel, 12–13
    disciple's connection with the, 3
    follow-ship, 148
    humanity of Christ, 99
    justice, 178
    mysterious agency of, 48–49
    obedience, 65, 88
    renewal, 25, 54
    self-denial, 62, 66–67, 199
    self-emptying of the Son of God, 21
    union through the, 151
Horton, Michael, 16, 19n58, 24, 25n84, 48n3, 149n70, 151, 153n86, 190–91
Hovland, C. Warren, 109
humanity/human nature of Jesus Christ, 17–23, 17n47, 86–90, 91n60, 93–94, 97–99, 108
human nature restored by grace, 151
Hume, David, 36

humiliation, 22, 87, 183–86, 187–88, 193, 194, 203–4. *See also* exaltation and humiliation; glorification and humiliation
humility, 42, 51, 98, 125–26. *See also* surrender
Hunter, James Davison, 24
Hus, John, 103

identification and incarnation, 86–89
identity
    in Christ, 69–70, 107, 123
    Christothentic, 51–54, 138, 199
    identity confusion, 32–34
    identity crisis, 122
    inconsistent self, 36–37
    new self, 48
    online identity, 3, 32–33
    and self-awareness, 169
    self-centeredness, 44–45
    and self-denial, 3, 199
    and self-understanding, 5
    view of self, 58
Idleman, Kyle, 31n1
Ignatius of Loyola, 192n45
image of Christ, 25, 58, 68, 122–23, 134, 151, 186–87, 188–90
imitation, 19, 85, 98, 102, 133–34, 138, 140, 148–52, 155–56, 202
The Imitation of Christ (Kempis), 149
immediacy and deliberation, 146–48
immediacy between friends, 171n62
incarnation of Christ, 18, 20–23, 86–89, 93–94, 94n71, 150
income, 143
inconsistent self, 34–39
individualism, 39n44, 158–59, 162
industrial progress, 19–20
inspiration in spiritual friendship, 161–62
intimacy, 52–53, 68, 144–46, 164–65. *See also* union with Christ
irresistible call, 136–38
Isaiah, 94, 121

Jacoby, Matt, 118
Jenson, Matt, 44

SUBJECT INDEX

Jesus Christ
  Arianism, 19
  befriending the world, 177–80
  call to discipleship, 135–38
  christological paradoxes, 17–23
  Christothentic identity, 51–53
  cross-bearing, 6, 79–96, 114–29, 200–202
  denying oneself, 5, 31–32
  discipline, 61n2
  dissonance, 58–59
  distorted ideas about, 23–26
  face of, 192–93
  fellowship through suffering, 119–21
  following, 6–7, 43n76, 133–56, 202–4
  forgiveness in spiritual friendship, 170–71
  friendship, 159–81
  as glorified friend, 183–87
  godforsakenness, 109–12
  Holy Spirit, 63n8
  humanity/human nature of, 17–23, 17n47, 86–89, 91n60, 93–94, 97–99, 108
  identity confusion, 34
  immediacy and deliberation, 146–52
  incarnation and identification, 86–89
  inspiration in spiritual friendship, 161–62
  and Johnson, 22n69
  love in spiritual friendship, 160
  loving God and neighbor, 152–55
  new self/newness, 48–51, 54
  obedience, 63–65
  opposition and persecution, 90–91, 102–4
  physical and spiritual suffering, 89–90, 100–102
  putting off oldness, 68
  putting on newness, 68–69
  relationships, 145
  renunciation, 141–44, 141n27
  sacrifice, 175
  sacrifice and forsakenness, 92–93
  self-awareness, 72
  self-centeredness, 44–45
  self-determination, 139–41
  self-emptying, 22n70, 97–99
  shapes of the cross, 115–18
  subjective value judgments about, 21n67
  sufferings, 85–93, 97–113, 174
  surrender, 127–29
  tensions, 5
  testing and temptation, 91–92
  threefold command, 1–4, 4n13
  transfiguration account, 182–95, 183n4
  transformation and contemplation, 187–89
  transformation through suffering, 122–25
  trials and temptations, 104–9
  uniqueness of, 21n66, 93–95
  unity in spiritual friendship, 162–63
  and Webster, 64n12
Jews, 178
Job, 110–12, 120, 124
John (apostle), 151, 159
John of Damascus, 186n14
Johnson, Bill, 22n69
joint suffering. *See* co-suffering, Paul's theology of
Julian of Norwich, 128

Kahn, Robert, 167
Kahneman, Daniel, 9–10, 11, 143
Kant, Immanuel, 19, 35–36
Kapic, Kelly, 70, 100, 118n14
Keener, Craig, 52–53
Keller, Timothy, 74, 120
Kempis, Thomas à, 149, 149n70
kenosis, 21–22, 22n70, 23n73
Kierkegaard, Søren, 53n30, 138n15
Kilby, Karen, 15
Kimber, Tom, 190n31
King, Jonathan, 184n5
Kirchenkampf, 115
Klein, Hans, 84, 84n29
Kohlberg, Lawrence, 122
Kolb, Robert, 51
Konersmann, Ralf, 34
Köstenberger, Andreas, 175n90
Kristallnacht (Night of Broken Glass), 114

lament, 95, 118, 119–21
law and gospel, 25n84
Lawrence, Joel, 99n6
Lecky, Prescott, 34–35
Lectio divina, 191
Lectio faciem, 192–93, 194–95, 204
Lee, Simon S., 187n20
legalistic disciple, 72
Leiper, Henry, 114–15
Leipzig, Germany, 179
letting go, 138, 139–46
Lewis, C. S., 16–17, 106–7, 163, 165
licentiousness, 72
Liebendörfer, Bernd, 7n17
life of the mind, 11–12
Life Together (Bonhoeffer), 191–92
Lippmann, Eric, 33
listening, 6, 70, 134–38, 160, 187, 191
Livingston, James C., 185n8
Lloyd-Jones, Martyn, 70, 73
Logos, 86–87, 97–98
loneliness, 143, 143n36, 157–58, 203
*Los Angeles Time*s (newspaper), 41–42
love
    befriending the world, 176–79
    denying oneself, 75
    emotional love *vs.* spiritual love, 162
    extraordinary deeds of, 153–55, 186
    of the friend, 164–67
    of God and neighbor, 152–55
    imitation of Jesus, 149
    and inspiration, 161–62
    Jesus's self-sacrificial love, 93, 99, 175
    reflection on, 180–81, 203
    in spiritual friendship, 159–60, 164–76
Love Letters from Cell 92 (Bonhoeffer), 145
Love Your God with All Your Mind (Moreland), 11
Lundgaard, Kris, 146n52
Luther, Martin
    communal aspect of discipleship, 70–71
    and confession, 172
    cross-bearing, 116n7
    God acting for us, 88
    godforsakenness, 109–11, 110n61

hidden God *(deus absconditus),* 184n6
intimacy between believer and Christ, 50, 52
Lutheran theologians, 2n4, 4n13, 7, 38, 105
outbreak of the plague, 175–76, 176n96
persecution of, 103
physical and emotional suffering, 100–101, 101n20
on self-centeredness, 43
sermons on the First Book of Moses, 110n59
tension between the old and new self, 56, 57–59
thriving in tensions, 2n4
trials and temptations, 105, 123
and weakness, 80
Lutheran theologians, 2n4, 4n13, 7, 38, 105
Luz, Ulrich, 85n32, 86n37, 103, 117, 117n10

Maaz, Hans-Joachim, 43
Macaskill, Grant, 65
MacCulloch, Diarmaid, 134
Macleod, Donald, 69n30, 85n35, 86, 86n37, 87–88, 89n52, 90–91
Mann, Thomas, 71
Man's Search for Meaning (Frankl), 81
Mark the evangelist, 154
Markus, Hazel, 36–37
martyrdom, 83, 103
materialism and consumerism, 141–44
maturation, 58, 81, 121–22
McCall, Thomas, 23
meditation, 189, 191–92
Melanchthon, Philipp, 15, 101
mental effort, 9–10
Meyers, Tim, 2n5
Migliore, Daniel, 16, 198n6
modalism, 14–15
modern Christology, 20–21n65
modern self, 38, 43–44
Moltmann, Jürgen, 43–44, 159, 166, 178, 178n107

SUBJECT INDEX

Monday Prayers for Peace
    (*Friedensgebete*), 179–80
Moo, Douglas, 52
moral development, 122
moralistic therapeutic deism, 13–14
Moreland, J. P., 11
Morris, Leon, 84
mortification, 55, 66–67, 73
Moses and Elijah, 182–88
Müller, Jac J., 101–2
Mummendey, Hans D., 38
Münsterschwarzach Abbey, 70
Myers, David G., 39, 39n46
mystery, 15–17, 88, 93

Nachfolge (Bonhoeffer), 7
naming of God, 137
narcissism, 41–44
"Narcissism beyond Gestalt and
    Awareness" (Nuttin), 41
Narcissus, 42–43
National Socialists, 81, 103, 114, 178
neighboring disciplines. *See* psychology
Nelson, Peter K., 57
new covenant, 188–89
new self/newness, 47–60, 197–98
    in Christ, 2–3
    Christothentic identity, 51–54
    Christ's self-emptying, 98
    comfort, 121
    cross-bearing, 127, 202
    denying oneself, 5, 199–200
    elements of, 47–51
    old and new self tension, 54–57, 71,
        165, 198
    putting off oldness, 65–68
    putting on newness, 68–71
    reflection on, 75–76, 96, 129, 204
    self-awareness, 39, 72–75
    Stuhlmacher on, 66n18
    thriving in dissonance, 57–59
    See also old self/oldness
New Testament, 20, 25, 39, 54–55, 58,
    89–90, 94–95, 138, 140n21, 146,
    150, 159, 161n20, 177, 182, 193,
    201
new vision of God, 2, 111, 113, 129,
    197, 202

New York, 114–15
Niebuhr, H. Richard, 2n4, 12
Niebuhr, Reinhold, 115
Noll, Mark A., 11
Nolland, John, 117
Nurius, Paula, 37
Nuttin, Jozef M., 41

obedience, 63–65, 65n16, 66n18,
    88–89, 98, 113, 146–47, 146n53,
    153–54, 200
obsession with self. *See* narcissism
O'Donovan, Oliver
    befriending the world, 176–77
    definition of virtue, 62
    and friendship, 160, 161, 161n21,
        163, 164, 165, 165n39, 167,
        167n48, 168n54
    self-forgetfulness, 74
old covenant, 188
old self/oldness
    baptism, 49, 199
    call to discipleship, 137
    confession in spiritual friendship,
        172–73
    denying oneself, 5
    and discipline, 61n2
    letting go, 139–40
    old and new self tension, 71, 165, 198
    putting off oldness, 65–68
    self-awareness, 72–75
    self-centeredness, 45
    self-denial, 200
    self-emptying, 98
    and suffering, 100
    temptations, 106
    thriving in dissonance, 57–59
    See also new self/newness
Old Testament, 35, 110, 120, 182
online identity, 3, 32–33
Open Doors, 102
opioid crisis, 34n12, 80–81
opposition and persecution, 84, 90–91,
    102–6, 200–201
optimistic bias, 40
orthodox teachings, 18, 21n66
The Other Side of Happiness (Bastian),
    80–81

Owen, John, 66
Oyserman, Daphna, 37

painful experiences, 80–81, 95, 120, 125
Pannenberg, Wolfhart, 49n8
Pass, Bruce, 4n10, 51n17, 97n1
Passion story, 95
passivity, 53, 135
Paul (apostle)
    baptism, 49
    and Barnabas, 168
    co-glorification with Christ, 186
    constant renewal, 55
    contemplation, 188
    costly gospel, 25
    co-suffering with Christ, 174, 186, 200
    on disciples, 17
    dynamic renewal, 59
    following after Christ, 197
    forgiveness, 50, 170–71
    imitation, 102, 150–51
    intimacy, 52
    on Jesus, 23
    law of Christ, 174
    new form of existence, 48
    new life, 49
    new self, 54
    old self, 45, 66–67
    possessions, 144
    pre- or post-conversion experience, 57n45
    putting off oldness, 65–66
    putting on newness, 68–69
    sacrifice, 175
    self-emptying of the Son of God, 21, 86–87
    sharing in Christ's sufferings, 85, 99
    sufferings, 123, 125
    surrender, 128
    thriving in dissonance, 57
    trials and temptations, 105–6, 116
    unification, 163
peace, 34, 107, 126, 138, 193–94
penal substitution model, 24, 24n81
Peppiatt, Lucy, 16n43, 26, 61n1, 89, 113, 118n13
persecution. *See* opposition and persecution
personhood, 14
Peter (apostle), 48, 92, 104–5, 108, 146–47, 165, 182, 194
Peterson, Eugene, 1, 67, 160
Pharisees, 72
physical and spiritual suffering, 89–90, 100–102, 201–2
Piaget, Jean, 122
pious self, 67
Piper, John, 73–74, 102n22, 160n18
Podmore, Simon, 110–11, 110n59, 112n67, 125n36
pop culture, 33
positive growth, 81–82
possessions, 141–44
postmodern relativism, 33n7
post-traumatic growth, 81
pretension, 172
pretentious disciple, 72
pride and self-admiration, 72
Prince Caspian (Lewis), 16–17
prosperity, 141–44, 202–4
Protestant church, 11
Protestant disciples, 171. *See also* Confessing Church movement
Protestant Reformers, 175
Protestant theologians, 19–20
pruning principle, 124, 129, 168
Psalm 42, 70
pseudo-disciple, 72
psychology
    facial expressions, 193, 199
    identity confusion, 32–34
    inconsistent self, 34–39
    as neighboring discipline, 7
    painful experiences, 80–81
    physical and spiritual suffering, 100
    psychological stress, 173–74
    rumination, 73–74
    self-centered self, 39–45
    self-understanding, 5, 73–74
    transformation through contemplation, 190
    transformation through suffering, 121
Purves, Andrew, 53n29, 150

putting off the old self and putting on the new, 65–70

quiet ego, 74, 74n56
quiet self-awareness, 5, 62, 65, 71–76, 134–35, 155, 169, 199–200, 204

radical denial, 141–42
radical discipleship, 1–4, 197–204
    Arianism, 19
    baptism, 49–50
    befriending the world, 176–80
    call to discipleship, 134–39, 135n3, 148, 151n75
    church-community, 99
    costs of, 183
    fellowship through suffering, 120–21
    friendships, 158–76
    and God, 14–17
    godforsakenness, 109
    humiliation and exaltation, 186
    imitation, 148–51
    immediacy and deliberation, 146–48
    Jesus's divinity, 21–23
    Lectio faciem, 192–93
    loving God and neighbor, 152–55
    obedience, 63–65
    opposition and persecution, 102–3
    positive growth, 81–82
    relationships, 144–46
    renunciation, 141–44
    self-awareness, 74–75
    self-determination, 139–41
    self-understanding, 53–54
    shapes of the cross, 116–18
    silence and solitude, 191–92
    surrender, 125–28
    tensions, 5, 25–26, 54–56, 112
    thriving in dissonance, 57–59
    transformation and contemplation, 187–91
    transformation through suffering, 122–25
    trials and temptations, 105–6, 108
    trivialization, 11–13
    See also cross-bearing; denying oneself; following

The Real Scandal of the Evangelical Mind (Trueman), 11
regeneration, 48–49, 48n4
Reimer, David, 142
reinvention and self-improvement, 33–34
rejection of the old self, 5, 74–75, 133, 200. *See also* denying oneself
relational networks between radical disciples, 162–63
relational sin, 44
relationships to intimacy in following Christ, 144–46
renaming of disciples, 48
renewal, 25, 49, 53, 54–56, 58–59, 62, 65, 150–51, 172, 178, 198
renunciation, 141–44, 141n27, 202
reordering of friendships, 165
representative vicarious action, 99
resurrection, 18–21, 127, 127n42, 129, 173
Revelations of Divine Love (Julian of Norwich), 128
Richmond, James, 20n64
Rievaulx, Aelred of, 159, 161, 163–64, 167
righteousness, 47, 50–51, 55n37, 65, 75, 150. *See also* forgiveness and righteousness
Ritschl, Albrecht, 19–20, 21nn66–67
Rittgers, Ronald, 95, 123n34
rumination, 73
Ruppert, Fidelis, 2, 7–8n22, 8, 70, 197n1

sacrificial love, 82, 92–93, 99, 159, 175, 177, 181. *See also* spiritual love
sacrificing in spiritual friendship, 175–76, 181
sainthood, 58–59
sanctification, 55, 73, 123, 150, 168, 168n52
Scandal of the Evangelical Mind (Noll), 11
Schlatter, Adolf
    Christ's resurrection life, 129n47
    church's confessions, 153
    decisiveness of disciples, 117n11
    on discipleship, 53n28
    disciples' hope, 194n51
    God as wholly other, 17n46

godforsakenness, 93n68
on grace, 151
imitation of Christ, 152
on Jesus's person, 23
on Jesus's priestly self-giving, 82n15
on new birth, 48n5
Pharisees, 72, 72n43
renewal, 53, 55
self-awareness, 170
on surrender, 126n40
tension of joy in suffering, 94–95, 94n75
unity and togetherness, 162n30
Schmeller, Thomas, 186n18
Schürmann, Heinz, 84n27, 141, 141n26
Schwöbel, Christoph, 20–21n65
Scriven, Joseph M., 159
Second Letter to the Corinthians, 188
self-assessment, 35, 45, 66–67
self-awareness, 5, 65, 71–75, 155, 169, 199–200
self-centeredness, 5, 34, 39–45, 47, 49, 73, 106, 164, 199, 203
self-congruence effect, 40–41
self-consistency, 35
self-denial. *See* denying oneself
self-determination, 4, 67, 139–41, 155, 202–3
self-discrepancy theory, 37
self-effacement, 170n59
self-emptying of the Son of God, 21–22, 22n70, 86–87, 93, 97–98, 112–13
self-esteem, 40–43, 60, 169
self-examination, 72–73, 73n48
self-forgetfulness, 73–74, 74n49
self-forgiveness, 173
Selfie (Storr), 37, 43
selfies, 42–44
self-illusions, 39–40
self-knowledge, 35, 68–69
self-reference effect, 40–41, 40n56
self-reliance, 32, 92, 106, 110–11
self-selection, 135–36
self-serving biases, 40
self-talk approach, 70, 138
self-understanding, 5, 31–46, 53, 56, 91, 111–12, 118, 159
self-worth, 137–38

servanthood, 98
sexual sin, 106
shapes of the cross, 115–18
shaping in spiritual friendships, 167–69
sharing in Christ's sufferings, 85, 86, 97–113, 186, 201–2
silence, 134–35, 191–92, 204
Silence (MacCulloch), 134
simplicity and immediacy, 146
simplicity of discipleship, 189
sin(s)
    confessing, 171–73
    forgiveness, 50, 170–71
    gospel distortions, 23–26
    Jesus's sufferings, 86–88, 93
    mortification of, 67
    relational sin, 44
    and sacrifice, 92
    sexual sin, 106
    sinner label, 58
    theological concept of, 43
Smith, Christian, 13
Smith, David Oliver, 85, 85n33
Smith, G., 37
snowflake generation, 81, 124
Social God and the Relational Self (Grenz), 38
social media, 37, 44, 117, 158
social networks, 173
social roles, 33
soliloquy, 70
solitude, 134, 191–92, 204
spiritual burnout, 61
spiritual disciplines, 61–62, 189–92
spiritual distress, 109
spiritual friendship, 134, 159–81
    affirmation in, 169–70
    befriending the world, 176–80
    confession in, 171–73
    expansion in, 163–64
    forgiveness in, 170–71
    fruitfulness in, 165–67
    inspiration in, 161–62
    love in, 160, 164–76
    sacrificing in, 175–76, 181
    shaping in, 167–69
    suffering in, 173–75
    unity in, 162–63

Spiritual Friendship (De spirituali amicitia) (Aelred of Rievaulx), 161
spirituality of North American teenagers, 13–14
spiritual love, 162, 165–66, 172, 174, 175, 176–77, 180–81. *See also* sacrificial love
Spurgeon, Charles, 73
Spurrier, William, 19
Stevens, Jennifer, 80
St. Nicholas's Church *(Nikolaikirche)*, 179
storage facilities, 142–43
Storr, Will, 37, 39n44, 41n62, 43
Stott, John, 1n1, 11, 123
Strobel, Kyle, 189–90
Stuhlmacher, Peter, 58–59, 66n18
suffering(s)
    of Christ, 85–96
    cross-bearing, 3–4, 6, 79–96, 200–202
    embodied, 101
    and evil, 106–7
    fellowship through, 118–21
    and glorification, 183–84
    godforsakenness, 109–12
    opposition and persecution, 102–4
    Paul's's theology of co-suffering, 174, 186, 200
    physical and spiritual suffering, 100–102
    sharing in Christ's suffering, 85, 86, 97–113, 186, 201–2
    in spiritual friendship, 173–75
    transformation through, 121–25
    trials and temptations, 104–7
superabundance and excess, 142
supernatural contemplation, 190
suppression, 3
surrender, 125–28, 129, 175, 202
susceptible saints, 59, 199
Swann, William, 44–45n86
Symbol of Chalcedon, 22, 89
Synoptics, 4, 49, 85, 182, 200

taking up the cross. *See* cross-bearing
Talaifar, Sanaz, 44–45n86
Talbert, Charles, 57

Tauler, John, 63
Taylor, Shelley, 39–40, 39n48, 173
technology, 33, 70
Tedeschi, Richard, 81
telos crisis, 3n9
temptation, 91–92, 91n60, 94, 101–2, 104–8, 105n41, 107n46, 109–10, 113, 116, 119n17, 123, 149, 201
Tend and Befriend Theory, 173
Teresa of Avila, 7
testing and temptation, 91–92, 105, 201. *See also* trials and temptations
theological anthropology, 48
Thinking, Fast and Slow (Kahneman), 9–10
this-worldliness of life, 26, 26n87, 28
threefold office *(munus triplex)* of Jesus, 2, 4, 4n13, 204
Tierney, John, 39
Tietz, Christiane, 51n19
transfiguration account, 182–95, 183n2, 183n4, 187n20
transformation, 3, 6, 62, 121–25, 134, 151, 159, 171, 187–91, 197–98, 204
Treatise of Human Nature (Hume), 36
trials and temptations, 91, 104–8, 113, 123. *See also* testing and temptation
Trinity, 14–16
tritheism, 14–15
trivialization, 11–13
Trueman, Carl, 11–12
Turner, Léon, 38n32
Twenge, Jean, 43

union with Christ, 5, 45, 49–50, 63, 68, 70, 149–51, 163, 199, 202. *See also* new self/newness; obedience
uniqueness of Jesus, 21n66, 93–94
unity in spiritual friendships, 162–63
unresolved contradictions, 59–60

view of self, 58. *See also* self-awareness
virtues, 42, 62, 63, 73, 166
Vlastuin, Willem van, 54n32
Volpe, Medi Ann, 63n8, 123, 197n2

von Wedemeyer, Maria, 145
Voorwinde, Stephen, 89n53

Walking With God Through Suffering and Pain (Keller), 120
Wayment, Heidi A., 74
weakness and vulnerability, 117. *See also* cross-bearing
Webster, John
    denying oneself, 63n9
    domestication of God, 64n12
    good causes, 149
    imitation of Christ, 150
    listening, 135–36
    loss of self, 139n18
    nature of discipleship, 136n9, 137n14, 139–40, 148n65
    on obedience, 146
    regeneration, 48n4
    renewal, 49n9, 54–56
    self-centeredness, 44
    surrender, 127n41
Weder, Hans, 91–92
Welker, Michael, 4n13
Weller, Matthias, 70–71

Wells, David, 33n7, 38
Wellum, Stephen, 18
Wengst, Klaus, 103n33
Wesleyan Perfectionist influence, 58n49
Western civilization, 1n2
Western Trinitarian reflection, 15
Westminster Shorter Catechism, 42
"What would Jesus do?" (WWJD) movement, 19, 25–26, 25n84, 150–51
Willard, Dallas, 2, 67
Williams, Rowan, 62, 169
Wills, Thomas A., 173–74
Wirth, Mathias, 64
Witherington, Ben, 79n2
Witten, Marsha, 13–14
The World's Unrest (Die Unruhe der Welt) (Konersmann), 34
worship of self, 39–45

Zachhuber, Johannes, 184n6
Zajonc, Robert, 190
Zimmermann, Jens, 65n16
Zwingli, Ulrich, 175–76

Scripture Index

OLD TESTAMENT

Genesis
1:3	136
5:24	148
6:9	148
6:14	10
15:12	110
22:2	110, 110n58
28:10–15	27
32:22–32	110
40:23	110
41:1	110

Exodus
4:4	117
13:21–22	182
33:16	148
34:4	188
34:28–29	188
34:29	188
34:33	188
40:34–38	182

Deuteronomy
6:4	17–18, 135

1 Samuel
20:23	167

Isaiah
35:5	136
45:15	121
53	87
53:3	89
53:5	94
54:7	109n52
55:2–3	135
55:11	136

Jeremiah
17:9	35
45	26

Ezekiel
36:25–26	50

Hosea
6:1	125

Psalms
6	109
6:1–3	109
16:2	128

Psalms (cont.)

18:1	202
22:1	92
22:8	92
23:2	4
42:5–6	70
62:5	191
73:25–26	128
103:14	45
119:57	128
133:1	163
147:4	126
147:5	17

Proverbs

17:27–28	134
27:17	168

Job

5:18	124
42:5–6	112

Song of Solomon

5:9	146

Lamentations

5:20	110

NEW TESTAMENT

Matthew

2:13	90
2:19–20	90
4:1	91
4:3	91
4:6	91
4:20	138, 146
5:9	194
5:13	12
5:13–14	177
6:6	20
6:12	171
6:13	105n41
6:21	156
8:17	112
9:9	146
10:12–14	104
10:24–25	104
10:37	144
10:39	75
11:29	82
12:34	90
13:16	136
16:21	184
16:24	4, 72n43, 79, 84n28
16:25	1, 32, 81
17:1–8	182
17:1–9	182–83
17:2	188
17:5	182, 187
17:9	183
18:15	166
18:22	170
19:16–23	142
19:16–30	64
19:21	142
19:22	142
19:29	145
20:28	92
21:12	90
21:18–22	124
22:1–14	95
23:25	72
25:24–30	124
25:35	174
25:40	152
25:53	92
26:26	95
26:26–28	95
26:38	90
27:40b	105
27:46	105
28:18	204
28:19	180, 204
28:20	204

Mark

2:14	146
3:5	193
3:17	48

4:38	86n37
4:9	135
6:3	89
7:6–8	45
7:34	136
8:12	89
8:17	112
8:29–30	183
8:31	184
8:34	4, 79
9:2	188
9:2–8	182–83
9:7	187, 191
9:9	183
10:37	43n76
10:38	43n76
10:39	43n76
12:13	91
12:30–31	152
15:30	92
15:34	92, 112

Luke

2:7	90
2:8–14	184
4:3	105
5:58	144
7:9	193
9:22	184
9:23	4, 79, 79n1, 82n17, 83n18, 84n29, 117
9:28–36	182–83
9:31	184, 186
9:33	194
9:35	182n1, 187
9:57–58	136
9:61–62	146
9:62	140
10:3	180
10:39	135
12:19	142
12:21	143
13:24	135
14:18	141
14:20	144
14:26	144
14:27	79n1
14:28	103, 116
14:33	141
16:3–6	140
17:3	66
18:14	42
19:19	141
19:41	89, 193
22:19–20	95
22:24–30	44
22:28	174
22:42	126
22:44	90
22:54–62	90
23:28	95
23:46	94
24:49	63

John

1:14	23
1:29	88, 92
1:38	192
1:39	27
1:46	27
1:51	27
3:3	49
3:8	48
3:16	126, 177
4:6	89
5:21	48
6	31n2
6:53	31
6:54–57	31
6:60	31
6:65	31n2
6:66	138
6:67	31, 193
6:68	137
8:57	91
9:3	117
10:3	137
10:5	133
10:10	2, 32
10:11	87
10:30	23
11:35	89
12:24–25	127

John (cont.)

12:28	184
13:1–17	87
13:10	54
13:15	150
13:34–35	174
13:35	160
14:12	22
14:15	64, 151
14:20	150, 174
14:27	34
15	124, 161
15:2	124, 160
15:4	67
15:5	63, 124
15:8	124
15:13	159, 175
15:14	160
15:15	163
15:16	136
15:20	102, 104
16:20–24	95
16:33	104, 112, 177, 201
17:3	127
17:14–18	180
17:14–19	197
17:23	150
19:1–3	90
19:30	92, 94
20:21	180
21:20	165
21:21	146
21:22	147n55

Acts

2:37	146
8:35	89
9:13	58n50
9:32	58n50
9:41	58n50
15:36–41	168
17:11	27
17:25	109
17:28	109
26:10	58n50

Romans

1:7	58n50
3:22	50
5:3	123
5:3–4	108
6:1	72
6:2	58
6:4	49, 50, 70
6:6	45, 49, 66
6:11	66, 68
7:7–25	57n45
7:15	57
8:1	150
8:7	186
8:13	66, 67, 166
8:14	54
8:14–17	75
8:17	85
8:17–23	197
8:26	99
8:27	58n50
8:29	199
12:2	180
12:5	99, 163
12:10	159, 164, 170
12:13	174
12:21	68
13:14	68
16:4	175

1 Corinthians

1:2	58n50
1:18	117
1:23	117
3:16	17
4:1	17
4:16	102
6:11	59
6:19	106
6:19b–20a	126
7:30–31	144
9:24–27	197
10:13	116
11:1	102, 150
11:26	204
12:27	99
13:4–6	166
13:12	194

15:31	55
15:44	18
15:57	201

2 Corinthians

1:1	58n50
1:4–5	121
1:20	63
3:7	188
3:18	68, 188
4:7	59
4:10–11	186
4:16	54
5:7	194
5:17	48
5:21	50, 87
12:7	125
12:9	117
12:10	125
13:5	23

Galatians

2:2	197
2:20	52, 150
4:5	75, 87, 92
5:7	197
5:13	141
5:16	56n42, 57n47
5:16–17	66
5:18	54
5:19–21	67
5:22–23	166
	5:24, 66
5:25	54
6:2	174
6:10	174
6:15	48

Ephesians

1:5	75
1:13	63
1:15	58n50
2:1	48
2:2	199
2:4	25
2:8	48
2:18	75
4:1; 3b	2
4:15	168, 203
4:22	45, 66
4:24	47, 68
6:10–18	105
6:12	106

Philippians

1:1	150
1:6	60
1:29	118
2:3	98, 170
2:5	98
2:7	21, 86
2:12	56
2:13	25, 57, 200
2:16	197
3:8	128
3:10–11	102
3:11	85
3:20–21	197
4:4	75
4:7	126, 138
4:11–13	75
4:22	58n50

Colossians

1:1	58n50
1:13	75
1:15	183, 198
1:15–17	88
1:17	23
1:19	198
1:20	180
1:24	99
1:27	150, 151
2:7	63
2:9	23, 185n11
2:12	50
2:14	92
2:15	107, 108, 121
3:2	69, 180
3:3	48, 52, 55, 128, 150
3:9	45, 65
3:10	47, 54
3:13	170, 171

2 Timothy

2:10–11	186
4:3	80, 135

Titus

3:5	50

Hebrews

1:3	23, 87, 183
2:7	122
2:10	122
2:18	108
4:15	86, 92
5:8	122
10:10	59
10:19–25	51
11:16	180
12:2	26, 95, 194
12:6	124
13:5	109
13:24	58n50

James

1:2	108
1:19	134
4:4	176
5:16	171

1 Peter

1:6	108
1:7	108
1:22	164
2:9	3, 178, 204
2:21	197
4:1	93
4:9	174
4:12	104
4:13	104
4:14	104
5:14	150

2 Peter

2:9	108

1 John

1:7	50
2:15	176
3:18	153
4:4	108
4:4b	107
4:10–11	159
5:3	151, 156
5:12	127

Revelation

21:1	180
21:5	204
22:4	194
22:20	194

www.ingramcontent.com/pod-product-compliance
Lightning Source LLC
Chambersburg PA
CBHW062012220426
43662CB00010B/1305